DEVON

— AT —

WAR

1939 — 1945

GERALD WASLEY

DEVON BOOKS

First published in Great Britain in 1994 by Devon Books

British Library Cataloguing in Publication Data

Data for this publication is available from the British Library

ISBN 0 86114 885 1

DEVON BOOKS
Official Publisher to Devon County Council

Halsgrove House
Lower Moor Way
Tiverton
Devon EX16 6SS

Telephone: 0884 243242
Fax: 0884 243325

Typeset by Exe Valley Dataset, Exeter
Printed and bound in Great Britain by Hillman Printers (Frome) Ltd

CONTENTS

Preface iv

Acknowledgements v

1 A Vignette of the Thirties............................ 1

2 Devon During the Phoney War 20

3 The Aftermath of Dunkirk 40

4 The Great Fire Raids on Plymouth 69

5 Exeter, Baedeker, Bombs and Beams 93

6 Focke-Wulf Fury 114

7 The Ivy Boys in Devon 143

8 Victory Celebrations 169

   Appendices 183

   Bibliography 198

   Index 200

AUTHOR'S PREFACE

The realisation, when writing my previous book on the intensive aerial raids on Plymouth (*Blitz: The Attacks on Plymouth*), that Devon was arguably the most military active county in the United Kingdom during World War Two, stimulated my interest in further research, resulting in the first ever publication of a history of wartime Devon.

It has been my intention to combine a military history with a social history of the county during the war. Major military events are covered only where they impinge upon Devon and the South West of England. Much of what is contained comes from contemporary sources and from oral accounts of people who were in the county at the time.

In my introductory chapter I have set the scene by describing the county during the thirties, leading up to the declaration of war. There were many who believed at the time that Devon would, in the event of war, be a safe haven. The consequences of the events of May 1940 were to dramatically change this view and to dispel any thoughts that Devon might play a secondary role. The evacuation of civilians to Devon, the first social experiment on such a grand scale, was to be just one feature of the remarkable history of movement of people in, through, and around the county during the war years.

I have also included much new information concerning the anti-invasion preparations for, whatever their military limitations, the planned defences in some areas were more extensive than may be realised.

The air war over Devon varied in intensity and duration. Plymouth's strategic importance inevitably led to extensive assault, while Exeter suffered largely as a result of the so-called Baedeker raids in which historic cities were targeted. But comparative studies show that almost every settlement on the South Devon coast was raided, often on more than one occasion. This was truly 'Front Line' Devon.

Perhaps of most significance is the American military presence, in the county. So great was this 'invasion' that the 'occupying' American forces often out-numbered local populations. In preparing for D-Day, vast Battle Training Areas were established through the compulsory evacuation of the South Hams. Linked to this was the North Devon Assault Training Centre where so many vital lessons were learned prior to the 'real thing'.

Part of the romance of the history of the US Army during those fateful days of early June 1944 is focused on the armadas that sailed from the five departure ports of South Devon. Less well known is the planning and activity associated with the US 4th Infantry Division in organising the huge marshalling areas in Devon, in the routes taken to the `hards' for embarkation, and the meticulous co-ordination achieved between the various armed services.

Throughout this work I have attempted to give equal balance between the dramatic military events and life on the Home Front. This was, after all, a `People's War' and it was through the resolution of the people at home that the Allies were ultimately victorious. Devon farmers, despite the frustrations of government regulations, made a significant contribution in producing essential food, as did the county's fishermen. Communities of all sizes contributed to the war effort and thousands not involved in the military fought their war as members of the Civil Defence, Home Guard, Fire Services and the vast numbers of volunteer groups that were called upon to do their duty. I also pay tribute to the work of those involved in essential wartime occupations, in factories, shipyards, transport services and as public servants.

Gerald Wasley
March 1994

ACKNOWLEDGEMENTS

Ihave been fortunate from the beginning in the preparation of this book to have had so many people and organisations respond to my request for information regarding wartime Devon. The subject specialists who have been so helpful, generously gave their time and advice, as did members of staff of the various public archives and other institutions. I am also indebted to the many people who sent me photographs from their family albums, particularly of VE and VJ street parties. My search for Devon wartime photographs led to Grispin Gill, Plymouth; George H. Lidstone, Torquay; David Murch, Salcombe; Leslie Lownds Pateman, Torquay; and Bernard Stephens, Exeter allowing me to use marvellous photographs from their personal collections. It is a pleasure to acknowledge below all those who have given their permission to use or refer to specific publications, documents or letters.

Included here are the names of contemporary wartime newspapers I also used as sources of information.

R. C. B. Ashworth, Air Historian; Richard T. Bass, Military Historian; Moyra S. Charlton, Wren Wartime Memoirs; A. J. Child, Royal Observer Corps; Peter Clare, Belgian Refugees; J. Gapper, Royal Observer Corps; Jane Hayter-Hames, *A History of Chagford*; Professor R. V. Jones, British Scientific Intelligence; Megan Keeble, WRVS Archives; R. J. Kennell, Librarian, Royal Naval College Dartmouth; K. Holland, Local Historian Tiverton; Arthur Lewis, Naval Historian; Pamela Mellor, *The Mystery of X5*; Leslie Lownds Pateman, Local Historian, Torquay; Miss M. Piper, Local Historian, Holsworthy; Dr Alfred Price, Air Historian; Pippa Pugh, *Henrietta's War*; James Rusbridger, *Who Sank Surcouf?*; Cyril Rushworth, Civil Defence Historian; Pete Southcombe, *Wartime North Devon*; Marcia J. Treece, *According to our Cloth*; Henry Wills, *Pillboxes: UK Defences 1940*; Freddy Woodward, Military Historian; Edna White, Local Historian, Torquay; Mrs A. Angus, Tiverton; Mr J. Ashley, Kingswear; George Baker, Catford; Miss K. Barber, Exeter; Mrs B. Barlow, Hanwell; Mrs Batsford, Sidcup; Mrs E. H. Blacker, Torquay; Irene Bond, Acton; Michael Bourne, Chivenor; Thomas Bradbeer, North Devon; Margaret Bradford, Plymouth; Eve Brett, Teignmouth; L. C. Brown, Acton; Sue Brown, London SE1; Mr C. L. Burden, Torquay; Mr K. Burridge, Torquay; J. Bryant, Honor Oak Park; Doris Chapman, Bristol; Mrs Chatherton, Ilfracombe; Mr A. L. Clamp, Elburton; Mr R. Coleman, Brixham; Irene Coles, Catford; Ken Coombe, Acton; B. J. Court, Exeter; Mrs J. Cox, Plymouth; Tony Cozens, Greenford; Maureen Craig, Leytonstone; Emily Crouch, S.E. London; R. J. Daniels, Erith; Jill Doney; The 1940 Association, Devon; Ken Doughty, Aveton Gifford; B. Duncan, Charlton; Ruby Durham, Witney; S. Dwyer, Roborough; Jenny Farmer, Kingswear; William T. Ford, Southwark; Mr Foxen, Eltham; Ray Freeman, Dartmouth; T. J. Furse, Bexley Health; V. Gatzias, Dartmouth; Ted Gosling, Branscombe; Mrs Gray, Exeter; Mr and Mrs Green, Torquay; A. Greer, Devonport; F. Gregory, Exeter; Mr Gunter, Tiverton; Tony Hallett, Exeter; F. Harris, Battersea; Ron Harris, Acton; Roy Hasset, Bristol; Derek Hayter, Woolwich; Ben Hick, Plymouth; J. A. Higgins, Kingswear; Mrs Hill, London SE1; J. Hodgson, Kingswear; Gladys Hook, Bexley Heath; Jean Hopwood, Bristol; Doreen Hyde, Eastbourne; George Courtney-Jones, Torquay; Mr Kella, Bristol; Barbara Kelway, Exeter; Mary Kizer, Tavistock; M. Knott, Exeter; Mrs B. Laidlaw, Exeter; Rene Liballeur, Teignmouth; Mr R. Little, Kingswear; J Lethernen, Exeter; C. H. Martin, Wetherby; Irene Martin, London SE1; V. R. Mason, Greenford; Mrs O. McMahon, Plymouth; Mrs B. Meir, London; Tony Merce, Exeter; Mrs A. D. Mercer, Exeter; V. R. Merman, Forest Hill; Mike Messer, London SE1; N. Minting, West Wickham; D. E. Moore, Yealmpton; Fred Park, Brixham; Mr W. G. Parkhouse, Exeter; Mr J. Patterson, London SE8; Vi Parr, Exeter; J. Peglar, Bristol; J. Petersen, Totnes; Jane Plifa, Cullompton; T. Porter, Burgh Island; Mrs F. Preston, Fremington; Mary Probert, Bristol; Ian Richer,

Blackheath; Mrs Round, Plumstead; P. R. Russell, Forest Hill; J. W. Saunders, Southend; D. E. J. Scattergood, Torquay; W. J. Scully, S. London; Geoff Sherratt, Bristol; J. K. Sinclair, Holsworthy; D. V. Smith, Exmouth; J. T. Snell, Yelverton; K. G. Southwick, Bath; Mrs G. Spencer, Bellingham; Jane Taylor, Acton; Paul Taylor, Bath; Leslie Thomas, London SE3; J. Thorburn, Lewisham; Mr and Mrs F. J. Tremlett, Dartmouth; D. Underdown, Ilfracombe; P. M. Vickery, Bristol; N. Vining, Crediton; Mrs Vospor, London SE1; B. M. Wall, SE17; Mr and Mrs Warren, Kingsbridge; E. Watson, Brockley; Norah West, Exmouth. I should also like to thank Isabelle Mear, and Rosemary Wasley for their secretarial skills. *Acton Gazette*; Aston Archives, Reading University, Berks; *Bath Star*; *Bideford and N. Devon Gazette*; Brixham Museum and History Society, Devon; Bundesarchiv Frieberg, Germany; *Bristol Evening Post*; *Dartmouth Chronicle*; Dartington Rural Archives; Devon History Society; *Exmouth Chronicle*; *Frankfurter Leitung*, 1941; Her Majesty's Stationery Office; Holsworthy Library Devon; Ilfracombe Museum, N. Devon; Imperial War Museum London; Aerial photographs, Australia War memorial, Canberra City, Australia; BBC Sound Archives, Reading Berks; British Newspaper Library, Colindale, London; Bundesarchiv, Frieberg, Germany; Bowden House, Totnes; Camberley Military Staff College, Berks; Dartmouth Library; Devonshire Association; *Das Reich* (Berlin), 1941; *Express and Echo*, Exeter; *Herald Express*, Torquay; HMS Britannia (RNC), Dartmouth; *Ilfracombe Chronicle*; *London Illustrated News*; *Kingsbridge Gazette*; National Archives, Washington USA; *North Devon Journal Herald* (Barnstaple); *Paignton News*; *Sidmouth Observer*; *South East London and Kentish Mercury*; *Tavistock Gazette*; Tiverton Museum Society; *Torquay Directory and South Devon Journal*; Torquay Museum; Trinity House, London; *Volkischer Beobachter*, Berlin; West Devon Records Office, Plymouth; *Western Independent*, Plymouth; *Western Times*, Exeter; The National Trust; *Okehampton Gazette*; Public Records Office, Kew; Society of Friends, London; *South London Press*; Teignmouth Post and Gazette; *Tiverton Gazette*; *Torquay Times*; *Wandsworth Borough News*; West Country Studies Library, Exeter; *Western Evening Herald*, Plymouth; Womens Royal Voluntary Service, London; *Western Morning News*, Plymouth.

DEDICATION

I toast the County of Devon;
The green sea and red earth of the south,
the rocky cliffs and yellow sands of the north,
and the heather covered countryside of Exmoor and Dartmoor.

The toast of 37 Devonians who met at the Palace Asmara, Eritrea, 25 February 1943.

A VIGNETTE OF THE THIRTIES

Twelve years after the end of the Great War (1914–1918) against Germany, the people of the United Kingdom wanted no more than to live in peace, to have a home, and a job. Throughout the thirties there were, in glorious Devon, halcyon days for some, the dole queue for others and for the majority a life of contentment based on a wage that was just above the breadline.

On the last day of January 1933 Adolf Hitler came to power. Whatever their lifestyle, people were now living in a period of phoney peace because of the politics of appeasement. Hitler, aided by his principal ministers Herman Goering, Dr Goebbels and Himmler, dictated the brutal political power of Nazi Germany. The expansive policy of *Lebensraum*, for the glory and good of Germany, was the cause of the gathering war clouds over Europe. Each passing year was but a prolonged countdown to World War Two.

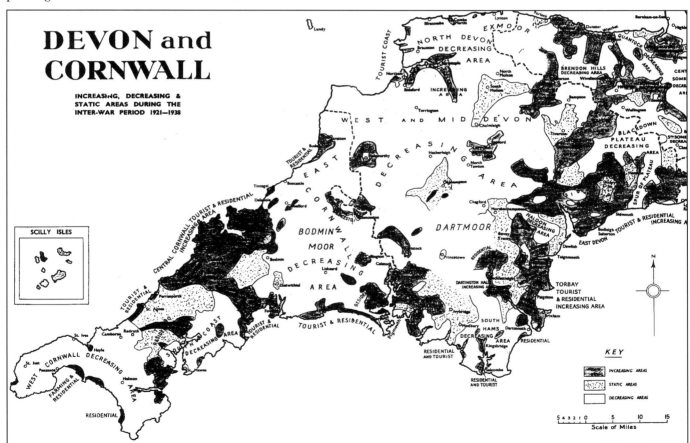

DEVON and CORNWALL

INCREASING, DECREASING & STATIC AREAS DURING THE INTER-WAR PERIOD 1921–1938

Devon's population in 1931 was 732 968, an average of 281 per square mile, less than half that of the rest of England and Wales. In order of population the eight largest communities were Plymouth, Exeter, Torquay, Paignton, Newton Abbot, Barnstaple, Exmouth and Teignmouth. Together, these accounted for 54 per cent of the total population of the county.

Population movements in Devon and Cornwall 1921-38: taken from a contemporary publication.

In 1931 Rear Admiral Sueter suggested that the British Government create a Ministry of Defence because of the vulnerability of Devonport Dockyard; the Rear Admiral believed AA gun defences could not prevent the bombing of ships.[1] Devon's population continued to increase by 1.2 per cent up until 1935, however the rest of the country increased in population by 3.2 per cent, indicating an unfortunate demographic decline for Devonshire. In the north and west the population of the county in the thirties was declining. In contrast, in areas of South and East Devon the number of people was increasing, with the exception of the South Hams area where there had been a reduction of inhabitants in some of the villages. Devon is a large county, but the size of its farms was small up to 1939, only twelve holdings were above 500 acres. After the agricultural boom of the Great War, when British farmers were looked upon as saviours of their country by producing vast crops to feed the island's population, there had been an economic decline in the subsequent years.

The cattle market Modbury, South Devon, June 1934.

Even with all the delicious Devon clotted cream that had been sold and consumed the county could not be considered as being predominantly a dairying region. The number of dairy cattle in Devon was no more than the average of the United Kingdom. The South Hams was famed for its 'South Devon' cow, a large animal capable of producing great quantities of milk of high butterfat content, but this was an exception. Devon before the Second World War was a place for raising beef and store cattle.

The average number of cattle on a Devon farm during the thirties was ten animals per holding. Few Devon farms had silos; farmers tended to grow fodder crops, rather than grain. The vegetable crops grown in the county were insufficient to satisfy local demand. At Exeter fifty per cent of the vegetables sold to the public were brought in from outside the county.

The already sparsely populated rural areas of Devon continued to decrease. Various factors were responsible for the exodus, one reason being poor communications; local public road transport ran a limited service, sometimes a bus was scheduled to call at a village or hamlet once a day. Others ran once a week and in some circumstances there was no nearby bus service at all. The low wages offered and sub-standard accommodation deterred men from working on the land. Farm workers' wives would persuade their husbands to refuse an offer of work if the tied cottage was not suitable to live in. Many estate cottages were unfit and these places remained uninhabitable. Cottages that fell into a state of disrepair were usually left by the landowner who could not afford to repair them. There was sometimes the paradox of new rural housing projects that had been completed; the farm workers could not afford to rent them, consequently the housing built for the agriculture workers was let to retired people and other approved tenants who could afford to pay the rents.

A view of Slapton in the 1930s. Many such communities were in decline in pre-war years despite a growth in tourism. This is the area eventually evacuated to provide a training ground for D-Day troops.

Crediton's Rural District Council built cottages in the larger villages of Newton St Cyres, Lapford and Sandford. At Newton St Cyres many of the cottage tenants were employed in Exeter, whereas at Lapford, employees at the Ambrosia milk factory rented the newly built cottages. The reason why the new property was built in the larger villages was the significant increase in costs incurred when transporting building materials to the remote villages.

As agriculture experienced a decline during the inter-war years, so Devon's sea fishing industry suffered economic misery. Brixham fishing fleet had 120 boats in 1919, this had been reduced to six boats in 1938. Westward, along the coast to Plymouth, 177 Cornish boats fished from Sutton Harbour during 1931, within a year the numbers were significantly reduced.

East coast drifters arrived but with small catches of fish only three boats remained. Steam trawlers fished from Plymouth, but their catches were also insignificant when compared with the immediate post-war years, when on one occasion half a million fish were landed on Sutton Quay.[2]

Education was another reason for people to move away from the rural areas. Many more Devon children attended school in the towns as the expectation of the younger generation, supported by parental ambition, began to rise. The children of the country communities attending the urban schools became town wise and began to reject the traditional ways of rural life.

Against the trend of population loss in North Devon was the increasing number of people who were settling in the small coastal resorts in what was the Rural District of Barnstaple. These included the communities of Instow, Westleigh, Combe Martin, Woolacombe, Braunton and Mortehoe. Barnstaple, said to be the oldest borough in England, maintained an almost static population between 1930–1941 whereas Bideford, by the River Torridge, was a town with a falling population due to the deterioration of industrial activity. The decline of the coal trade with Swansea, the closure of the nearby shipbuilding yards and redundancies from three local factories that had given employment to many local people, were detrimental to Bideford. At Appledore the decline of the boatyards resulted in local men moving away from the area. Men found work at Devonport, others travelled to Middlesex, Hertfordshire and Kent. The economic problems of Appledore also influenced the economy of South Molton which served as a shopping centre for the area.

Ilfracombe, North Devon. At the time this photograph was taken in the early 1930s the North Devon resorts were catering for large numbers of summer visitors. The bandstand and the Victoria Pavilion, seen in the centre of the photograph surrounded by deckchairs, were amongst Ilfracombe's attractions. Many visitors arrived in the resort from South Wales on paddlesteamers, one of which, the *Devonia* was later damaged and abandoned at Dunkirk.

Whereas large areas of Devonshire were declining in population certain others were increasing. Those places that attracted people to take up residence created a climate of developing employment for hotel, catering and retail trades, as well as the transport services. Certain South Devon coastal resorts between Seaton and Salcombe, particularly the Torbay area, were showing a rapid increase in the density of their population.

In this area of South Devon, where the scenery is so attractive and the climate usually so mild, there were opportunities for golf, fishing or yachting. Newly built properties attracted considerable interest from the growing numbers of would-be home owners. The detached house, semi-detached, or bungalow had all the essential public services and latest household features. Jade-green-painted half-tiled kitchens, power points for an electric cooker or Hoover, iron radiators for central heating, door chimes, and space in the kitchen for a refrigerator. Each property had a garden to grow roses and a lawn to sit out on and enjoy the sunshine. At Torbay, communications were good, as were the educational and social facilities. A wide choice of shops and the opportunity to attend a theatre or concert were available. Of particular importance was the wide range of many places of worship.

Travel across Devon in the thirties was time consuming; people would tend to shop and meet in a nearby town. A visit to a city would be on a weekly or monthly basis, when the sales were on, or when an individual had a day off. In some rural areas, for example in East Devon, visits to Exeter would be once or twice a year.

Town entertainment meant little to those people who lived in the rural areas, with the exception of agricultural shows, travelling fairs and, for some, professional football at Exeter, Plymouth or Torquay. For the country dweller, the cost of a cinema seat would be matched by the bus fare into town; then there was the problem of returning home.

Inns and public houses were the traditional social meeting places for many of the men. Here the finest ciders, cheap in price, were drunk down with relish, sometimes in preference to beers and ales.

Rural communities continued to organise their own entertainment, skittles, socials, dances, fetes, coach outings, or a walk down to the travelling picture show held at the local village hall. Religion maintained its influence on rural social life with varied activities associated with the local village church. A common cry of the local youth, however, was that their village was dead, resulting in many young men rushing off on their motorcycles, to where grass was supposedly greener.

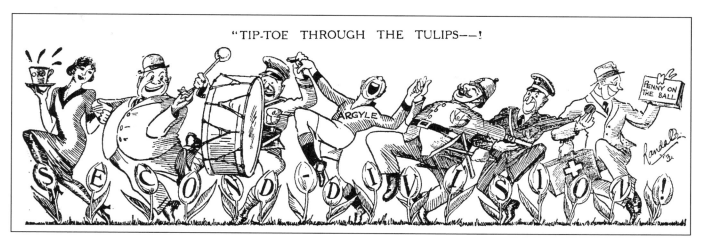

"TIP-TOE THROUGH THE TULIPS--!"

A contemporary cartoon celebrating Plymouth Argyle's promotion to the Second Division of the Football League in 1930.

Exeter, mother city of Devon, smaller in size and population than Plymouth was able to successfully compete commercially with the naval city, for Exeter with its active market and good shopping facilities attracted people from a wide radius. Farmers came to Exeter on market day for here they could also buy their clothes, and other items associated with agriculture. These men would gather in taverns, while their wives enjoyed a meal in one of the many restaurants before continuing their shopping. The magnificent Exeter Cathedral, the many old timbered buildings, together with the narrow passages and alleyways, conveyed to the observer that the city was a place steeped in history. The cathedral's presence exuded a dignity, making Exeter a tranquil city.

If Exeter was the Jewel of the West, then Deller's Cafe, was a magnificent gem, for Deller's was the choice of affordable pleasure, eating, relaxing and sometimes dancing in a civilised environment offered by a courteous and efficient management. Deller's Cafe was one of the few genuine art nouveau buildings in the United Kingdom, constructed in 1900. The elegant interior décor and the placing

The interior of Deller's Cafe, Exeter. Built in 1900 it was one of the few genuine art nouveau examples in Britain. Sadly it was to be destroyed in the Exeter Blitz.

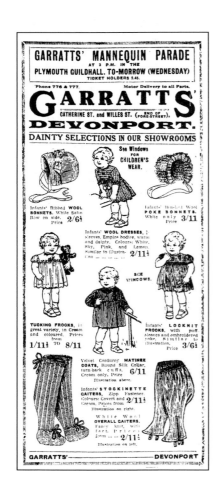
of the tables created a tasteful setting for the enjoyment of the customers who could dine up on the balcony or on the ground floor.[3]

Polo was played on the green lawns at Topsham Road, a privileged pastime. For more popular taste the city had the Theatre Royal and its cinemas. One of the older picture houses charged 1½d (less than 1p) for admission. Entrance was via an old rickety staircase, there to sit on a platform called the 'Jam Shelf'.[4]

While the adults went to work, children went to school, but for one young Exeter girl during the thirties, she would first have to go to Weston Bakery to buy stale bread and cakes. On occasions a visit would also be made to Slugget the butcher to buy a pig's bladder for her mother to make faggots and sausages. Her mother earned money, washing, starching and ironing the surplices of a local church choir in Mary Arches Street.

For Exeter families who were very poor there were farthing breakfasts and soup kitchens where children would bring a jug to be filled with hot soup. The majority of families lived on a low but regular income and by their thrift, good housekeeping and self denial they managed to be suitably fed and attired.

Buckland Abbey, the Dartmoor home of Sir Francis Drake, caught fire early in 1935 and the west wing was almost destroyed. Drake's Drum, his sword and portrait were saved from the blaze. This was one of nine major fires that occurred in the county within a period of two weeks. Flames of a different source were seen lighting the night sky when the magnificent spectacle of the Aurora Borealis was observed by people along the coast of North Devon.

A visitor's experience of Devon life during the thirties was often completely different from the people who lived in the county. Preconceived ideas were often taken from images depicted by picture postcards, music hall comedians, and current comedy radio programmes. Men in white smocks, red nosed villagers drinking from a flagon of cider, and every girl a Devon milk maid, was far from the reality. During the thirties, light music concerts and the songs of Sir Edward German were very popular. His songs of Devon *Four Jolly Sailor Men*, and the *Devonshire Song* gave pleasure and a reminder of a bygone Devon and, for many, the words and music of German's *Glorious Devon* conveyed the spirit and romance of the West Country.

Mutley is a quiet and respectable area of Plymouth, most of the houses are built in long terraces with bow-fronted windows and small front gardens. The Mutley community in the early thirties was self-sufficient with a variety of shops located on Mutley Plain. The Royal Dockyard and naval base was a tram ride away, as was the main shopping centre of Plymouth.

Home for one family was a top flat in one of the terraced houses in Mutley. The kitchen had a scrubbed table, where the family ate their meals or played, as they did on many occasions, games of ludo or cards, and completed their jigsaw puzzles. The small front room had a polished table, used on occasions when visitors arrived. Later, when the children grew up, the front room table was allowed to be used for homework, with mother being very upset whenever ink was accidently flicked on the tablecloth. The neighbours downstairs were quiet people, below them was a basement flat, where a succession of tenant naval families lived.

For the children, playing in the park was preferred to hanging around the streets. Nearby was Freedom Park, where the park keeper would not allow the boys to play cricket or football. The tennis courts were there to poke little fingers into the wire mesh fence, watching the grown ups playing tennis. When winter came, the children played in the streets nearer their homes; paving stones were ideal for playing hop-scotch, five stones and 'off-ground'. The gas-lamps in the streets held a fascination as the lamplighter arrived with his long wooden pole and with a 'pop' the light would blaze.

Part of life for one young girl, when not at school was running errands to the corner shop, the money wrapped in a piece of paper that listed the goods. Sometimes she would be told what to buy and this meant running all the way to the shop, repeating 'one loaf, a tin of black boot polish and two gas mantles'.

Meals for this Mutley household were plain and wholesome, but very tasty. Roast dinners and stews were made from the cheaper cuts of meat. Pasties were cooked using skirt of beef. The meat was eked out with plenty of vegetables with butter, or suet pudding. Sunday dinner was usually beef, and the pudding, spotted-dick or jam roly-poly tied up in a cloth carried steaming from an iron saucepan. Food was never wasted; stale bread and cakes became spicy Nelson squares or were used in trifles. During the week, breakfast was cereals, in the

A publicans' dinner held at the Palm Court Hotel, Torquay c. 1930. Despite the Depression years such opulence was not uncommon in the resort which continued to enjoy its 'Riviera' status.

winter porridge, with thick slices of bread, butter and marmalade. Sunday's breakfast was a marvellous fry of potatoes, slices of fried bread, a small piece of bacon and beaten up egg. Supper was thick, strong sweet cocoa with a home made currant or coconut bun. The greatest pleasure of life was a fresh scone spread with clotted cream and strawberry jam.[5]

In the thirties more people were employed in the personal services industry at Exeter and Torquay than anywhere else in Devon. These two communities had a higher ratio of people in the upper income group than elsewhere in the county. The thirties was a wonderful decade for some sections of Devon's society, even if clouded by the talk of war. Residents and visitors could take coffee or morning tea in Torquay's Marine Spa, a civilised way of 'enjoying a morning break'.

The small sandy bays, the beaches and sub tropical foliage of Torquay helped to give it the name of 'The British Riviera'. The Torquay palms, posh hotels and general environment made the resort different from others in Britain.

Here lived the rich, and others who were very rich, drawn like a magnet to the resort, if only to sail on their ocean-going yachts. Such visitors would travel first class from London on the GWR Torbay Express, enjoying the ride along the South Devon coastline, arguably the most splendid train journey in the United Kingdom. Torquay was a smart resort, even the cliff railings were painted a deep terracotta with the rims light-pink, that seemed to match the deep red loams of the earth. Quality and fashion was part of Torquay, in some areas of the town a women was considered improperly dressed if she was seen on the street not wearing gloves. Chanel on the Strand was always in vogue. At this shop the Torquay debutantes selected their gowns in preparation for their being presented at the Royal Court.[6]

Everyone seemed to dress for dinner in Torquay. The Palm Court Hotel had an outdoor orchestra that would play from a bandstand on the hotel's roof, while some visitors thought it most romantic to go midnight bathing at Torre Abbey Sands.

Few Torquaians could, or would wish to live in this lavish style. The general quality of life for the local residents was good but working in the tourist industry

'Remaking the World'. A packed meeting at the Drill Hall, Devonport in the mid 1930s. The Nazi Party flag is just visible to the right of the Union Flag above the podium.

involved hard work and long hours. Owners of boarding houses were pre-occupied during the holiday season assuring their clients received satisfactory service; whatever the financial rewards, it was a demanding life.

For a brief period in the thirties there were elements of fascism in the West Country. The British Fascists first arrived in Plymouth during August 1933, holding meetings on the pavement outside Plymouth's Post Office. The active members of the party wore a black beret with a gilt badge and a black blouse.

The official party paper *The Blackshirt* sold 2000 copies per week in Plymouth. In November 1933 a Fascist Headquarters was opened in Lockyer Street, Plymouth. They cleared away all the flowers in the back garden of the premises and laid concrete for the local Blackshirts to practice their drill. In the building were offices with other rooms let out to party supporters. The fascists were interested in the tithe problems of the West Country farms that had resulted in the British Union of Farmers being established.[7] Meetings were held at various places throughout the county; for example at Exeter, Exmouth, Tiverton and Torquay. Sir Oswald Mosley the leader of the British Fascists spoke at the Guildhall, Plymouth in September 1934. The following month a fascist meeting was arranged at the Drill Hall Millbay, Plymouth. Mosley arrived and so did many communists singing the 'Red Flag'. There were scuffles and the meeting finished in uproar.

Discordancy set in at Plymouth when some of Mosley's men arrived from London and another meeting of the fascists held at the city's Corn Exchange was a disaster. The West Country membership of the Blackshirts significantly dropped, it seemed that almost overnight they had completely lost their supporters. In 1935 few members of the British Union of Fascists[8] remained in Plymouth. An infamous fascist visitor in that year was William Joyce. He spoke at Heathcoat Hall, Tiverton and spent six weeks in Plymouth during 1935. Joyce was unpopular among the remainder of the Plymouth Blackshirts and would have possibly been forgotten but for his 'Lord Haw Haw' broadcasts during the war. Eventually the Fascist Headquarters in Lockyer Street closed. The rise and fall of the Blackshirts in the West Country covered a period of two years.[9]

Two of the most well known people in the United Kingdom during the early thirties were associated with Devon. They were Lady Astor, the member for Parliament for the Sutton Division of Plymouth, who with Lord Astor owned a grand terraced house on Plymouth Hoe. The other was T. E. Lawrence (Lawrence of Arabia) who in the early years of the decade was an RAF mechanic (extra-ordinaire) stationed at the RAF seaplane base at Mountbatten, Plymouth. These two famous people were also good friends. Lawrence was known to take Lady Astor riding pillion along the narrow Devon lanes on his powerful Brough motorcycle, a present from Mr and Mrs Bernard Shaw.

Another friend of T. E. Lawrence was the author Henry Williamson who at this time lived in a cottage at Croyde Bay, North Devon. Lawrence had written a long and detailed critique regarding *Tarka the Otter*, and was known to travel cross Dartmoor on his motorcycle to visit Henry Williamson and his wife. On 12 May 1935, Henry Williamson wrote to Lawrence asking him that if he, Williamson, could arrange a meeting with Adolf Hitler, would Lawrence accompany him to Germany to meet the German dictator, for Williamson believed Lawrence could influence Hitler.

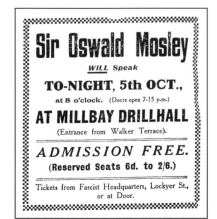

Lawrence decided to reply to Williamson's letter by telegram — it was while travelling on his motorcycle from his base in Dorset to a Post Office to send the telegram that Lawrence was involved in his fatal accident.[10]

In 1935, the Silver Jubilee year of King George V and Queen Mary, it seemed that every Devon community was decorated with the Union Flag and flags of the British Empire. There were services of thanksgiving, dinners and dances, bonfires, fireworks and street parties for children. Devon schoolchildren were given a Silver Jubilee beaker. A twenty-one gun salute was fired from Plymouth's magnificent Citadel, with the massed bands playing and marching on Plymouth Hoe. A special attraction in the Torbay area was the Jubilee Arch built near the seafront at Paignton.

Jubilee year was the time the Southern Railway decided to close down some of the passenger services in North Devon as traffic receipts did not justify expenditure. There was however money to be spent, for example at Barnstaple the new art déco Odeon was planned to hold 1330 customers. A significant event in

Crowds of bathers enjoy the summer sunshine at Tinside, Plymouth c. 1935.

Barnstaple's Pannier Market in 1932. Almost all the stallholders are women.

South Devon was the opening of the Plymouth Tinside open air bathing pool. Its gracious curved perimeter made it a lasting landmark in the city, more so than any other Plymouth building. Events seem to attract large crowds; at Home Park football ground in 1934, when Plymouth Argyle played Huddersfield Town, over 44 000 people attended the match.

Changes were taking place in Devon if not always obvious. Tradition was broken at Exeter and formal disapproval expressed when a young married woman was appointed to become a full time teacher, something that had never happened before at Maynards School.[11]

Barnstaple's Pannier Market was as busy as ever on a Friday, when the country communities arrived from a wide area of Exmoor, South Molton and Ilfracombe to sell their produce directly to the customer. This large market accommodated five hundred stalls run almost exclusively by women stallholders. Political meetings were held at the market; Lloyd George was known to have attracted 10 000 people when he spoke at a rally. At Ilfracombe, there were more than 450 unemployed people, yet a coal merchant publicly stated he could not obtain four local men to shovel coal for 18 shillings and 6 pence per week. The result of this public statement was that he received five hundred applications from unemployed men throughout the country.

The Imperial Hotel, Torquay, the premier establishment of the resort, even with its luxury and grandeur, was having to make improvements to maintain its status. A magnificent lounge ballroom opened in 1935. The event was a glittering

An artist's impression of the Grand Opening of the Imperial Hotel Ballroom, Torquay, 1935.

occasion for Torquay, with dancing to the music of two orchestras, one having been contracted to travel down from London. Superb food, wines, spirits, vintage champagnes and forty-year-old Brandy were consumed. After the cabaret, dancing continued until 2am the following morning, with the fashionable ladies swirling around in their long evening gowns and the debonair men in white ties and tails.[12]

In the years leading up to the Second World War the move away from arable farming continued and farmhouse produce, including Devonshire cream, began to disappear from the market. The working horse, for so long seen on the land, was gradually being replaced by the mechanical tractor. The thirties was a peaceful life for many Devon villagers. There were some farmers who were fortunate not to be affected by the decline in agriculture and this was reflected in each succeeding year at harvest festival celebrations. Sunday school outings for many children were usually visits to the seaside. In contrast church outings for many Plymouth children were to the moorland areas.

AN ENGLISHMAN'S HOME IS HIS CASTLE

A contemporary illustration of the contentious gasworks proposal, published in the *Sidmouth Observer*, 1936.

But the clouds of war were gathering. Notices, meetings and occasional exercises relating to civilian Air Raid Precautions were being drawn to the attention of the local communities. In the Autumn of 1935 a black out exercise over Plymouth took place when aircraft flew over the city to check the effectiveness of the black out in the event of an air raid.

The first month of 1936 saw a solemn and important event for the nation with the death of King George V. In Devon meetings were cancelled and prayers were said in church. At Torquay massed bands marched through the town playing solemn music.

But life went on: in select Sidmouth, set amid red sandstone cliffs, its conservative, mainly retired population, was stirred into activity by proposals to improve the Sidmouth gasworks. Meetings were held that attracted large numbers of people and the proposed move became an electoral issue. Election day came and the Sidmouth Councillors in favour of the removal of the gasworks won the day.[13]

Shipwrecks off the Devon coasts are part of the county's history. In April 1936 considerable publicity was given to the Finnish barque *Herzogin Cecilie* that ran aground after striking the Ham Stone off Sewer Mill Cove in a dense fog. The four-masted barque was a graceful sight even as she lay wrecked. Thousands of people made their way to the Bolt Head area on the south west coast of Devon to view the wreck. Attempts were made to save her, but she was eventually broken up for scrap.

If the year 1936 started with the death of the king, it ended with the abdication of the uncrowned King Edward VIII. Many regretted the situation, but it meant long live King George VI who, with Elizabeth, was crowned on 12 May 1937. Decorations were again put up in the streets. At Newton Abbot the town was transformed overnight with a blaze of red, white and blue bunting all made in waterproof material, the finest coronation street decorations in the whole of South Devon.

Schoolchildren had a day's holiday, there were street parties and celebrations. Iced cakes, fancy dress costumes, all were in the national colours. There being no television service at the time, the recording of the coronation was done on film for the newsreels, a feature of current cinema. One aircraft landed at Haldon with a film of the coronation for screening at the Riviera Cinema, Teignmouth.[14]

Herr von Ribbentrop, the German Ambassador in London, later Germany's Foreign Minister, arrived by train at Torquay on the 16 April 1937 to inspect the crew of the *Schlesien*, a German Naval training ship that was paying a courtesy visit to the resort. Ribbentrop was greeted on arrival by the Mayor of Torquay and

The wreck of the *Herzogin Cecilie* off Salcombe, South Devon.

The visiting German Ambassador, Herr von Ribbentrop (left), is received by the Mayor of Torquay in April 1937. Second on the right of the picture is Admiral Wassner of the German Fleet.

given a civic reception at the Marine Spa. While at Torquay the German Ambassador stayed at the Imperial Hotel.

Two days before Ribbentrop's visit, a football match had been played between Torquay United and the Germans at Plainmoor football ground; before the kick off the German team lined up and gave the Nazi salute. In the evenings the Germans would parade through Fleet Street, Torquay, chanting 'Heil Hitler' and giving the Nazi salute.

On another occasion, Ribbentrop stayed at Moretonhampstead, at the Manor House Hotel. He arrived in a huge bullet-proof Mercedes Benz saloon. The car was so large it would not fit in the hotel's garage and was parked instead at a local garage that could accommodate the Mercedes. A tall uniformed German chauffeur with swastika buttons on his coat drove the powerful car.[15]

Later in 1937 the British Home Fleet visited Torbay, followed by units of the American fleet that included the warships *Arkansas, Wyoming* and the USS *New York*. Thus the spectre of war continued to develop. Civil defence, in terms of plans and preparations, was activated by government notices that were to be actioned by the local Devon authorities. Some were more advanced with their decision making and planning than others. The Air Raid Wardens service at Torquay was, for example, formed with a small number of volunteers in 1937, rapidly expanded the following year and comprised twelve groups, with a further sub division of ninety sectors.[16]

In South Devon the beautiful River Dart was an anchorage for redundant merchant ships that were laid up by the international surplus of shipping.

Even as Torquay's civic dignatories welcomed the German Ambassador, South Devon was preparing for a war that was thought sure to come. This 1937 newspaper photograph shows Torquay policemen training for gas warfare.

Dartmouth Harbour in the mid 1930s where three Bibby troopers the *Lancashire*, *Dorsetshire* and *Somerset* lie at anchor.

Harbour dues were paid, a small source of income for Dartmouth that did not unfortunately reduce the town's unemployment problem. The river port had public health problems affecting a small part of the community. In one residential area ten families shared two water taps and two outside toilets.

1938 was the year of the Munich crisis, and in many ways was an eventful year for Dartmouth. The town appointed its first ARP controller, while the Royal Castle Hotel succumbed to the current fashion by opening a cocktail bar. Later in the year Dartmouth had its first milk bar. Dartmouth Town Council decided at a meeting that their small town would not be a target for the German Luftwaffe on their way to attack Plymouth. Many still believed that South Devon would be totally immune from enemy air attacks.

Dartmouthians were told that in the event of the enemy air raid the town would be warned by the sound of a steam whistle that would be blown from the local gasworks. Later on an electric air raid siren was installed.

The arrival of the cruise liner *Slamat* at Dartmouth bringing 330 young Dutch students gave an army officer the idea to approach the German Embassy in London to enquire if it was possible for a German 'Strength through Joy' ship to make Dartmouth a port of call. The German Embassy replied indicating the proposal would be passed to the proper department. There was some fascist activity at Dartmouth with painted slogans on the road at Warfleet two miles outside the town's centre. The town's population in 1938 was in the order of 6000 people.

Chagford a small community on the edge of Dartmoor, had a population of 1579. It had started planning its Air Raid Precautions (ARP) in 1938. A census was made of the number of bedrooms and sitting rooms in each property. The ARP headquarters was based at the Three Crowns Hotel, an old building with an impressive porch and mullioned windows.[17]

Slapton Beach, July 1938. A rare photograph of the amphibious exercise organised by Brigadier Bernard Montgomery. A Fairey Swordfish, playing the role of a bomber, flies over the beach from HMS *Courageous* anchored in the bay.

May 1938 was also the time recruitment began for the Womens Voluntary Services, to be known as the WVS, for ARP. This organisation would be closely involved in many events concerning Devon during the next eight years.

Perhaps the most significant occurrence in Devon during 1938 was largely unheralded and has been overlooked ever since. Yet it was prophetic in terms of the forthcoming war. On the coarse shingle of Slapton beach an amphibious military exercise was held in July involving all three of the armed services and was the first of this type to be held since the disasterous events at Gallipoli during the First World War.

The planning of the Slapton exercise was given to Brigadier Bernard Montgomery. Two models of the Slapton beach and the immediate hinterland had been constructed with an accurate representation of the topography. All military personnel involved with the beach assault were instructed using the models, each soldier being told what role he was given for the exercise.

The troops practiced during the day and night, disembarking from the deck of a ship down Mediterranean ladders into cutters and whalers. Each serviceman had been allotted a place on board a specific boat, he always sat in the same place in the boat and in no other. A drill was devised which meant the men could get to their seats easily and quickly. This training enabled the troops to reach a high level of proficiency in embarking, rowing and landing silently on a beach during darkness. The first troops to land would be rowed to the shore with muffled oars to maintain silence.

Service-dress jackets, trousers, puttees and caps were required to be worn by the troops throughout the exercise who also carried a gas respirator, fifty rounds of blank ammunition and a greatcoat slung like a bandolier across the shoulders. The backpack carried by each soldier comprised one shirt, one pair of socks, towel, a holdall with washing kit and razor. Each also carried a waterproof sheet, mess tin, cardigan, knife, fork and spoon, and two filled water bottles along with landing rations. The latter contained one piece of cake, an apple, chocolate, and six large, meat sandwiches — on landing on Slapton beach there would be portable cookers and food stores.

The advanced party of assault troops embarked on to the troopship HT *Lancashire* on 30 June 1938. The ship was one of three Bibby Troopers, a familiar sight at anchorage off Dartmouth (see page 13). The other boat used for transporting the troops was the MT *Clan MacAlistair*. When it was known this ship was commissioned for carrying troops, the lascar crew threatened to strike if they were required to wear gas masks. Another problem with the crew was their mistaken idea that they were destined to sail to Spain, which at that time was involved in the Civil War.

The 9th Infantry Brigade involved in this exercise included men of the Lincolns, The King's Own Scottish Borderers (KOSB) and the Second Battalion of the Middlesex Regiment.

The transport ships sailed from Portsmouth across Lyme Bay to Start Bay. Warships participating in the exercise were HMS *Southampton*, HMS *Sheffield*, the battleship HMS *Revenge* and a flotilla of destroyers. Air co-operation was supplied by the Fleet Air Arm flying twelve Swordfish aircraft acting as bombers from the aircraft carrier HMS *Courageous*.

Part of the planned exercise was for the assault to take place on three designated beaches (Beach C was an area nearby the Royal Sands Hotel). The main assault force would land in the early morning light.[18]

People in Kingsbridge and the surrounding villages were aware that something unusual was taking place. Throughout the previous night continuous noise of aircraft disturbed the sleep of many local inhabitants, while in the daylight anyone on the clifftops could see the warships steaming across Start Bay.[19]

The defending force of the exercise was designated the Wessex Army; there was also a theoretical Wessex Air Force. The main objective was for the invading forces to capture Dartmouth as a preliminary to the capture of Plymouth, the 'capital' of Wessex. On the day of the exercise the Swordfish aircraft from HMS *Courageous* were much in evidence. People began to realise something was happening in the South Hams area and flocked to Slapton to watch the 'Landing Exercises'.

In the evening the weather broke and a gale developed. It became apparent that because of the risk of some ships being blown towards the shore it was impossible to re-embark the troops in the heavy rain. The exercise was abandoned.

At first there appeared to be no alternative accommodation for the troops who were now wet and hungry. The situation of over 1100 military personnel without food or shelter appeared to be desperate, when a naval officer suggested the Royal Navy College, Dartmouth should be contacted as they may be able to assist. The naval officers of the college were assembled at 11.15pm that night and told to expect 1100 men and 80 army officers who needed to be dried, fed and billeted.

The Naval College employees, many living in Dartmouth, were called from their homes and by midnight the College was ready to house the troops. The Brigade Headquarters composed of the Middlesex Regiment were the first to arrive in lorries, with troops continuing to come in throughout the night. The East Yorks were billeted in Plymouth.

Never before in the history of the Naval College had there been such remarkable scenes, the quarterdeck, gun room, cinema and many other rooms were packed with troops, 'like sardines in a tin'. The men dried their uniforms on

Supplies are offloaded from an early version of a landing craft during the Slapton exercises of 1938. Visible in the background are two naval rowing boats of the type used to carry assault troops from ships out in the bay.

A contemporary ink sketch by a Royal Naval College Cadet showing infantry being transported to Dartmouth following the cancellation of the Slapton exercise.

radiators, hot pipes and in the drying rooms, using the rugs and oilskins of the naval cadets to cover their naked bodies. The order 'tea for a thousand' was given, and this, with beef and biscuits, was issued.

The Naval College was completely cleared by 8am the following morning, the troops marching off to Dartmouth. At 10am, by the hard work of the college cleaners, no traces of the overnight occupation remained.

The Slapton exercises had ended disappointingly. The episode however had not been forgotten, for Major General Montgomery (promoted on the day he visited Dartmouth) returned to the Naval College in October 1938 and presented the Commander of the College with a silver and bronze statuette of a British infantry soldier, dressed and equipped in contemporary style, as a token of gratitude for the hospitality received on the night of the 6 July 1938.[20]

Rain came to many areas of Devon on New Year's eve 1938. An estimated 2000 people welcomed in 1939, the last year of peace, at Wolborough, Newton Abbot in the most appalling weather conditions, but this did not deter the people from dancing and singing in the rain.

Large crowds gathered too on Bideford's ancient Longbridge, singing, as is the tradition, as the clock struck midnight.

On the western edge of Dartmoor, at the town of Tavistock, early in 1939 there was 'Council talk' of supplying the small Dartmoor village of Princetown with piped water to replace the existing shallow wells in the district. The local Civil Defence welcomed the proposals for without piped water firefighting would be severely restricted.

Throughout the county, the looming spectre of war in Europe, provided an impetus to thoughts of civil defence at home. At Woolacombe in North Devon a proposal had been made to build an underground car park that could always be used as an air raid shelter if necessary. A county-wide appeal was made for people to volunteer to participate in the Government's Evacuation Scheme by offering to billet young evacuee schoolchildren. Barnstaple schoolteachers organised a census concerning the availability of accommodation for the Scheme, one returned form stated: 'Why can't they fill Buckingham Palace with children before they ask us to take them in'. The general response to the questions regarding billeting was however very sympathetic. The Air Defence (of Great Britain) announced early in the year that Dartmouth and the South Hams was a safe area with regard to possible enemy air attacks.[21]

But it was not all gloom. Early in March, the latest dance craze came to Dartmouth when they started doing the 'Lambeth Walk'. So many people were on the floor of the Dartmouth Guildhall, that the wooden boards of the floor began to move up and down resulting in the local authority limiting the number of people to 250 when a dance was held.[22]

Devon seemed to delight in dancing, although the traditional step-dancing of the rural and moorland communities was seen on fewer occasions in the thirties. The popular form of dance was ballroom dancing inspired by the strict-tempo music of Victor Sylvester.

Devon had dance halls built not only on land, but over the water. During the thirties there was considerable interest in going dancing at 'pier' ballrooms. Plymouth Pier, and Teignmouth Pier, the latter having dances every night except Sundays, were very popular. There were at Plymouth in 1939 at least twenty-five halls used for dancing, and the city had at least thirty dance bands. By fashion rather than dictate, there was a uniform code of dress, the young men all would wear a dark jacket, grey flannel trousers with a knife-edge crease, a clean white shirt with a starched collar, and always a tie, the more fashionable tied with a Windsor knot. The dedicated ballroom dancer would travel considerable distances, discriminating as to the quality of the dance floor; only a sprung maple floor would satisfy some dancers. Serious devotees brought their own dancing shoes, lightweight black patent pumps for men, and silver or gold shoes for women.

But the merriment of dances belied the impending fear of conflict. The increasing threat of war stimulated Tavistock to prepare its civil defences. The local air raid sirens were tested and the town received 16 000 sandbags to be filled and forty steel helmets for the wardens' service. A sand dump was prepared for fire fighting. Extra lengths of hosing were required for the rural areas where distances between properties and known hydrants were usually much larger than in the town. Tavistock Police Station became hidden under sandbags, while fresh white ARP paint was to be seen on all kerbs and corner stones.

In March 1939 the German warship *Schleswig Holstein* called at the Cornish port of Falmouth. While there, an approach had been made to the Mayor of

Dartmouth regarding the possibility of the Nazi warship visiting Dartmouth on its return voyage to Kiel, northern Germany. The advantage of the visit to the River Dart town, would, it was suggested, be to bring much needed trade to the town's shopkeepers. The leading citizens of this ancient borough met to discuss the possibility and consequences of the proposed visit. It was decided that the time was not opportune for the invitation to be extended despite earlier arrangements that had been made for the German naval officers to dine at the Royal Castle Hotel, Dartmouth.

The *Schleswig Holstein* departed from Falmouth and sailed up the English Channel direct to Kiel. Six months later she was ordered to Danzig, and it was here the first salvo of enemy shells were fired on to the Polish battle port to herald the outbreak of the Second World War.[23]

The summer of 1939 was fine and warm. With crowds of visitors arriving in the county, many of the resorts experienced record numbers of holidaymakers. Yet it was a strange summer that combined the normality of any holiday season with preparation for war.

Many Devon seaside resorts held band concerts every day throughout the season. Paignton for example had engaged fifteen military bands during the summer. Thousands of people sat in their deckchairs on the beaches of Devon in July 1939 unaware that twenty-one warships of the Home Fleet had left Devonport and had sailed to their action stations; or that thousands of men of the Fleet Reserve had been called to Plymouth to man the warships.

The political crisis in Europe was deteriorating and showed no signs of abating when the annual holiday for Devonport Dockyard began on the 6 August 1939, less than a month before the outbreak of war. The 15 000 dockyard workers went

'Come Listen to the Band'. An open air concert on Plymouth Hoe attracts over three thousand people on a warm spring afternoon in 1938.

17

on holiday with more money than they'd ever had; it was the biggest pay day in the history of the Dockyard.

Torquaians had been encouraged to stock their larders with emergency stores, but by the end of August, some of the townspeople, only doing what they had been requested to do, were accused of hoarding food. Holidaymakers had arrived in their thousands at the resort, sitting out in the sun relaxing with tea and toasted tea cakes, or the most delicious fresh 'tuffs' with cream and strawberry jam. At Addison's Cafe, an orchestra played in the morning, afternoon and during the evening.

The scene was similar at the North Devon Coast resorts, where the golden beaches, some larger than on the South Coast, were packed with visitors taking in the sun. At Ilfracombe all accommodation had been taken, and many people slept in their cars at night or out on the hills that surround the town. On August Bank Holiday eight thousand deckchairs were hired out at Ilfracombe.

Royal watchers would have observed the royal yacht the *Victoria and Albert* sail from Torbay and arrive at Dartmouth. Crowds waited on the Dartmouth embankment to greet the royal family and Lord Louis Mountbatten. Rain poured down but this did not deter the people who lined the roads all the way to the Royal Naval College gates. This was a significant visit as here the young Princess Elizabeth first met the naval cadet Philip Mountbatten, a meeting that was eventually to lead to their wedding at Westminster Abbey.[24]

As the jollifications of holiday-making continued, communities throughout Devon were becoming more active with their civil defence preparations. The Regional Commissioner Scheme was made public. This required the appointment of Regional Commissioners in time of war within the United Kingdom. The hypothesis was that enemy attacks could create destruction and social problems on a scale far exceeding anything that had been experienced in the past. The regional posts would thus convey and exert Government authority throughout the county.

The concept of Regional Commissioners had previously been kept secret. The political crisis in Europe now made the Government announce the names of those people who would be appointed. These posts were mustered in two levels of authority that were appropriate to differing wartime conditions. One level would be required to co-ordinate activities of, for example, civil defence. The other would cover the result of enemy activity, for example invasion, which might cause the disruption of communications with the headquarters of National Government. In this case the appointed Commissioner would take executive control in a designated area.

The Regional Commissioner Scheme was divided into twelve Regions. The South West Region, that included Devon, was listed as No. 7 Region and the Regional Headquarters were located at Bristol.[25]

The British Government announced that local civil authorities should appoint their ARP controller without delay; some Devon local authorities had already done this. Among the qualities expected for an ARP controller was someone 'likely to inspire confidence under conditions of strain'.

The Air Raid Precaution Scheme, renamed the Civil Defence, but referred to by either title, was closely associated with the Air Raid Wardens Service. Important as these gallant people were, there were many arms to the Civil Defence Service that during the war were also to play a critical role. The structure of the local civil defence varied according to the size of the population the passive defences served. Like so many of the wartime organisations, changes occurred that refined and strengthened the civil defences.

Exmouth had formed seven squads of civil defence workers and had been experimenting with positioning their air raid sirens at different locations. The Exmouthians heard, no doubt with some relief, that the Royal Marine Corps were to establish a camp at Littleham covering an area of 58 acres. Summer holiday trade was good at Exmouth during 1939. Exmouth has sandy beaches that not only attracted the visitor, but also the sand artist. As soon as the sea began to recede and enough sand was uncovered, the sand artist started work. Out of the wet sand, as if by magic, there was a church, a castle or a lion; some artists were opportunists and would, if there was a royal event, produce a royal portrait or perhaps build Buckingham Palace.

But the sand now had a more sanguine role to play. Exmouth had piles of sand and 49 000 sandbags to fill; the seaside town had also received its quota of civilian gas masks that were assembled and distributed.

Throughout the county, men of the Territorial Army were being called up. Although most accepted the inevitability of this eventuality it did not make it easier for those of the family who remained at home. Devon communities were beginning to receive information that they should prepare to accept government sponsored evacuees. Sidmouth had sandbagged its shelter on the seafront as a place to go if an air raid occurred. A London theatre repertory company had to terminate its Sidmouth engagement at the Manor Hall Theatre which was required to be used for the reception of one thousand evacuees.

During the third week of August 1939, Southern Command received a cipher telegram informing them that an airborne landing against the RDF (RADAR) Station at Prawle Point was possible.[26]

The demand for ARP material in Plymouth at the end of August 1939 was so heavy that most of the supplies had run out as people shopped in their thousands to buy suitable black out material for their windows. Local suppliers wanted at least three weeks to cope with the demand. One Plymouth shop had sold at least 10 000 yards of black cloth, and 1000 paper blinds. Another shop had sold 30 000 yards of black out material. Black paint or black distemper was also sold in large amounts. There was a growing demand for food, being bought up on government advice. One Plymouth store handled several thousand food deliveries in one week during August.

Plymouth, as did other certain Devon towns, tried out an experimental bus that produced its own gas as fuel. The bus could reach a speed of 30 mph, but had problems pulling up hills.

At Tiverton two days before war was declared there had been an exceptional number of people in the town. Everyone seemed to go about their business, there was no undue excitement, but the local police were involved in presenting call up orders to many of the local men. The following day a more wartime appearance prevailed, as the police appeared on the streets wearing their 'tin helmets' and carrying gas service respirators slung over their shoulder. Sandbagging had started; large numbers of men arrived at the Territorial Drill Hall. The town on this night was blacked out and already the police were searching out offenders. One Tiverton resident had adequately blacked out his house, and then went into his garden and lit a bonfire!

On the eve of the declaration of war, some villages in the vicinity of Stokenham, near Slapton Sands, may have thought the Germans had already invaded the county. Nine aircraft flying from Aberdeen to Plymouth were compelled to land in a field at Stokenham because of bad weather.

Chapter 1 — References
(PC = Personal Communication)

1. *Western Morning News*, 1931.
2. *Sutton Harbour* (1970), Crispin Gill.
3. *Deller's Cafe* (1961), A History of Architecture of the Comparative Method.
4. PC: Mrs V. Par.
5. *According to our Cloth* (1984), Marcia Treece.
6. PC: Mrs E. White.
7. *North Devon Journal*, 1934.
8. *Western Evening Herald*, 1934.
9. *Western Evening Herald*, 1935.
10. *A Touch of Genius* (1988), Malcolm Brown.
11. PC: Mrs A. E. Green.
12. *The Story of the Imperial* (1982), Garbor Denes.
13. *Sidmouth Observer*, 1935.
14. *Exeter Airport* (1988), Geoff Worral.
15. PC: Mrs B. Kelway.
16. *Torquay ARP, History of Civil Defence organisation*. Torquay Library.
17. *History of Chagford* (1981), Jane Hayter-Hames.
18. Report: Staff College Camberly (Camberly).
19. *Kingsbridge Gazette*, 1938.
20. *The Britannia magazine* (Summer term), 1938.
21. *Dartmouth Chronicle*, 1938.
22. *Dartmouth Chronicle*, 1938.
23. *After the Battle (1989)*, The First Shots of World War II.
24. *Royal Sisters* (1990), Anne Edwards.
25. *Civil Defence* (1955), Terence H. O'Brien.
26. WO 126; 1252; Southern Command Diaries, PRO.

DEVON DURING THE PHONEY WAR

The lights went out all over Devon on the 1 September 1939, although there were exceptions where lights were dimmed and not extinguished. The 'blacked out' county gave the people the first indication that their peaceful way of life was going to be transformed. This was the beginning of their war on the Home Front.

Local civic authorities throughout the country had been aware since 1938 of the government's black out restrictions that would be implemented at the onset of hostilities. The black out was not just a matter of switching the lights off, removing electric light bulbs, or not lighting gas mantles. It meant the compulsory requirement of preventing any interior lighting from being seen from outside the premises. The occupier albeit civic authority, domestic, industrial, or military was responsible to impose and maintain their blacked out premises. If for any reason they failed they were liable to be prosecuted. The purpose of the black out was to prevent enemy aircrews from identifying their position and targets.

Off went the street lights at the beginning of September, so did all outside illuminated signs and lighted shop windows. Motorists and other transport drivers were required to ensure their vehicle lamps were fitted with regulation approved masks.

Those familiar lights that twinkled from the portholes of the ships that silently glided across the waters off the Devon coast were no longer visible from the land. The homely harbour lights were either dimmed or extinguished. A solitary moving coloured navigation light was sometimes the only evidence that a maritime vessel was passing nearby.

Coastal towns were required to be blacked out not only to prevent them from being detected from the air but also to ensure they did not silhouette any ships at sea.

There was for the Devon coastal dweller a double hazard, that of being knocked down by a car while crossing the road in the black out, or falling off an embankment or quayside into the water. Many such tragic accidents occurred throughout the war.

In the rural communities of Devon, the gentle soft shadows of an oil lamp stealthily being carried by a silhouetted figure were no longer to be seen through a cottage window. The room would need to be blacked out before lighting the oil lamp. Many people used curtain material of suitable light-proof quality to screen their windows. Boarding, shutters or constructed frames were also used as a black out. Preventing interior light from showing out on to the streets when an exterior door opened was a particular challenge for some shopkeepers.

In the early period of the wartime black out there were difficulties experienced by the responsible officers whose job was to check the efficiency of the black out in a community. One weakness in the system was the difficulty in detecting loft lights that many people would overlook to black out. To assess the effectiveness of the Plymouth black out, the city's Chief Constable flew over the city in a Sunderland flying boat of the Royal Australian Air Force to observe the situation.[1]

On a clear night, with a moon shining down on the buildings, streets and lanes of Devon, communities were distinctly visible. In contrast on a dark night, with reduced visibility, perhaps due to drizzle or a rolling mist, the county appeared deserted. For those walking out at night the white-painted kerbstones steps and corners of buildings helped in navigating the dark streets. The use of a battery torch, fitted with an approved mask was a useful aid to prevent an accident. To step on to a black cat in the black out was frightening for both the human and feline, but perhaps not so scaring as bumping into an unseen stray animal when walking in the darkness of a Devon lane.

Painting the kerb with white ARP paint at Duke Street, Dartmouth, opposite the Butterwalk. The black out caused many civilian injuries and deaths.

Being in an unfamiliar town or village and having to hurry to catch a bus or train in the black out, with no real knowledge of the layout of the streets, caused problems throughout the war years. Boarding a bus or a train meant travelling in a dimmed, almost forbidding, interior, often having to depend on the goodwill of others to confirm if one had reached one's required destination.

Infringing the government black out regulations was quickly and often emotively dealt with by an air raid warden or policeman, the latter having the power to bring about a prosecution. Even lighting a cigarette by striking a single match would bring about the earliest of war cries 'Put that light out!'.

In the railway stations, goods yards, marshalling yards, bus stations and the shipyards of Devon, restricted lighting was imposed. As a result these places became dimmer, resulting in a more forbidding look than being completely blacked out.

During the last days of peace and the early days of the war the people of the county were faced with the physical and emotional changes wrought by the face of war. Men were being called up to serve in the armed forces. At Ilfracombe many people were up and out early on the streets to see the local company of the 6th Devons march to the town's railway station. One young soldier who had overslept started his war by being delivered in a baker's van in time to catch the waiting train.[2]

On the eve of war the resorts were still full of visitors. At Exmouth, as the holidaymakers were strolling through the town, the local council workers were busy applying white ARP paint. Many reasons have been given to explain the busy holiday season up to the outbreak of war. There was for example a belief throughout the country that Britain would not go to war; others were oblivious to the political situation, while a minority went on holiday realising it would be their last vacation for sometime. The Exmouth shops were very busy on 2 September 1939, there were picnics on the beaches, cricket on the greens, the local cinemas were full, as were the dance halls. Yet on this fine sunny Saturday, local volunteers, many of them women, had been busy at the town's community hall preparing for the reception of London schoolchildren evacuees that were on this day travelling en route to Exmouth. Similar preparations were being made in other Devon communities, indeed some Devon towns and villages had already received Government sponsored evacuees.

Schoolchildren evacuees at Ealing Broadway railway station, Middlesex, about to board their train for the West Country.

On Sunday 3 September there were eighty people in the congregation at morning service at St Augustine Church, Plymouth. As the collection plate was being offered by the verger he whispered to the vicar conducting the service that war had been declared. A hymn was sung, then the vicar made a short statement to the congregation about the declaration, after which the National Anthem was sung. The solemn faces of the congregation showed there was no enthusiasm for war.[3] For most people, though, the news was not unexpected and, knowing that the Prime Minister Neville Chamberlain was to make an important announcement over the radio at 11am on Sunday, many people had decided to be at home by their radio set.

Teachers and their young evacuees had assembled at Smethurst Hall, Moretonhampstead to listen to the Prime Minister's broadcast. At Exmouth on this fateful morning visitors were on the beach and some had gathered around a small radio. In the afternoon as the sun came out more people arrived on the town's beach. Adults sat pensively in their deckchairs watching children splashing in the sea or making sandcastles.[4]

Many Devonians at this period still retained vivid memories of the dreadful trench fighting of the First World War and in particular the casualties sustained by the Devon Regiment. In addition there was the long list of Devon sailors who were lost during the naval battles. Thousands of Devon families were bereaved; the grief and mourning continued for years. Disabled servicemen were not an uncommon sight in the streets of the Devon towns and cities during the period between the wars. Monuments for the dead and missing of the Great War were to be seen in nearly every Devon town or village.

A belief, almost a conviction, that the West Country would be immune from enemy air attack was held by many people, this based on the supposition that the performance of the enemy bomber and the flying distance was a limiting factor. However, there had been a re-evaluation by the air staff of what could be forthcoming in the event of a war, and this presented a forbidding picture. Even so, the Air Council's assessment of the threat was largely based on the concept of long-range bombers flying from German bases. The prospect of a defeated Europe, with German airfields on England's doorstep was almost inconceivable, as was the thought that Devon would eventually become so closely associated with the conduct of the war that it would be the most military active county in the United Kingdom during the Second World War.

Air attacks were considered the most likely form of aggression to be used against the United Kingdom, but it was recognised that the county could also be attacked by seaborne troops. The spectre of the U Boat menace, with the severance of the island's sea communications, also haunted the British after the experiences of the disastrous effects of German submarine attacks on shipping in the First World War.

On the first day of the war giant silver barrage balloons were hoisted high up in the Plymouth sky as a defence against enemy air attack. Balloons were to become a familiar sight, not only at Plymouth, but at various Devon harbours where merchant ships, naval boats and amphibious invasion craft would be seen flying a balloon as a means of protection. Anti-aircraft guns, searchlights and sound detectors were part of Plymouth's air defence and were located at sites away from the centre of the city.

The air raid warden service throughout the county had been alerted, if not fully recruited. Civil defence lectures and demonstrations were being arranged. The air raid warden's posts were manned by full and part time members of the wardens' service. The possibility of the Germans dropping gas bombs meant the Devon civil defence had to prepare gas decontamination services. The day following the declaration of war an announcement was made that petrol rationing would be introduced in two weeks' time; private motorists on application would be issued with petrol coupons. There would be only one grade of petrol 'Pool'; all commercial brands would go.

An early Government order, just two days after the declaration of war was the impressment of horses in North Devon. A similar order had been issued two days after the outbreak of the First World War when the British Army made a compulsory purchase of horses. At Kingsbridge in 1914, some eight hundred horses were gathered in from the surrounding farms for Army inspection. The horses deemed suitable would be trained to haul heavy field artillery before being transported to France.[5].

In addition to the numerous visitors in Devon during the summer of 1939, thousands of civilian evacuees had or were arriving in the county. The influx of these people was the beginning of the remarkable history of the movement of people into, out of and across Devon throughout the war.

One of the abiding images of wartime England was that of the government wartime evacuee. The reason why schoolchildren were evacuated to Devon and elsewhere in 1939 was the belief by the British government that London and other cities were vulnerable to enemy air attacks. The government of the day expected London would suffer an immediate devastating air raid by an all-powerful enemy airforce. Such anticipated attacks were based on the 'Big Bang' theory, with the capital sustaining high numbers of casualties. This (mistaken) belief, of the enemy air force focusing its attention on London and the East of England, formed the basis for the planning of Britain's air defences.

The reception of the arrival of government sponsored evacuees in Devon was by no means an ad hoc arrangement. The government had, in 1938, recommended a scheme that in time of war meant that certain classes of the civilian population from large and densely congested industrial areas could be voluntarily evacuated. Special provision was given for the evacuation of young children accompanied by teachers and voluntary helpers, but not the children's parents. Such places were designated 'Evacuation Areas'.

Communities where evacuees were sent were officially known as 'Reception Areas', while communities that were not allowed to officially evacuate people, or act as a Reception Area, were referred to as 'Neutral Areas'.

In the pre-war planning of the Government's Evacuation Scheme a map and lists of Reception Areas were prepared with the proposal that the status of Plymouth would be an Evacuation Area in time of war. The plan indicated that

Table 1
Classification of UK Civilian Evacuees in Devon
during the Second World War

1 **Crisis period – outbreak of war (1939)**
   (A) Government sponsored schoolchildren
        i   Essex
        ii   London County Council
        iii Middlesex
        iv   Surrey
   (B) Private families and individuals
   (C) Staff of commercial organisations
   (D) Staff of public organisations

2 **London Blitz (1940)**
   Trickle Scheme
   Schoolchildren and families

3 **Bristol Blitz (1940)**
   Schoolchildren

4 **Plymouth Blitz (1941)**
   Schoolchildren and families

5 **Exeter Bædeker (1942)**
   Schoolchildren

6 **South Hams Villages Devon (1943)**
   Families

7 **London/SE England (1944)**
   Missile attacks, V1, V2
   Schoolchildren and families

Evacuation Areas would send their evacuees to the nearest convenient rural communities. London evacuees would for example move out to Reception Areas in the home counties. Plymouth would send its evacuees to its hinterland.[6] Within a matter of weeks government plans were changed and Plymouth was classified as a Neutral Area. This decision on the status of Plymouth caused considerable debate before the war which continued up to the time of the intensive air raids on the city in 1941. The Government's sponsored scheme of evacuation also include other priority classes: mothers with young families, expectant mothers, the elderly, the blind and disabled.

Prior to the war some Devon councils had prepared their reception schemes. Committees had been formed, billeting officers appointed. Public notices were displayed and placed in local newspapers inviting people to offer billets to evacuees if and when the time came. Notification and numbers were decided by the Ministry of Health. Early in 1939 Teignmouth Council were notified that 2400 evacuees would be accommodated in the district.[7]

A payment would be made to each household who billeted evacuees. The allowance for the first child would be ten shillings and sixpence, with nine shillings and sixpence per week for each additional child. This payment was made in advance at the local post office and was expected to cover full board. The response by the Devon communities in offering homes to evacuees was usually very good; there were people who were reluctant, and some people adamant they were not going to offer accommodation. Devon County Council notified the local community when to expect a batch of evacuees to arrive at a stipulated time. This did not always happen. At Paignton for example notification was received to expect a trainload of evacuees to arrive on a specific date, the reception committee were on the railway platform to greet them, but there were no signs of the anticipated evacuees.[8]

The departure journeys of the official evacuees were arranged by the Ministry of Transport. Schoolchildren were assembled at their school, perhaps wearing their

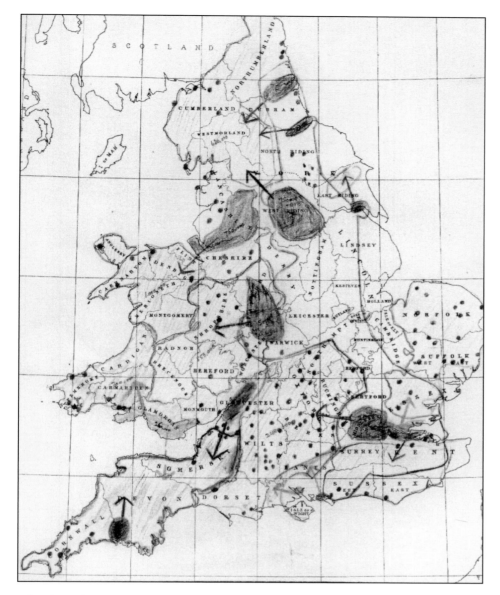

A secret pre-war (1938) government map of areas proposed for evacuation, or to become Reception Areas. Note that Plymouth is shown as an Evacuation Area.

school uniform, with their gas mask carried in the regulation cardboard box. Many of the children carried a small case, perhaps a carrier bag or a 'tied bundle' to carry their spare underwear, socks, night attire, and other personal items. The Ministry of Education had provided a list of possessions that each child should take, but the Ministry recognised that social circumstances prevented many of the children from having all the recommended items. Small stitched-up blankets to act as sleeping bags were also carried by some children. Each young person carried an identification label pinned on to their coat or jacket. Other than the teachers, members of the WVS were present for they were closely involved with administration of the Evacuation Scheme.

Children walked to the railway station, or were taken by bus. The government evacuees whose reception areas were in South West England boarded trains that departed from Paddington or Waterloo, the trains often stopping at suburban stations down the line to collect more children.

One of the first of many schools to arrive in Devon was the Acton Central School, Middlesex. Acton, a small town with a concentration of factories and an important rail network, would be involved in essential war production. The school travelled from Acton (mainline) Station on the morning of the 1 September 1939. One young school girl thought it was a practice run until she realised the train was travelling further and further into the country away from home.[9] Journey's end was at Kingsbridge, a small hillside town, the 'capital of South Hams'. As the Kingsbridge reception committee were arranging billets for the girls, the boys of the school were driven by bus to Dartmouth to be greeted by a reception committee at the Town Hall.

Government sponsored evacuees arriving at Torquay station, September 1939.

(Right and below) Evacuees in a painting group at Dartington in the summer of 1940. These children were from the Blackfriars and Southwark areas of London.

The school being billeted in two towns twelve miles apart meant some of the Acton schoolteachers having to commute between Dartmouth and Kingsbridge. Until rooms could be found to be used as classrooms, certain lessons were taken out in the open. The geography lesson would be a walk to a nearby village and the route mapped out on the return journey.

The schoolteachers made every effort to maintain social behaviour. Morning assembly was usually a lecture on how to behave in other people's houses. The young girl evacuees had to be aware of their own behaviour as any local disturbance in Kingsbridge was usually attributed to the evacuees. On occasions the students of the two sections of Acton Central School would meet up, and on one such visit the combined school went to the Royal Naval College. This was the first time the all-male domain had allowed so many young ladies to use their extensive sports facilities.[10] The Naval College was very co-operative for they also offered the Dartmouth evacuees the use of their indoor swimming pool, with naval instructors teaching the boys to swim.

Life for a young schoolgirl evacuee living at Kingsbridge during the latter part of 1939 was very much a matter of conforming to a set routine. The days were spent at lessons in local rooms that had been made available. Nearly every evening there was homework; being an evacuee did not excuse one from this particular task. Any free time was spent knitting or reading, some girls were allowed to listen to selected radio programmes. Week-ends would include helping with household shopping and going out for long walks, which for many girls was

a constant delight. Walking in the Devon lanes, then through wooded areas, finding flowers and plants that for them were seen for the first time, was a new dimension to their lives.[11]

Further inland at historic Totnes, built by the upper tidal reaches of the River Dart, the boys from Berrymede School Acton were detrained after their long journey and taken by bus to the nearby villages of Bittaford, Wrangaton and Ugborough. Two of the boys were billeted in a manor house, near Ivybridge. The manor house to them was 'out of this world' with a staff of five servants, a cook, kitchen-maid, two housemaids, parlour-maid, three gardeners, two grooms and a chauffeur; and this was the wartime staff. The boys lived with the servants. The master of the manor was a huntsman and eventually introduced the young evacuees to the hunt.[12]

Two brothers evacuated to Totnes were billeted with a well known Totnes family, the father of which owned a garage and was always referred to as 'God'. The two brothers were always in trouble with the police; they had five different billets and on one occasion fell into the River Dart, yet somehow they managed to enrol for ballet classes at Dartington Hall![13]

On the day the Acton Central School arrived in the South Hams, over four hundred children from the Priory School Acton arrive at Teignmouth station, some of whom were transferred by bus to Dawlish.

At Paignton and Torquay evacuees from the London County Council area began to arrive. One young evacuee travelling with her school from New Cross, London reacted with disbelief when told that some of the cliffs in Devon were red, for she had only seen the white cliffs on the south coast of England. Disbelief turned to wonderment when travelling along the beautiful coastal rail route from Exeter past the red cliffs of Dawlish Warren.[14]

The evacuee children arrived at their safe havens to be introduced into an entirely new way of life, and into a completely different environment. How the children settled into their billets, and their subsequent social behaviour, varied. The term 'culture shock' was not in the general vocabulary but many children experienced it, and soon began to return to their homes. Similarly, those households who had taken in evacuees responded in various ways. The experience for them of taking in young persons was also something entirely new. Two publications relating to evacuees in Devon are recommended reading.[15,16]

Friday, 1 September 1939 is a date associated with the arrival of the government schoolchildren to Devon. They were not however the first evacuees to arrive in the county, with many known examples of earlier arrivals.

The National Association of Local Government Officers moved during August from their London offices to the holiday camp at Croyde Bay, North Devon.[17] At Crediton, the finance staff of Gaumont British News, so well known at the time for its weekly newsreels seen on many cinema screens, arrived during August 1939 to occupy 'Newcombe', a Georgian house.[18]

One week before the outbreak of war, a special train arrived at Torquay with the staff of the Prudential Assurance Company, Holborn, who used the Victoria and Albert Hotel, Torquay, and the indoor bowling green Paignton as the company's offices. The staff were given temporary accommodation in local hotels.

Considerable publicity has always been given to the government sponsored evacuees to Devon, yet it was the private evacuees that first made a significant addition to the wartime population.

Private evacuees, had previously arrived in Devon at the time of the Munich crisis (1938) only to return home. Some twelve months later they appeared again to seek refuge. Such evacuees were accommodated by friends or relatives, others rented accommodation.

One London woman with her young family rented accommodation at Paignton. Her husband, exempt from the forces, was a coalman and drove down in his company's coal lorry once a month to visit his family. The two eldest sons, both under ten years of age, were on one occasion trapped on the rocks with a

Springtime: picking primroses at Lustleigh on the eastern edge of Dartmoor. These children were evacuated from Derwentwater Infant School, Acton, Middlesex in 1940.

Employees of the Prudential Assurance Company were evacuated to new offices in Torquay, prior to the outbreak of war, August 1939.

The spectre of hunger was ever present for many throughout the war. This London schoolboy evacuee has found the answer - a Devon pasty!

rising tide before being rescued. Getting trapped by the tide, was to be a common evacuee escapade. Every evacuee retains strong memories of their wartime experience. The fondest memory of this London woman was to visit the Louville Arms public house, buying a hot baked potato in its jacket that had been cored with an apple corer, with a fried sausage inserted.[19]

Another private evacuee arrived very late at night with her mother, aunt and grandmother at a home in Newton Abbot. The lady of the house was apparently well off and kept two resident servants, a gardener, and owned a Rolls Royce. The evacuated family had the use of a drawing room with dark-green heavy velvet drapes and shutters on its windows. The air was pervaded with a musky smell of books and upholstery. The hall was imposing; black and white tiles, with a large hat stand and an aspidistra plant. The evacuees slept in the same dark bedroom on the first floor, with hot water jugs and basins supplied for washing.

The lady of the house had a habit of roaming around the house barefoot with her long grey hair flowing down her back. Although simply eccentric, to a young girl evacuee she presented a frightening sight. The master of the house died while the evacuated family were in residence and was laid out for all to see on a four-poster bed.

The great treat for the young girl was to visit a mobile fish and chip bar that resembled a steam-roller. Painted green and gold it had polished brass barley-sugar twist columns and the hot fried chips were shovelled into a bag with a small brass shovel.[20]

At the end of September 1939, four weeks into the war, over 82 000 evacuees had arrived in Devon. The private evacuees outnumbered the government evacuees by approximately 700 per cent.

The official history of the war records there were an estimated 71 800 private evacuees in Devon during this time, compared with 10 200 government official evacuees.[21] These figures are not adjusted to account for the number of people who returned home.*

If the arrival of the evacuees was producing social problems, the declaration of war at the height of the summer holiday season created others. Whatever the reason for all the visitors being in Devon on the outbreak of war, the reality was that many of them were in the wrong place at the wrong time. At Ilfracombe the

*As a guide to the status of the evacuees associated with Devon a 'Classification of UK Civilian Evacuees' is shown on page 24. To refer to all such people as 'evacuees' is misleading and the list will help to dispel any myth that all the wartime evacuees in Devon originated from London.

Post Office handled a record number of telegrams and the sudden departure of holidaymakers from the town produced long queues at the railway station to the extent that passengers were only allowed on the platform in controlled groups. Other people were leaving by car or coach as quickly as possible. As this exodus was in progress, Ilfracombe's estate agents were being inundated with telephone calls from people in London and the east coast of England with enquiries as to the availability of rented houses or furnished apartments.

One golfer staying on at Ilfracombe was not to be denied his pleasure, not without a temporary fright, however. He was about to chip on the third green, when he heard what to him was an explosion. In his worst moments he thought the invasion of England had begun, but he continued to play on. At the nineteenth hole he learnt he had heard the rocket discharged as a signal for the Ilfracombe lifeboat![22]

One of the announcements made after the Prime Minister's broadcast to the nation on the 3 September 1939 was an order forbidding the gathering of people in places of public entertainment, resulting in the immediate closure of cinemas, theatres, dancehalls and the cancellation of football matches, horse and dog racing. The annual Barnstaple fair was cancelled, although the town council was permitted to allow the fair's honoured guest to drink the traditional spiced ale.

At Bideford the annual regatta was cancelled. North Devon dart players were informed that owing to the international situation *Braunton's Darts Notes'* would no longer be published. The British government soon realised the ban on entertainments had no practical value and was possibly affecting the morale of the people. The order was relaxed on the 14 September 1939.

Only two weeks of the war had passed when a major disaster was suffered by the nation and, in particular, by Devon. The Devonport manned aircraft carrier HMS *Courageous* was torpedoed by the German submarine U29 and sank with the loss of 519 men. The carrier had only a few days earlier sailed from Devonport to the Western Approaches where the ship met her fate. There were anxious scenes at the main gate of the Royal Naval barracks Devonport as relatives scanned the list of the survivors. Many Devon women were widowed and many children lost their fathers.[23]

A remarkable photograph taken as the aircraft carrier HMS *Courageous* sinks within fifteen minutes of being torpedoed by U29 to the west of Ireland, Sunday 17 September, 1939. A total of 519 members of her crew perished, many of them Devon men.

Residents of the moorland town of Tavistock had some welcome news for, within a month of war being declared, the town's domestic rate had been reduced. With all the upheavals the war had caused, many domestic and social rural events continued if only in a modified form. The grouse shooting season coincided with the first wartime Tavistock Goose Fair. The latter event was organised on a restricted basis; gone were the popular roundabouts and most of the favourite amusement stalls, mainly because of black out restrictions. Visitors to the fair were carrying gas masks while some also carried steel helmets. Recently introduced petrol rationing saw many farmers arriving at the market on horseback. The weather was dreadful, and being wartime, the number of people attending the Goose Fair was significantly reduced.[24] In North Devon, the councillors of Combe Martin were asking 'When are the evacuees coming?'. Villagers were claiming they had lost hundreds of pounds by keeping their accommodation in reserve for evacuees, and refusing visitors.

The war effort on the Home Front of Devon had got underway. Individuals at home and groups, meeting perhaps in the village hall, were busy knitting and making garments for servicemen. Knitting was actively being pursued not only by women but by schoolchildren and men throughout the county.

Contributions were made in response to appeals by local voluntary organis-ations and this important Home Front activity gave many civilians an opportunity of doing something they felt was worthwhile. A knitting circle was also a social meeting point, particularly for the women who were now often alone.

The small South Hams village of Ugborough had in the early months of the war adopted the warship HMS *Impulse*. This pastoral-like interest was welcomed by the crew and echoed similar 'adoptions' by other Devon communities. The Ugborough adoption had been organised by the local WVS and included the provision of 'comforts' for the ship. Production was high, for the village women had, within a period of two months, knitted twenty-five pairs of bedsocks and mittens, and made altogether some five hundred garments.[25]

The first serious wartime fire in Devon occurred three weeks after war was declared when a well known furnishing store on Torquay's harbourside was set alight. The fire, not caused by enemy action, spread rapidly and the popular departmental store of Bobby's was soon ablaze.

In East Devon, at Budleigh Salterton, 'Henrietta's War' began in the form of humorous letters and sketches from the hand of an anonymous lady resident writing news on the Home Front.[26]

The familiar, perhaps over-used phrase 'Don't you known there is a war on?' was put to an individual who lived alone outside Newton Abbot. The local air raid warden visiting the man, was told he was not aware the country was at war! Another visit was made to a cottage in a remote village near South Molton in order to tell the occupier to comply with the black out regulations. The woman who lived in the cottage apologised and told the warden she was not aware of the war as she did not possess a radio, and never read the newspapers.

A wartime knitting circle at Torbay, South Devon, 13 August, 1940.

A newspaper photograph of the fire at the Williams & Cox furniture store in Torquay on 21 September, 1939. This was the first serious civilian fire to occur in Devon following the declaration of war.

Two illustrations from the popular wartime series 'Henrietta's War'.

The old women of Britain who will break Hitler's heart in the end

The Home Guard looked a little uncomfortable

The call up of men to the armed services had a severe impact on the local community; shops reduced staffing levels, and small businesses were, on occasions, closed down for the duration of the war. Personal problems were also far reaching. With a wife it went beyond the emotion of missing one's husband; there was also the adjustment to be made in coping with a family of children and having to budget on a reduced income. Many servicemen did not have their service pay supplemented by their peacetime employers, consequently their family at home lived in reduced circumstances.

Local doctors also often went off to war. An Exeter General Practitioner took on the entire medical practice of his brother-in-law and that of two other doctors who had been called up to serve in the armed forces. The practice had over 4500 patients, with only an elderly woman GP to give support. The surgery was always full with patients and at the time of an influenza epidemic over seventy people arrived, with patients having to sit on the stairs because of the overcrowding. Visiting patients in the black out was a nightmare as there were no lights to identify specific homes. Arrangements were made for someone to stand by the roadside with a torch outside the house to be visited, although this contravened black out regulations.[27]

At the outbreak of war there were no RAF fighter stations operational in South West England. The only active base was RAF Mountbatten, later associated with Coastal Command operations carried out by the Australians flying the large, graceful Sunderland Flying boats. Throughout the war people would watch from Plymouth Hoe as these giant aircraft skimmed gently across the surface waters of the Sound to become airborne.

Work had started on constructing RAF St Eval in North Cornwall that would rapidly expand to become an important RAF station. But this airfield did not

A RAAF Sunderland flying boat over the South Devon coast c.1940.

become operational until October 1939. Exeter's RAF fighter base began its operations in July 1940, in time for its fighters to participate in the Battle of Britain.[28]

Just two months after the declaration of war Southern Command Diaries record that a warning had been received that enemy airborne landings may be attempted by parachute troops to seize an 'aerodrome' or secure open spaces on which aircraft-carrying troops could land. The enemy troops would attempt to seize a port. The main target was Plymouth.[29]

The presence of the enemy, or what was believed to be the enemy, had been reported off the South Devon coast ever since the beginning of the war. One official report stated a U Boat was sighted near the Plymouth breakwater on the 13 September 1939. Other reports of their presence off the South Devon Coast were frequently made.[30]

With German peace proposals being rejected by the Allies, unrestricted warfare was anticipated. The British Admiralty notified the Commander in Chief, Western Approaches that there was now the possibility of air raids on Devon dockyards.[31]

The popular Warner's Holiday Camps at Paignton and Seaton were re-opened during October 1939 as internment camps for classified alien subjects. The smaller camp at Paignton was for those who were compulsorily interned, it was referred to as a 'privilege' camp. The larger camp was of wooden huts built close to the sea and when it rained the camp ground became waterlogged. The Seaton internees were subject to restrictions and were guarded, but the internees were allowed visitors. Seaton camp was a most remarkable congregation of alienated people. The British government had brought together Jewish refugees, Germans who had

Painted grey, the ill-fated Blue Star liner *Arandora Star* lies at anchor in Dartmouth harbour just after the outbreak of war.

fled from Nazi Germany, together with German Nationals and known Nazi's. This strange mix living in the same compound resulted in an unofficial truce between the Jews and the Nazis, although fighting sometimes broke out.

Later, at the time of the expected invasion of England, the government decided on the mass internment of alien subjects, including Italians. A decision was also made to deport many aliens to Canada. The pre-war luxury liner the *Arandora Star* was ordered to Liverpool to transport 1600 internees, including 185 aliens from Seaton Camp, across the Atlantic.

During the early weeks of the war, many Dartmouthians would have been familiar with the *Arandora Star*, for having returned from New York in September, now painted in a wartime grey, the liner was ordered to Dartmouth to await further orders.

The *Arandora Star* sailed from Liverpool on the 1 July 1940. But in the Atlantic she was torpedoed and sunk by a German U Boat commanded by Gunther Prien who had also been responsible for sinking the Devonport-built battleship HMS *Royal Oak* at Scapa Flow. Among the survivors of this wartime tragedy were several internees from the Seaton camp.[32]

As 1939 wore on many visual changes could be seen on the Home Front. The familiar red-painted fire engines were now coloured grey, as were saloon cars and lorries of the civil defence. Small compact trailer pumps, used for fighting fires, were a common sight.

Many more buildings were protected with sandbags, the white ARP paint now an accepted part of the environment. Signs directing people to air raid shelters were stencilled on walls or painted on buildings. Military signs, meaningless to most civilians, gave indications to service personnel as to the direction of a base or store. Government information posters, artistically designed and colourful, sometimes humorous, were displayed at railway stations, bus shelters, and other public places. Nearly every Devon town now had a small forces canteen.

Contracts for brick-built public air raid shelters had been signed and these were hastily being erected in the streets, local parks, school playgrounds and on sea-front promenades. Whatever protection these shelters were to give during air raids they were a model of how to destroy the local environment. The public shelters were forbidding places, out of bounds for children, were usually damp, sometimes flooded, and often a target for the local vandals. They needed to be thoroughly cleaned out once enemy air raids started.

Public air raid shelters, Plymouth 1940. Local contractors were responsible for constructing brick-built air raid shelters to government specifications, although corners were sometimes cut for the sake of extra profit.

Air raid wardens posts were established in most local communities. Some of these were purpose built of brick or concrete, others utilised existing buildings. Inside, they all had a familiar look about them: a polished wooden table with at least two telephones, one or two chairs, an assortment of official forms and a log book. Depending on the size of the area served, the post would have stirrup pumps, rattles to warn of gas attack, gas decontamination clothing, steel helmets, pick axes, at least one made up bed with grey blankets for the night duty warden, and a sacred place to make a cup of tea.

At Totnes some local humorist made it known that a warden's post of a particular sector was called 'Hotel Splinters', the Ambulance Station 'Hotel de Blast' and the town's soup kitchen 'Hotel Fritz'.

The Ministry of Agriculture did little to humour the Devon farmer, or make him happy. The Ministry had indicated to the farmers the need to increase their yield and change their ways. There was already a shortage of male farm workers in the county. The Women's Land Army (WLA) were beginning to recruit and although the attitude of Devon farmers to employ women on the land would eventually change, farmers in the early period of the war were reluctant to employ women as agriculture workers. In Devon there were only twenty-four Land Army employed on farms at the end of 1939.[33]

There were people in the country who believed that the war would soon be over, probably by Christmas. The Royal Air Force had been flying missions over enemy territory dropping bombs and propaganda leaflets. On the Western Front in France there had been skirmishes between the opposing forces, with some ground won or lost, but no real land offensive with what could be described as heavy fighting had occurred.

The BBC radio was an important means of national communication and entertainment, as were the local cinemas that showed weekly newsreels of the progress of the war. The news media were censored and the conduct of the war was expressed in a tone of guarded optimism. One of the popular comedy shows was ITMA (*It's That Man Again*) starring the comedian Tommy Handley. Some of the most popular comedy characters of the time were created by Jack Train, a Plymouth born comedian.

Early wartime songs had silly lyrics, for example *We're Going To Hang Out the Washing On the Siegfried Line* and *Run Rabbit Run*. However, they were very popular with the nation. Despite the impending crisis people were still looking for breaks in the country. The catering and hotel trade was picking up as more people were booking to take a holiday, if only for a few days. A sense that things might not be so bad was reflected in the government's decision to reduce civil defensive capability in some areas. At Newton Abbot there was a reduction, while at Plymouth, the Government ordered a fourteen per cent cut back in the city's civil defence.[34]

The first wartime Christmas was approaching. Devon shops were stocked with Christmas presents, with plenty of toys for the children. Ilfracombe sent 350 Christmas parcels to local servicemen. The North Devon post offices handled more Christmas mail than the previous year of 1938. In East Devon it was a similar story as the traders of Tiverton were very pleased with their increased sales. Many but not all of the evacuees had returned home to be with their families. The evacuee children who remained joined in the local family Christmas festivities. It seemed that every Devon community that had received evacuee children had organised some form of Christmas celebration for them.

At the Royal Oak Hotel and assembly rooms, South Brent, there were parties and concerts organised for the children, while at Moretonhampstead the children were entertained with a Punch and Judy show. In contrast the Ashburton Charities distributed cash, coal and bread to the needy. There was, it seems, at the time plenty of goodwill among the people of Devon. The Christmas holidays were celebrated without any interference from the war, with the exception of the absence of relatives and friends who were serving in the armed forces. Towns large and small held their Christmas dances. The Imperial Hotel, Torquay, that closed down at the beginning of the war had re-opened and held a grand gala fancy dress ball with crackers and balloons on Christmas night. On boxing night the hotel organised a huge party.[35] At Tavistock town hall four hundred people danced in the hall that had been decorated in red, white and blue with a GR monogram displayed on the balcony.

The New Year of 1940 was the time that the Death Watch Beetle was discovered in Lifton Church. At Tavistock three gas indicator boards were placed in the town for the detection of mustard gas, if it was used by the Germans. The presence of this gas would be detected by the formation of red spots on the indicator boards.

Local people filling sandbags at Dartmouth, 1939. Nearby the ancient Guildhall was surrounded with a wall of sandbags as protection against bombing.

Tavistock residents were informed that their town hall noticeboard would in future be used for important civil defence notices, not as it had been, for weather records.[36]

The Mayoress of Dartmouth had, with the help of many local people, organised a New Year's treat at the small, sandbagged Guildhall for all the town's evacuees. Up the road from the Guildhall a motorist had been apprehended by a policeman for not having his car bumper and running board painted white according to the black out regulations; the motorist was subsequently prosecuted. The summer of 1940 seemed a long way away but, even with so many men called up, Dartmouth Cricket Club planned to field three cricket elevens in the coming season.

But the realities of war were beginning to intrude upon the normalities of life in the county. The activities on land, air and off the Devon coast resulted in the loss of both friend and foe. An early image of the ferocity of war was seen by hundreds of people on the 16 January 1940 who watched from the North Devon coast the scene of the blazing oil tanker *Inverdargle* on fire in the Bristol Channel after hitting a mine off Foreland Point near Lynmouth. As the tanker burned an aircraft circled the stricken vessel. Lifeboats were launched from Ilfracombe, Lynmouth, and Minehead to search for survivors. The crew of one of the lifeboats was at a funeral when it received the urgent message to put to sea. The oil tanker, that was sailing to Avonmouth from Trinidad, eventually sank with the loss of 42 crew members.[37]

The first winter of war was as bleak as anyone could remember, yet in Devon one could not have wished for a more picturesque scene. At Dartmouth it seemed as if a large white carpet had descended on the town. The narrow streets of the town were dark and silent. What little traffic there was moved silently on the deep snow, while footsteps were muffled.

The very cold winter had an adverse effect on the town's trade, with the exception of the local plumbers who were in great demand to unfreeze water pipes. The warmest outside spot in Dartmouth was at the baker's shop off Foss Street. The bakery wall exuded a soothing warmth and children and adults would stop to press their hands on the warm bricks.[38]

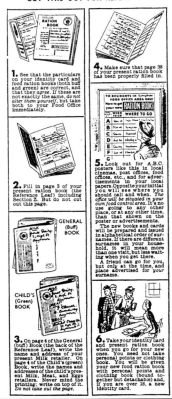

The River Dart traffic was not affected; the GWR steam ferry continued to glide back and forth across the river from Kingswear to Dartmouth. Ice formed in the town's boat float; further up the Dart the river froze over at Old Mill Creek trapping swans in the ice.

At Slapton Ley, the freshwater froze from one end to the other, allowing people to skate over the ice, one person even producing a bicycle and riding it over the entire length of the frozen Ley. Local bus services were suspended, vehicles stranded. At the remote village of South Pool the local hunt met, but because of the frozen ground the hunt was abandoned and everyone went home.

The month of January 1940, was the time food rationing was introduced for civilians. Butter, sugar, bacon and cooking fat were the first foods to be rationed. The Ministry of Food placed notices in the local newspaper giving details and instructions on how to apply for ration books. The buff coloured books (green for children) were issued from the local food office or public hall. Children under the age of six years had a different food allowance, as did certain categories of manual workers. Later, in March 1940, meat was rationed by a stated price for each person. Sausages and other processed meats were not placed on ration, but there was no guarantee of availability. Brawn and sausages were examples of 'under the counter' availability. This was seldom a fair way of distribution and the system caused problems for the butcher.

The distribution of certain rationed foods was not always efficiently organised. The quality of meat was not of the same standard throughout the county, and butchers, farmers and local authorities complained to the Ministry of Food.

At Sidmouth, over 11 000 ration books were issued at the local food office. This office also publicly announced that there would be no additional food allowance granted to vegetarians or Jews in lieu of the bacon and ham ration.[39] There was the wartime paradox that at the time food rationing was introduced, the local Dartmouth fishermen were throwing their catches of sprats back into the sea as the prices offered were so low.[40]

The attention of the nation was directed to the arrival of HMS *Ajax* at Devonport on the 30 January 1940, and later to the homecoming of HMS *Exeter*. These two warships, together with a New Zealand cruiser, had been involved in the dramatic South Atlantic naval encounter with the German battleship *Graf Spee*, and the engagement known as The Battle of the River Plate at which the German warship was scuttled. This was the first British naval victory of the war.

The news of the arrival of the Chatham-manned cruiser HMS *Ajax* at Plymouth, had been announced over the local Rediffusion service. At daybreak naval tugs towed the warship to her berth at Devonport. Crowds assembled along the sea-front to welcome her and as the cruiser approached the dockyard the 'yardies' dropped their tools and joined in the welcome. The warship had been damaged in action and had suffered casualties.

It was two weeks later, on the 15 February 1940, that the Devonport built and manned cruiser HMS *Exeter* arrived with an escort into Plymouth Sound. The *Exeter* was extensively damaged in action and was compelled to sail to the Falkland Islands for temporary repairs before attempting the long Atlantic sea voyage back to Plymouth. The *Exeter* was fitted with false gun turrets in the fore of the ship so as to deceive the enemy.

On the cold grey morning when the *Exeter* arrived, every vantage point had been taken up by the huge crowds of people who came to welcome back their conquering heroes. Winston Churchill, the First Sea Lord arrived on a naval barge for the official welcoming ceremony. The ship's company were assembled on the quarterdeck as they listened to Churchill, who stood on a capstan, offering the nation's tribute.

Sixty of the ship's company were not at Devonport for they had lost their lives and were buried in the South Atlantic. The following day the men of HMS *Exeter* marched through the streets of Plymouth to the Guildhall where they were entertained to a civic luncheon by the city fathers.[41]

Shortages of consumer goods and restricted services were a growing source of frustration for many people: razor blades, cosmetics, and torch batteries were a few of the many items that were difficult to obtain. It was however still possible to buy a suit off the peg or to pay extra and have it measured to fit. Shopping at Exeter, with sufficient money to spend, one could purchase coffee ground from freshly roasted coffee beans, or enhance the weekend 'mini roast' with French beans and asparagus, with fresh pineapple for dessert. Those women who considered their figures were able to have their corsets made to measure.

Exonians had now received evacuees into their homes. One Exeter family had

HMS *Exeter* sails triumphantly into Devonport, February 1940, after her gallant action at the Battle of the River Plate. Fitted out with dummy guns in order to mislead the enemy, she limped back to port after temporary repairs in Falkland Islands.

two evacuees billeted with them with the surname Hitler. With such a name they were too embarrassed to tell their neighbours. Mr Hitler, the evacuees' father was in the RAF.[42] On the day when two hundred parents of evacuees had travelled to Exeter to visit their children, the city's surveyor presented his scheme for the provision of public air raid shelters. A unique, if somewhat sombre play was staged at Exeter based on the effect a 500 lb bomb exploding. The production, open for the public to attend, was for more realistic civil defence training. Exeter people were led to believe that Sunday cinemas would soon be opened, and the local watch committee would be recommending a relaxation in the Sabbath ruling. The proposals were debated, but the city's cinemas remained closed on Sundays.[43]

The warm weather of spring 1940 encouraged people to venture outside. Great Torrington held its traditional May fair with a wartime May Queen and dancing in the streets. Exmouth, in more serious mood, posted notices throughout the town ordering the local townspeople to have their gas masks inspected at the Civil Defence Headquarters. An inspection held at Sidmouth by the council's Gas Committee was to decide what shade of green the town gasholders should be painted. Sidmouth people were reminded that an order had been introduced requiring all householders to clear their lofts and that it was an offence for civilians to camouflage their cars.[44]

Prosecutions continued throughout Devon regarding the breaching of the black out regulations. Even the City of Plymouth was not immune and pleaded guilty when the Lord Mayor, Alderman and Citizens of the City were fined for a black out offence at the City's Guildhall.[45]

Notification was received that more government evacuees would be arriving in Devon. Ilfracombe was advised that two hundred schoolchildren from Dagenham would be coming, and the assembly hall was to be used as the reception area, while at Barnstaple at least 2500 children were expected and were to be billeted in the area.[46]

Early in 1940 a decision had been made that Plymouth would be used for training crews and equipping the massed-produced Fairmile Motor Launches

Winston Churchill, as First Sea Lord, delivers the nation's thanks to the crew of HMS *Exeter* after their long and dangerous voyage from the South Atlantic (15 February, 1940).

(ML's) to be used for harbour defence and anti-submarine escort duties in coastal waters. A number of the contracts were given to various small Devon shipbuilding yards for the construction of these craft. This work was taken up by Blackmore, Bideford; P. K. Harris, Appledore; and Morgan Giles of Teignmouth. Other Devon ML boatbuilders were S. B. Hall, Galmpton; J. W. Upham, Brixham; and Mashford Bros at the Cremyll Yard, Plymouth. The important contribution made by these Devon boatbuilders is part of the remarkable story of Fairmile Motor Launches in the various theatres of war.[47]

Government regulations and directions that were issued to farmers were having the effect of causing anger and frustration among the farming community. The expected yields, restrictions on marketing, and on what or what not to grow were still unclear to the farmers. Poor prices of mutton and corn resulted in large acres of arable land reverting back to grass. The Government Agriculture Scheme encouraged farmers to plough up; Devon farmers were urged to plough for milk, plough for beef, plough for pigs, even to plough for victory. Devon farmers had the largest task of any county in the United Kingdom under the ploughing scheme. Tractors were being made available to the farmers to replace the horse-drawn plough to enable as much land as possible to be ploughed up in time for seed sowing. North Devon farmers were asked to plough 80 000 acres of land for growing corn and potatoes.

Many of the 12 000 holdings in Devon were under 100 acres. The people who worked these small units mainly depended on poultry and pigs and in the early months of 1940 there was a shortage of feed.

Wild rabbits were a common pest and a major problem for Devon farmers. The Agriculture Committee, aware of the problem, impressed on the owners and tenants of agricultural land the importance of destroying these vermin. Good prices were paid for rabbits, a much sought after meat by the wartime housewife, cooks and hotels. The offer of a rabbit was never refused. The meat, a texture not unlike chicken, was cooked in a stew, prepared in a pie or baked in an oven. The skin of a rabbit was also useful and was used for making gloves and other articles of clothing.

Land Girls were being recruited in growing numbers by the reluctant Devon farmers. This had been a slow start, but eventually the significant contribution they were to make was acknowledged. The Land Army Girls were recognised by their distinctly attractive uniforms: fawn corduroy breeches, stockings, green pullover, heavy brown shoes, all requiring clothing coupons. This uniform was not suitable for daily work on the land and the girls usually wore overalls, with perhaps a sack wrapped around the waist to serve as an apron. The essential rubber boots were often difficult to obtain.

The open air life on a farm involved harvesting, cleaning pig-sties, muck-spreading and milking cows, along with many other tasks. There were the specialists too, one job being to catch rats.[48]

The life of the Land Army Girl could be rough and tough. One young woman who chose to work on the land was sent to a forty acre moorland farm, seven miles from Tavistock. The farm had no electricity or drains, not even a septic tank. The water was hand pumped from a well. A bus called at the farm once a week on market day, otherwise it was a five mile walk to the main road to catch a bus. One day off was given every two weeks. On the eve of the day off there was the five mile walk to Mary Tavy railway station, and there being no station staff the train had to be waved down to stop. On a winter evening a lighted hurricane lamp was left in a little blacked out waiting room for use by any passenger to get the train to stop at the station. The hill-farms on Dartmoor were governed by wartime regulation, but being so isolated and not particularly fertile they tended to escape the closer scrutiny of the Ministry of Agriculture.

Farms that kept more than fifty hens had to send all their eggs to the Ministry. Many of the Dartmoor hill-farmers therefore kept forty-nine hens or less and did not bother to register. Farmers were encouraged to grow potatoes as a crop and received a subsidy, and with the good rainfalls over Dartmoor the potato crop did well. Other crops grown were oats, rye, turnip, cabbage and kale. The neighbouring farms being scattered there was limited social life in this moorland area. The farming communities often consisted of elderly or middle-aged farmers, their wives, and hordes of young children, including evacuees.[49]

Sunday was a solemn occasion. Best clothes were worn and most people attended church. Local authorities would chain and lock the swings and roundabouts in the parks and recreation areas. Cinemas were closed; nearly every shop was closed.

On fine and dry Sunday evenings the community would be out all dressed up, looking extremely smart, performing the ritual of slowly walking up and down and across the town's streets, or along the sea-front. This traditional Sunday parade was of great social benefit as it gave the local people the opportunity to stop and gossip and catch up on the latest war news.

The long winter nights of 1940 had passed. The black out, knitting woollen socks, listening to variety shows on the radio, the restricted BBC programmes, the presence of evacuees, propaganda posters, being made aware of what it is like serving on a minesweeper or the hazards undertaken by the Merchant Navy, letters from relatives away serving in the forces, produced a strange wartime social climate. Up to the Spring of 1940 few shots had been fired in anger. The days passed, the weeks passed by, then on one morning in May 1940, everyone woke up from sleep to find everything had changed.

Chapter 2— References
(PC = Personal Communication)

1. *Australia in the War* Herington.
2. PC: Mr P. G. Southcombe.
3. *St Augustine Church War Diary*, Plymouth, West Devon Record Office.
4. *Exmouth Chronicle*, September 1939.
5. *Around Kingsbridge* (1988), Kathy Turner.
6. HO 186; 128; Evacuation. PRO.
7. 'Evacuation to Teignmouth' (1992), C. Channon and M. Channon. *Rep Trans Devon Assc. Advmt Sci.*
8. 'Evacuation to Torquay' (1992), J. Whitcher. 'Reaction in Devon to Invasions'. Dev Ass.
9. PC: Mrs E. Mason.
10. PC: Mrs A. Warren.
11. PC: Mrs E. Mason.
12. PC: Mr I. Richter.
13. PC: Mr R. Harris.
14. PC: Mrs B. Ducan.
15. 'Evacuation to Teignmouth' (1992), C. Channon and M. Channon. *Rep Trans Devon Assc. Advmt Sci.*
16. 'Evacuation to Torquay' (1992), J. Whitcher. 'Reaction in Devon to Invasions'. *Rep Trans Devon Assc. Advmt Sci.*
17. PC: Mrs S. Brown.
18. PC: Mrs N. Minting.
19. PC: Mrs G. Spencer.
20. PC: Irene Martin.
21. *Problems of Social Policy* (1950), R.M. Titmus. HMSO.
22. *Ilfracombe Chronicle*, September 1939.
23. *It Came to Our Door* (1945), H. P. Twyford.
24. *Tavistock Gazette*, October 1939.
25. *Totnes Times*, October 1939.
26. *Henriettta's War* (1939), Joyce Dennys.
27. PC: Mrs A. S. Gray.
28. *Action Stations 5.* Chris Ashworth.
29. WO 166; 1252: *Southern Command Diaries*, PRO.
30. WO 166; 2060; *Plymouth fixed Defences*, PRO.
31. WO 166; 1252; *Southern Command Diaries*, PRO.
32. *Collar the Lot* (1980), Peter and Lini Gillman.
33. *Women on the Land* (1990), Carol Twinch.
34 Plymouth Emergency Committee No. 39 (1939), West Devon Records Office.
35. *The Story of the Imperial* (1982), Garbor Denes.
36. *Tavistock Times*, January 1940.
37. *Britain's Sea War* (1989), John M. Young.
38. PC: D. Wassell.
39. *Sidmouth Observer*, January 1940.
40. *Dartmouth Chronicle*, January 1940.
41. *The Story of Plymouth* (1950), R. A. J. Walling.
42. PC: Mrs V. Parr.
43. *Express and Echo*, Exeter April 1940.
44. *Sidmouth Observer*, April 1940.
45. *The Phoney War on the Home Front* (1961), E. S. Turner.
46. *Ilfracombe Chronicle*, March 1940.
47. *Allied Coastal Forces of WW2* (1990), J. Lambert and Al Ross.
48. *The Land Girl, 1940 PRO.*
49. PC: Mary Kizer.

THE AFTERMATH OF DUNKIRK

O n the 10 May 1940, the German Army using blitzkrieg ('lightning war') tactics in an attempt to bring about a rapid victory, invaded the neutral countries of Belgium and Holland. The Germans' objective was to defeat the Franco–Anglo armies. In London the King had invited Winston Churchill to become Prime Minister, who was now to be the 'Nation's Supremo' for directing the war against Hitler. From this date the conflict would become a war of attrition.

Anticipating the likely course of events the Commander in Chief, Western Approaches, requested that Southern Command should send detachments of troops to Exmouth, Paignton, Brixham, Torquay and Dartmouth to prevent the landing of aliens from refugee ships at unauthorised ports.[1]

The manner of the German airborne forces' invasion of the Low Countries, and the subsequent enemy advances, had the immediate effect of concentrating the minds of the British military on a possible invasion of England.

Four days after the German offensive, the Secretary of State for War, Sir Anthony Eden, made a national appeal for men between the ages of 17 and 65, who were not liable for military service, to join a newly created defence force, the Local Defence Volunteers (LDV). The force was not a resurgence of the British Legion, although many men who had previously served in the First World War were to have an important role in the training of this new defence force.

Within five days of the national appeal a quarter of a million men had volunteered. The response in Devon was immediate. Among the 135 men who had presented themselves at Tavistock were veterans of the Boer War; one man who asked to be recruited was 79 years of age.[2] At the time of its formation this was a force without a uniform, only an armband indicated that the wearer was a volunteer. Firearms were scarce. The husband of Agatha Christie joined an LDV unit at Brixham and shared a rifle with ten other men.[3] For some units there were no arms at all.

The German advance across Europe resulted in the most dramatic wartime events; each day there was news of significant enemy gains. Three days after their initial assault the German army had reached the outskirts of Rotterdam. With Dutch resistance broken, Holland surrendered to the Germans on the 15 May 1940.

In response to the Germans, British and French forces advanced into Belgium, a move anticipated by Hitler. The trap had been sprung, resulting in German armoured units and motorised divisions outflanking the Allied forces. This was the start of a general retreat; there were gallant defensive actions that held up some advancing German units, but it was to end with thousands of British soldiers driven on to the beaches of Dunkirk, while other troops fought a gallant rearguard action through North West France.

The British Cabinet authorised Lord Gort to effect his plan (Operation Dynamo) for the withdrawal of troops from the Dunkirk beaches on the 26 May 1940. Civilian refugees were, however, arriving in the United Kingdom before this date. On the 20 May 1940, a Belgian ship arrived at Brixham and attempted to land two hundred Belgian refugees. Disembarkation was refused and the ship was ordered to Weymouth.[4]

More than 800 vessels of all shapes and sizes were involved in the Dunkirk evacuation. In South Devon a fleet of small craft were assembled and sailed to

Let us brace ourselves to our duty

Upon this battle depends the survival of Christian civilisation .... We shall do our duty and so bear ourselves that, if the British Commonwealth and Empire lasts for a thousand years, men will still say "This was their finest hour."

THE PRIME MINISTER

BOROUGH OF BARNSTAPLE

IMPORTANT NOTICE.

ALL PERSONS willing to enrol as **Voluntary Workers** to **Carry Out Defensive Measures Against Possible Landing by Enemy Aircraft** are requested to Register their names and addresses at any Post Office, or with the Borough Surveyor at The Castle.

F. J. BROAD, Town Clerk.

Three of the North Devon and Bristol Channel paddlesteamers which went to withdraw troops from Dunkirk. (Top)The *Glen Avon* , a familiar sight at Ilfracombe before the war, returning to England, her decks laden with soldiers. (Centre) The *Brighton Belle* in distress after striking a submerged rock having successfully rescued 800 troops. (Bottom) The beached *Devonia* abandoned at Dunkirk after an attack by enemy aircraft (taken from a German postcard of the time).

Dartmouth where they stayed overnight. There a decision was made not to use them for this venture.[5] The GWR steam ferry the *Mew* that glided to and from Dartmouth and Kingswear, steamed up the English Channel to offer its services at Ramsgate Harbour. The ferry's draft was to deep to allow it to get close enough to the French coast to embark troops and subsequently it returned to its work on the River Dart.[6] Two small South Devon boats known to have participated in the Dunkirk evacuation were the motor launch *Lady Cable*, based at Teignmouth, and the *Seymour Castle*, built at Dartmouth and used for trips up the River Dart. The

Lady Cable transported five hundred men from the beaches of Dunkirk to the larger ships anchored off the French coast.

Those glorious paddlesteamers that before the war had delighted holidaymakers on excursions from Ilfracombe to Swansea, and elsewhere in the Bristol Channel, were closely involved in the Dunkirk evacuation. The paddlesteamer *Waverley*, that early in the war had been commissioned by the navy under the name of HMS *Snaefell*, went to Dunkirk. Later she was sunk by enemy aircraft in July 1941. The well known *Devonia* that paddled on the Ilfracombe to Swansea service sailed to Dunkirk but was damaged by an enemy air attack and abandoned on the beach at La Panne. The beached paddlesteamer later excited the interest of the Germans who photographed it, producing a postcard of it stranded on the beach.[7]

Bayonet practice on Slapton Sands 31 August, 1940. Soldiers of the Durham Light Infantry were based in South Devon following their return from Dunkirk.

(Top) Smiling British soldiers rescued from Dunkirk land at Millbay Dock, Plymouth, July 1940. (Bottom) Transferred to smaller tenders, such as the *Sir John Hawkins*, the troops arrive at the quayside, their mixed emotions evident on their faces.

Wartime censorship restricted the reporting of sensitive news. Only with the passing of time was the fate of Devon servicemen known. Eventually information, and sometimes a photograph, appeared in local newspapers giving news of Devon men who were at Dunkirk.

Many injured and exhausted servicemen who arrived from the beaches of Dunkirk were sent to Devon to recuperate before reporting back to their units. For example, four thousand soldiers arrived by train from Dunkirk to convalesce at Exeter, Crediton and Ilfracombe.[8] The warm summer of 1940 was long afterwards associated with the memory of wounded Dunkirk troops in the Tavistock area, lying in the fields basking in the sunshine. In one home nearby, soldiers would pay a halfpenny to have a bath; there only being a coldwater tap meant heating water in a washhouse boiler. Every week five soldiers visited the house for their bath and at no time did the family have any trouble with the troops.[9]

Men of the Durham Light Infantry were sent to the South Hams after Dunkirk, using part of Slapton Sands to practice their bayonet drill.

The last day of May 1940 was very hot. A train arrived at Plymouth packed with French troops, the first of many troop-trains that were to carry over 60 000 French soldiers from Dunkirk to the city during a period of eight days.

Some of the troops were detrained, fed at the dockside, before embarking on to a ship. Others were marched away and accommodated at Raglan Barracks, Seaton Barracks and Plumer Barracks, while some were sent to the Citadel Fortress on Plymouth Hoe, or to a staging camp at Marsh Mills.

The presence of the French in Plymouth became more apparent to the local citizens when some of them bathed nude in one of the city's reservoirs. Some Frenchmen were kitted out with new uniforms having barely survived their ordeal at Dunkirk. Eventually, the soldiers embarked on to ships at Millbay Dock, walking up the gangplank to the music of *La Marseillaise* played by the band of the Royal Marines.

It all seemed to happen so quickly: no sooner had the French soldiers appeared in Plymouth than they had departed, many returning to their country to continue the fight.[10]

The consequences of the rapidly declining military situation in North West France began to manifest themselves in Devon. On the 14 June 1940, the 1st Division of the Canadian army embarked on their troopship at Millbay Dock, Plymouth.

These two rare photographs show French troops in Plymouth after their evacuation from Dunkirk in June 1940. Over 60 000 French soldiers arrived in Plymouth from where many returned to North West France to continue the fight against the advancing German army.

Hours passed and the ship remained docked. It seemed there was a problem. Eventually moorings were slackened and the ship moved slowly away to anchor in Plymouth Sound. The news of the collapse of the French Army had been received and there was no longer a need for the Canadians to be sent to France; they returned to the dock, disembarked and moved out of Plymouth.[11]

As the Canadian troops departed, so large numbers of civilian refugees and members of the Allied forces flooded into the South Devon coastal ports. Across the English Channel two hundred Belgian trawlers of various sizes departed from Ostend in some panic and sailed to Dieppe. On arrival at the French port they were surprised to learn of the speed of the German advance and so set off again, sailing directly to Brixham and Salcombe. Many of the Belgian fishermen had used the port of Brixham before the war and they now arrived with their boats crowded with relatives, friends and numerous household possessions.

Refugee Belgian fishing trawlers tied up at Brixham, June 1940.

A Belgian fisherman, Brixham, July 1940.

The Brixham community welcomed them, supplying them with food and accommodation.[12]

The Belgians were ordered to sail their boats to Dartmouth to await instructions by the Royal Navy. At Dartmouth the boats were tied up abreast alongside the Embankment. Immigration officers had the task of investigating the possibility of enemy agents attempting to infiltrate the country by passing themselves off as refugees.[13]

A meeting of the Belgian fisherman was held at Dartmouth Guildhall and a decision was made that the largest fishing boats were to sail to Fleetwood (Lancs), the next largest to Newlyn (Cornwall) and the smallest vessels, some 160 in number, would stay at Brixham. After the meeting all the boats were ordered to return to Brixham under a commanding officer. Thereafter the various boats sailed out to their new destinations. The Belgians at Brixham commenced fishing, and were eventually to be armed as a result of attacks by enemy aircraft. Three of the boats were sunk by mines.[14]

Throughout the war a Belgian community remained at Brixham, with its own school and social amenities. To continue the traditional skills of fishing the Belgians opened up their own school of fishing. One young evacuee became very interested and puzzled by the people who lived next door to her, who spoke a strange language (Flemish), and hung fish out on the washing line to dry.

Plymouth was already overcrowded but now French civilian refugees were arriving in large numbers at the port. This resulted in the city's emergency social

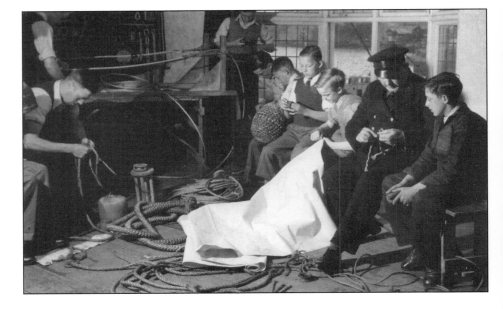

Brixham 1940: (Top) Many Belgian families arrived with their household goods and family possessions, setting up home in the temporary accommodation provided for them. (Bottom) In order to continue the traditional maritime skills, a school of fishing was set up for the Belgian children.

services opening. The rest centres were originally prepared to care for people made homeless by air raids but the city rose to the occasion in a magnificent way by offering the refugees shelter and food. Eventually the refugees were sent to Liverpool and then on to a camp at the Grand National race course at Aintree until arrangements were made to repatriate them to France via the North African port of Casablanca.[15]

The influx of people into South Devon seemed never ending, for there now arrived at Plymouth Allied servicemen, mainly British, who also had been evacuated from North West France under another rescue plan, code name Operation Cyclone. This too entailed a fleet of merchant ships and small craft assembling and sailing from Plymouth and Portsmouth to various ports in North West France.[16] Brixham and Paignton also received French refugees who remained in these two towns throughout the war.

At the Atlantic port of Saint Nazaire were two of the Bibby Line troopships, the *Dorsetshire* and *Somersetshire*, both now converted to hospital ships and each painted with large red crosses. The *Somersetshire* was the last ship, with a thousand wounded on board, to leave Saint Nazaire along with the Cunard White Star Line passenger ship *Lancastria* with over nine thousand servicemen on board. The *Lancastria* was attacked outside the harbour and hit by a bomb. She caught fire and sank within fifteen minutes. The death toll from this single bomb was more than the total number of British fatalities suffered at Dunkirk. Survivors from the *Lancastria* were landed at Plymouth and taken to the Royal Navy Hospital.[17] Another group of survivors from this catastrophe were men of the Royal Army Pay Corps who arrived at Ilfracombe. Many were bandaged around the face, arms, knees and hands; badly shocked and suffering severe burns.[18]

Under Operation Cyclone a further convoy of ten ships sailed overnight from the North West ports of France to Plymouth carrying 23 000 service personnel.[19] An army officer on the hospital ship *St Andrew* records that he was given a cabin and settled down on his cross-channel journey. On arriving at Plymouth he noticed the Sound was full of ships. The *St Andrew* docked at Millbay where the Royal Marine band was on the quayside playing 'Soldiers of the King' as he disembarked. On the quay he was offered a cup of tea and a sandwich and was then given a form to complete advising the War Office of his safe return. He then sent cards to his wife and mother. Later he was ordered to sit at a table by the dockside registering the men who were disembarking from the convoy; to him this seemed never ending.[20] The servicemen were conveyed from the larger ships by the GWR passenger tenders that prior to the war had serviced the ocean-going liners that anchored in Plymouth Sound.

As this grand reception of troops was taking place, one trooper had been ordered to Devonport Drill Hall to help prepare thousands of sandwiches, all the bread having to be cut by hand. Eventually, after working for hours on end without a break, the trooper collapsed with exhaustion, becoming an unusual non-combatant casualty of war.[21]

Plymouth was bursting at the seams with people. All the service barracks were full and there was an acute accommodation problem. For example, three hundred Polish men had arrived from France to enlist in the exiled Polish Navy. These men were scheduled to move on to a camp at Westward Ho! when, with a last

The French battleship FS *Paris* at Devonport, July 1940, following her escape from France laden with servicemen and civilians.

Survivors from the French vessel *Meknes* arrive in Plymouth, 25 July 1940. Their ship was torpedoed by a German E Boat while crossing the Channel laden with repatriated servicemen.

minute change in orders, it was decided to accommodate them at the United Services Orphanage being used at the time by the Canadians (HMCS NIOBE). The Canadians moved out and the orphanage was henceforth known as the Polish Naval Barracks, Stoke. A Polish passenger ship the SS *Koscirsz* had been converted into a depot ship at Devonport for the Polish Navy and renamed ORP *Gydnia*. She accommodated five hundred Polish officers and men.[22]

French warships were also arriving in Plymouth. Among them was the battleship FS *Paris*. She arrived in Plymouth Sound having been towed across the English Channel from France packed with naval personnel and civilian refugees.

The FS *Paris* required to be docked to make good a leak caused by a bomb exploding near the ship before arriving at Devonport. Eventually consideration was given by the British Admiralty to how the battleship might be used. One proposal was that the *Paris* could be used in Atlantic naval operations, but an Admiralty survey revealed she was in a very poor condition and unsuitable for this form of warfare. Requests were made by the Vichy Government to return the *Paris* to France. Later in the war the Allies wanted to use the old battleship as a blockship for the Mulberry harbours at Normandy; eventually near the end of the war, the *Paris* was returned to the French Navy.[23]

Along with the fleet of French warships at Plymouth was the giant French submarine *Surcouf*. She had sailed into Plymouth in the early hours of the morning of 20 June 1940. This vessel, launched in 1928, was at the time the largest submarine in the world. The *Surcouf* was armed with two eight-inch guns mounted in a power operated twin turret. She also carried a seaplane housed in a cylindrical watertight hanger immediately aft of the conning tower. The vessel was crewed by 130 officers and men, with space allotted to accommodate forty prisoners of war.

Rumours had circulated of expected trouble by French sailors wanting to be out of the war and anxious to return with their ships to France. Although General de Gaulle was rallying exiled Frenchmen and women to join the Free French Forces, some Frenchmen declined to support De Gaulle.

The Franco–German Armistice had questioned the future of the French naval ships in Britain and certain North Atlantic ports. The French fleet at Oran, Morocco, was under the command of the pro-Vichy Admiral Darlan. He was someone the British believed could possibly collaborate with Hitler and use the French Navy to attack the British.

The Prime Minister, Winston Churchill, announced on 4 July 1940 that, as the French warships at Oran had refused to surrender to the British fleet, and were not prepared to scuttle their vessels, a force of British warships had shelled them inflicting considerable damage and preventing the warships from being a viable fighting force. During this operation 1500 French sailors were killed.[24]

At Devonport on 3 July 1940, prior to the premier's statement, Royal Navy and Marine task forces boarded French naval vessels in Plymouth. The warships had,

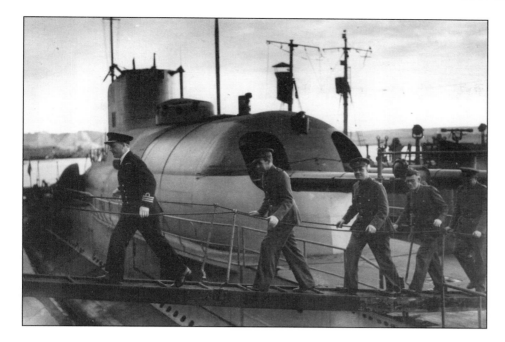

A British naval officer leads others off the giant French submarine *Surcouf* tied up in Plymouth, July 1940. Note the two huge guns and the massive upperworks in which a seaplane was housed.

on some pretext, been moved from anchorage in the Hamoaze to alongside jetties in the naval dockyard. The British boarding party that had been sent to take over the *Surcouf* experienced a most difficult operation. Three launches carrying the boarding party swept up to the *Surcouf* and within a short time the submarine was under British command. However, three British and one French sailor had been killed and other seamen were wounded during the shooting that had occurred.

At Dartmouth, crews of French naval ships, including two tugs, were taken from their vessels by armed naval cadets of the Royal Naval College. The French sailors were marched to Dartmouth Guildhall where they were given the option of joining the Free French Force or being returned to France.

As a consequence of the bombardment of the French fleet at Oran, and the events at Devonport, few of the *Surcouf* crew chose to remain with the Free French Navy. Those who declined to stay were eventually repatriated to France. The giant *Surcouf* remained for a time at Devonport with replacement members of the crew. The submarine became a topic of speculation and was shrouded in mystery. Eventually, she sailed from Devonport and docked in Newfoundland. Later, on a voyage from Bermuda in February 1942 the *Surcouf* was sunk.[25]

German victories changed the mood of the British people. Local Devon newspapers reflected the nation's concern of an anticipated 'invasion of England'. Relevant government announcements and propaganda concerning the war were published alongside the local social events. The prospect of German parachutists dropping out of the sky on to Devon soil, or the enemy landing on a local beach, did not prevent people from arranging marriages, playing cricket or going away on holiday.

The official military thinking was, if the Germans were to attempt a landing, it would be on the beaches in South East England. Home defence was the priority throughout the country. In Devon plans went ahead for the defence of the county. The public were asked to be vigilant regarding enemy parachutists being dropped from troop-carrying aircraft. Silhouettes of enemy aircraft were published in the Devon newspapers as an aid to their recognition.

At Exeter any person observing enemy aircraft or parachutists over the city was asked to immediately telephone the city's police.[26]

The national plan for the defence of the United Kingdom included 'stop-line defences'. Planned constructed defence lines within designated towns and villages were earmarked as strongpoints, reinforced with a chain of fortifications. The Taunton stop-line followed the estuary of the River Parrett, crossed Somerset (828 pillboxes) into Devon, ending at Seaton. The shorter Devon sector of the stop-line had 26 pillboxes. This defence system was built in 1940.[27,28]

As early as January 1940, before the invasion of Holland, German strategists discussed the possibility of landing in England and believed this was possible once the Allied forces were defeated on the Continent. Later, on 20 June 1940, the German Admiral, Raeder, mentioned the subject of invasion to the German

Aircraft identification charts were regularly published in local newspapers.

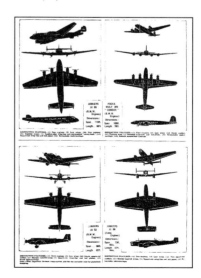

Prepared defence lines in Devon, 1940. Part of a national system of strongpoints and chains of pillboxes, including stop-lines at which the invading forces would be held. The major defences in Devon were sited at likely landing grounds around the coast.

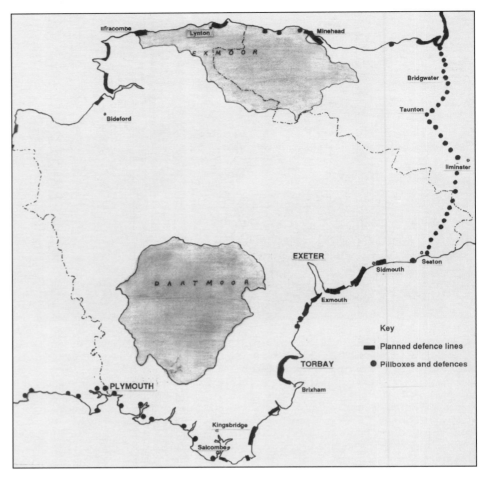

Führer and two weeks later Hitler approved plans for a seaborne assault to be made against England, code name Operation Sealion. As the High Command prepared their plans, the German Luftwaffe, as a prelude to the final assault, set out to gain mastery of the sky. The ensuing aerial conflict became known as the Battle of Britain.

The invasion plan was for the Germans to land on the beaches along the narrowest sections of the English Channel. The German 6th Army Group B would depart from Cherbourg and attempt landings in the Weymouth — Lyme Bay area. Units of the 6th Army would, if necessary, occupy Devon and Cornwall. The Germans proposed to establish minefields off the Devon Coast at Start Point and

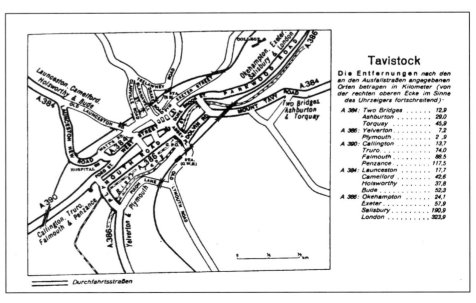

Example of a German map of Devon towns prepared for the invasion of England.

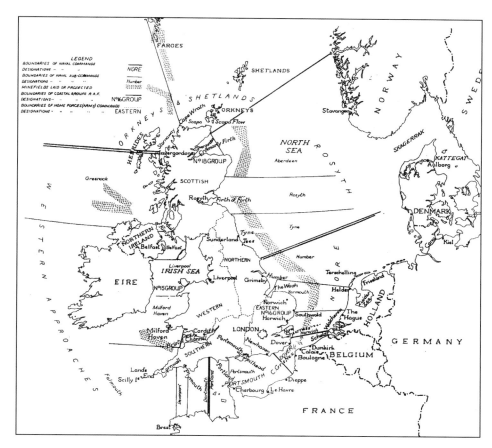

A contemporary map (mid 1940) showing the organisation for the Home Defence of the United Kingdom.

concentrate U Boats in the Channel waters between Plymouth and Start Point.[29]

The military defences of Devon, at this particular period, were limited by a shortage of available troops and equipment, much of which the British Army had abandoned at Dunkirk.

The order of battle for the defence of the United Kingdom placed Devon under Southern Command, with the 48th Division committed for the defence of the county, a fact known by the German Army (see map on page 65). The 48th Division HQ was based at Lydford. The LDV were to be the first line of defence and would be responsible for holding the coast until the arrival of the regular army troops.

The main role of the LDV was defence and information. These volunteers, their name being changed to the Home Guard in June 1940, were under no illusions as to what was to be expected of them. Many of the Home Guard would have seen in wartime newsreels, shown in every cinema, the ferocity of the German Panzer

Seven of Torquay's Local Defence Volunteers guarding Greathill reservoir, May 1940. These were early recruits to what was later to become the Home Guard. It is interesting to speculate what the invading German army might have made of such 'troops', but the threat of invasion was very real and it took some courage to volunteer when equipment and arms were almost non-existent.

Better equipped than early recruits, these members of a Home Guard detachment march through Sandford, a small village north of Crediton. Often too old or too young for active service, and including those in 'reserved occupations', the Home Guard was sometimes led by officers who had seen service in the First World War.

units. To add to their concerns, members of the non-uniformed LDV would, the Germans said, be shot if captured.[30]

LDV training in the early stages of its formation was an ad hoc affair. The weapons, if they had any, varied from rifles shared between men, broomsticks, muskets, shotguns, swords, pistols and pikes. They were organised in a manner similar to the British Army, with battalions, platoons and sections. For the definitive list of Devon Home Guard (LDV) Battalions see Appendix A. From 1940 the men were issued with unsightly denim overalls as their uniform, but as supplies improved they gradually progressed to battledress, webbing equipment, service respirators, boots, gaiters, forage caps, and steel helmets. In 1942 the Home Guard were issued with sten guns, a light automatic weapon. Later in the war their responsibilities increased to include anti-aircraft defence. Along with their duties of standing guard and being out on night patrol, the men were required to give up their free time to undergo training.[31]

The military defence of the whole of the North Devon coast was impracticable. The area was divided into sections for purposes of defence, the 50th Warwickshire Regiment having the responsibility of holding the area between the border of Somerset and Westward Ho!

Sea defences were urgently prepared. Concrete bollards, 'tank traps' and pillboxes sprang up. A pillbox, essentially a mini fortress, was a means of static defence against enemy infantry forces. They were sited along the coastline and inland. Telegraph poles were implanted into the sand of certain North Devon beaches so there would be no clear runway for enemy aircraft to land as they had been able to do on the beaches of Holland.[32]

Entrances to beaches or slipways had concealed 'tank traps' to prevent or hold up the landing of enemy mechanical transport. Long lengths of tubular-steel scaffolding were erected on and along the seafront and beaches, often sited to be covered by tidal waters. Minefields, almost as dangerous to the defenders as they were to the enemy, were buried in sand or shingle.

The army believed the enemy's objectives in North Devon would be Barnstaple, Bideford and Cleave airfield, the latter a small RAF airfield perched on a clifftop four miles from Bude (Cornwall).

Seaborne landings could also be attempted at Ilfracombe, Barnstaple, Instow, Appledore, Bideford and Bude. Other North Devon beaches where it was thought the enemy could attempt a shore landing were at Saunton, Croyde, Woolacombe, Westward Ho! and Widemouth.

Possible inland landing places were identified (see Appendix). In North Devon any captured German troops were to be taken to the Royal Artillery Camp, Okehampton or the Drill Hall, Barnstaple.[33]

For the defence of the North Devon ports, emergency gun batteries were established and manned by the Royal Artillery Special Battery with its group headquarters at the Marine Hotel, Instow. A 4.7-inch naval gun protected the entrance to Appledore, with 4.0-inch guns installed at Instow and Ilfracombe. The guns at Appledore and Instow were placed at points overlooking the mouth of the River Taw and the River Torridge.[34] Preparations were made to engage every boat that approached the coastline. At Ilfracombe armed motor launches were based in the harbour as part of the defence force.

The Bideford 5th Battalion Home Guard were responsible for the infantry defence of the district, while the Appledore Home Guard platoon was placed on standby to occupy any strategic position.

Orders were issued to immobilise or, if need be, to destroy the existing dock facilities. In North Devon this included the docks at Barnstaple, Bideford, Ilfracombe and Appledore. The objective was to deprive the enemy of a foothold on British soil pending the arrival of sufficient defence forces. The orders also directed the destruction of public utilities of electrical and water supplies. To implement the orders a 'most secret' signal would be given to proceed. Arrangements had also been made to immobilise the railways of North Devon by the removal of existing rolling-stock and sections of the rail track between Mortehoe station and Ilfracombe. The railway points were also to be destroyed.[35]

North Devon had an armoured train manned by Polish soldiers. The train was equipped with two 6-pounder guns, two anti-tank rifles and six Bren guns, and was capable of firing on enemy troops, aircraft and shipping. Its primary role was to operate as a mobile unit on either side of the Barnstaple estuary.[36]

The hot summer months saw an army Lysander spotter-aircraft flying from the large flat field at Folly Gate Okehampton, carrying out dawn-to-dusk coastal patrols over Lyme Bay and a stretch of the North Devon coast. Similar patrols over other areas of South West England for Southern (Army) Command used aircraft of 225 Squadron based at RAF Roborough (Plymouth). These daily coastal watches were to look for any evidence of attempted enemy landings.[37]

The watching of the Devon skies was monitored by the (Royal) Observer Corps. The Exeter Corps Centre, Group 21, became operational at the end of July 1940. These observers were relied on to detect and recognise any aircraft approaching their designated area of responsibility and to plot the course of such aircraft.[38] Observer posts were established throughout Devon and were managed in groups of three linked to a controller at 21 Group Centre located in the basement of the library at Exeter.

In North Devon one group included Torrington, Barnstaple, and Horns Cross. The Torrington observer post (L1) was a large hut sited on Furzebeam Hill next to Torrington Golf Club. The facilities and any comforts were provided by the initiative of the post's crew who included an ironmonger and plumbing contractor who obtained secondhand materials and built a heating system for the hut that made life tolerable while the men were on duty during the cold weather.

BOROUGH OF OKEHAMPTON
A Defence Committee
exists to deal with the situation on
INVASION
and is now concerned in making preliminary plans to deal with it.
Until it comes the Committee does not possess any Executive powers.

The PROBLEMS to be covered by such Committees include:—
Co-operation with the Military.   Arrangements for Casualties.
Arrangement for Sheltering and Housing Homeless.
Cooking and Distribution of Food.   Conservation of Water.
Making provision for Labour and Transport to assist the Military.

The Committee includes Representatives of :—
The Local Authority. The Police. The A.R.P. Authority. Public Assistance Authority.
National Fire Service. Ministry of Information. Ministry of Labour and National Service.
Local Transport. Women's Voluntary Service.
and if you are in need of advice you should apply to the Committee.

What the Civilian should do now.
Join the HOME GUARD.
Volunteer for EMERGENCY DUTIES.

What the Civilian should do when Invasion occurs
Avoid spreading rumours.
STAND FIRM, and carry on your ordinary work.
STAY PUT, and obey orders of Military, Police and A.R.P. Authority.
Keep off the roads, and do everything to help the Military and impede the enemy.

The threat of invasion continued throughout the early war years and each major town organised a Defence Committee for the dissemination of information to the local populace.

A Lysander. This aircraft was used for coastal patrols at the time of expected invasion, flying from RAF Okehampton and RAF Roborough. Later in the war such aircraft flew clandestine missions from RAF Winkleigh and RAF Bolt Head, taking agents and equipment into occupied France.

A contemporary map shows the aerial patrols operating over the Channel and North Sea in 1940. Later, the establishment of the Chain Home radar system would partly replace the need for such reconnaissance.

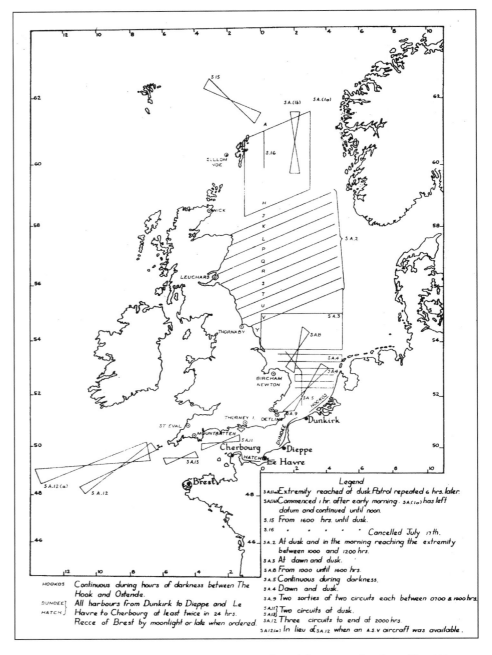

Legend

SA11 *Extremity reached at dusk. Patrol repeated 6 hrs. later.*
SA11 *Commenced 1 hr. after early morning. SA(1a) has left datum and continued until noon.*
S.15 *From 1600 hrs. until dusk.*
S.16 *" " " " Cancelled July 17th.*
SA.2 *At dusk and in the morning reaching the extremity between 1000 and 1200 hrs.*
SA.3 *At dawn and dusk.*
SA.8 *From 1000 until 1600 hrs.*
SA.5 *Continuous during darkness.*
SA.4 *Dawn and dusk.*
SA.9 *Two sorties of two circuits each between 0700 & 1000 hrs.*
SA11 }
SA13 } *Two circuits at dusk.*
SA.12 *Three circuits to end at 2000 hrs.*
SA12(a) *In lieu of SA.12 when an A.S.V. aircraft was available.*

HOOKOS *Continuous during hours of darkness between The Hook and Ostende.*
DUNDEE } *All harbours from Dunkirk to Dieppe and Le Havre to Cherbourg at least twice in 24 hrs.*
HATCH } *Recce of Brest by moonlight or late when ordered.*

Outside, the primitive structure was camouflaged by gorse bushes. The L1 post was crewed by a chief observer with a full and part time staff that manned the post on a 24 hour basis with 4 hour and 8 hour shifts. To defend the post, the crew were issued with two Canadian rifles. Rockets were issued to be let off if Allied aircraft were in danger of flying into the nearby high ground. All the members of the Observer Corps were submitted to aircraft recognition tests in which proficiency certificates were awarded.[39]

Although some radar equipment had been established in the West Country, this did not include the Chain Low (CHL) System, capable of detecting low-flying enemy aircraft, which meant that cover was incomplete. This made the work of the Observer Corp even more important. An emergency programme to build six CHL stations had been agreed to rectify this situation and to extend the chain to the West of England. A radar site at West Prawle (South Devon) was proposed as early as March 1939 on land requisitioned in November 1939. Radar equipment, transmitters and a wooden tower had been constructed at East Prawle, but during the summer of 1940 the cover between Prawle and Portland was inadequate.

To the east, at Kingswear, a prototype CHL station with 43 gantries was erected in a field at Coverton Farm, on land owned by Rupert D'Oyly Carte. The site selected was 400 feet above sea level, but it was criticised as being unsuitable due

Scaffolding erected along the beach at Sidmouth in the summer of 1940. Such makeshift measures were typical of the early war years. Many beaches were also mined although the dog in this photograph indicates this had not happened at Sidmouth.

to the difficulties of camouflaging the station. Later in July, No. 13 Radar Station built at Branscombe, near Sidmouth, became operational, obvious to all with its wooden tower and masts. In the North Devon area a radar tower 87 feet high was erected at Northam, near Appledore, while in south-west Devon a radar station was built at Hawks Tor, Shaugh.[40]

The government ordered that all road signs and milestones were to be removed so they would not be of assistance to enemy airborne troops. At Torrington, North Devon, shopkeepers were incensed when police decided to remove their trade signs and property signs.

Dartmouth became a borough without a name, well almost. The obliteration or removal of the word 'Dartmouth' on all public noticeboards, shop signs, and commercial vehicles had been undertaken. Brass plates outside public offices, companies and other buildings had also been removed. The local estate agents had been busy visiting all the properties for sale to change the advertisement boards. Even posters publicising a dance required the word Dartmouth to be deleted. The most difficult problem was removal or hiding of names that had been engraved in stone or wood. Then there were foundation stones, water hydrants and the name Dartmouth on gravestones in the cemeteries. The major task however was to deal with the very large lettering in the harbour, the remains of publicising the Royal Dartmouth Regatta of 1939. This required two coats of paint to cover up all the words. With all the effort to erase the town's name, many local lorries and motor-vans persisted in driving around the town with the name Dartmouth still painted on the vehicles.[41]

Beach and coastal defences were erected and established along the South Devon coast. In the south-east scaffolding and barbed-wire was erected from Exmouth to Budleigh Salterton and Sidmouth, with some beach areas laid with land-mines. Seaton was guarded with two 6-inch naval guns of No. 402 Coastal Battery. For the defence of the approach to Sidmouth Town, No. 389 Coastal Battery was equipped with one naval gun, one French gun, both of First World War origin, and a 16-pounder gun, as well as Bren guns and rifles. At Exmouth the swing bridge was partially immobilised each night, as was the town's timber jetty.[42]

In the Torbay area, most of the beaches were considered possible landing places for enemy assault troops. The anti-invasion defences on the Torquay beaches and Preston sands included rolled barbed-wire erected along the seafront. Fishcove, Goodrington Sands, was protected by tubular scaffolding. Churston Cove and Elberry Cove were also mined as were Broad Sands (Churston) and Saltern Sands, where it was considered the enemy could attempt to come ashore.[43]

Babbacombe beach and Oddicombe beach were guarded by the LDV. Above the cliff tops, barbed-wire was placed across the golf and race courses. Anti-tank positions were established to the north-west side of St Marychurch, and trenches dug at the backs of houses there. At the Greathill reservoir, Torquay, three men dug a trench to be used as an observation post. One Sunday morning LDVs were called out to defend Greathill reservoir having been issued with one rifle and five rounds of ammunition. One young fifteen-year-old LDV member had an air rifle and his father possessed a sword stick.[44]

Torquay harbour was partially closed by the siting of two block ships and the harbour's entrance guarded by two torpedo tubes. The small harbour at Paignton had a boom defence placed across its entrance. Two naval guns of Japanese manufacture, manned by 363 Coastal Battery, were sited at Corbyn's Head. The battery also had two coastal searchlights.

Hope Cove, South Devon c. 1940. A newly constructed pillbox and three concrete tank traps, known as 'dragon's teeth', can be seen on the slipway.

At Brownston, near Kingswear, there were counter-bombardment batteries of two 9.6-inch guns that were to be used to engage the enemy farther out to sea.[45]

Brixham harbour was guarded by two 4.7-inch naval guns, manned by the Brixham 362 Battery, that later was to become 378 Battery and eventually was manned by members of the Home Guard. Brixham defenders were ordered to be economical with ammunition as supplies were short, and for this reason it was thought more desirable to shoot to disable many enemy boats, rather than sink a few. Brixham harbour had a boom defence and a controlled minefield.[46,47] Strict control was imposed on all ships entering Brixham harbour between sunset and sunrise. No merchant vessel was allowed to approach at night within three miles of the coast and port, with the exception of ships that were in an organised convoy. Roadblocks were placed in position to prevent access inland from the Brixham breakwater. Throughout the South West, road blocks were set up at five mile intervals. Ever since 1936, in anticipating the war, a store of four million gallons of aviation fuel had been established at Brixham, and in 1939 the Air Ministry had decided to increase the storage capacity. To speed construction, special permission was given to use floodlights during the black out to work through the night.

The base spirit was converted into high-octane grades suitable for training and operational aircraft use. The stored fuel was pumped from Berryland, Brixham to a rail loading-bay close to the Brixham (GWR) branchline. The four-track sidings accommodated forty fuel carrier tanks. Twice a week during the early evening each of two trains hauling forty tanks were sent to Islip near Oxford. The tank trains were assembled at Goodrington as the Brixham branchline was limited to taking ten tankers at a time. The trains were given air cover as they passed Teignmouth and Exeter. Fuel was also sent to RAF Exeter, and the airfields of Chivenor and Winkleigh. Motor torpedo boats stationed at Brixham were also supplied with fuel.

As a defence measure the Brixham breakwater beach was covered with tubular scaffolding and barbed-wire. Inside the breakwater quarry, small tanks were built to hold a mixture of petrol, diesel oil and creosote for feeding flame-throwers placed at the approach to the breakwater.[48]

A boom defence of steel cable and nets held up by wooden floats was placed across the River Dart to prevent the incursion or a suprise attack by enemy coastal craft. The defence barrier was controlled by a boom vessel to regulate river traffic in and out of the harbour. History thus repeated itself at Dartmouth, for in 1434 a great chain stretched across the entrance of the river from Kingswear to Dartmouth as a protection from marauding forces.

At Dartmouth Castle, two 4.7-inch guns were installed to cover the entrance of the River Dart, along with two torpedo tubes.[49] On the riverside at Dartmouth, there is a thick walled battery at Bayard's Cove, constructed in the mid sixteenth century as a fortification to defend the town. The inward splay embrasures for the guns made it obsolete by the time it was completed. In 1940 the Royal Engineers adapted the ancient battery as a machine gun strongpoint only to abandon the fortifications after a few weeks for the same reason as the Tudor military force.[50]

All the small beaches in the area were considered likely places for the enemy to land. Mill Bay Cove, Kingswear, and across the waters of the Dart at Castle Cove, and Sugary Cove, were blocked and barbed-wire defences erected.

A special College Defence Company was set up and trained to fight enemy paratroopers and to defend the Royal Naval College, Dartmouth. Later, all senior staff were involved in the defence of the college. Barbed-wire was erected throughout the grounds of HMS *Brittania* and college officers were issued with hand grenades and ammunition to be kept in their cabins in readiness for a sudden enemy attack. The threat of an invasion and the possibility of the Dartmouth Naval Cadets being rounded up by the Germans resulted in two boats being kept at standby, with provisions, to transport the cadets up the River Dart out of the danger zone.[51]

The orders to immobilise or completely destroy the dock facilities in North Devon, extended also to the South Devon ports of Brixham, Dartmouth, Exmouth, Plymouth, Teignmouth and Torquay. The men of Dartmouth who had rallied to the call to join the LDV would have to bear the brunt of defending their town. The Commander in Chief of the local defences indicated that in the event of an invasion there would be no troops available for their support.[52]

Men of the Buffs, East Kent Regiment, surveying the existing Slapton beach defences between the villages of Strete and Torcross, found one First World War gun and several telegraph poles mounted on axles and intended to resemble guns to mislead the enemy. The Commanding Officer had thirteen rounds of ammunition for the gun. He had one shell fired out to sea only to be rebuked by his General for wasting ammunition. Ten-foot-high poles were erected in fields where it was thought enemy aircraft might land.[53]

All along this coastline concrete pillboxes were erected by the roads and on cliffs. The most southerly pillbox in Devon was constructed at East Prawle. The entrance to Salcombe harbour was guarded with two 4.5-inch guns and search-lights manned by 329 Battery, garrisoned by three officers and seventy-six ranks. Salcombe harbour had a boom defence; most of the jetties and landing places in the small town were blocked and had barbed-wire defences erected.[54]

Nearby at Kingsbridge one young lad who had joined the LDV as a messenger was given an order to jump on his bike as soon as the warning clamour of church bells was heard, and to report to Fore Street to join up with the older members of

Anti-invasion beach defences overlooking Plymouth Sound, July 1940. The steel scaffolding appears somewhat flimsy but supported by the pillbox (left) provides a considerable obstacle.

These three remarkable photographs show a detachment of Indian troops who were stationed at Modbury, after Dunkirk in 1940. Among their duties was the erection of barbed wire defences along the shoreline near Mothercombe. Mules were an important form of transport for forces on both sides throughout the war and thousands of horses and mules were requisitioned.

the force. Among the Kingsbridge LDV weapons for the defence of the town included a pitch fork, air rifle, and a twelve-bore shotgun. The main routine was to spend all night on Churchstow church tower watching for the 'presence of the enemy'. At Slapton village one member of the LDV was armed with a pike.[55]

At Woodleigh, a former monastery near Modbuy, a mounted unit of the Indian Army was accommodated. The Indian troops were a familiar sight to the local villagers as they slowly moved with their mules to collect rations at Loddiswell railway station. One young Acton evacuee, walking down a quiet South Devon lane, was astonished to pass Indian soldiers with mules going towards Mothercombe beach. The soldiers were wearing turbans and their mules carried coils of barbed-wire to erect as part of the local beach defences. The evacuee had never seen anything like this in his life.[56]

At Burgh Island the military were in residence in the art déco Hotel, with two pillboxes built as part of its defences.[57]

Plymouth was recognised by the military as a key position in the West of England. A direct frontal attack on the city was thought unlikely, but a boom defence was installed to prevent enemy amphibious craft from attempting to land directly in the city. Coastal batteries were sited to cover the approaches to Plymouth Sound. The gun batteries were divided into three fire commands, Wembury, Drake and Rame.[58] The defences included six 9.2-inch guns, six 6.0-inch breech-loading guns and eleven quick-firing 12-pounder guns.

An attack by the enemy in strength, landing at several places, would present a serious danger. It was thought probable that enemy landings would be made to the east and west of Plymouth, with the east side being more vulnerable. The belief was that enemy landings on beaches would be made in conjunction with German airborne troops dropped over Dartmoor. The stretches of open water on the rivers Tamar, Lynher and Plym caused concern as it was believed that enemy troop-carrying flying boats could land there. An appeal was made to owners of small boats to moor their craft across the rivers to act as a barrier to prevent any enemy seaplanes from landing.

Armed farmers on mounted patrol in the Exmoor Area, North Devon, July 1940.

LDV parachute patrols out on Dartmoor, 1940.

A watch was set up by Dartmoor farmers, hunts and the Home Guard for enemy parachutists being dropped on the moors. Among the patrols were women riders, armed with binoculars, riding through the bracken and gorse ready to report back anything suspicious. At night the vigil was continued by Home Guard patrols. The No. 5 platoon of Whiddon Down, with its headquarters at Drewsteignton, operated in the moorland area, one of the loneliest places to patrol in England. Armed mounted patrols were also organised to watch over Exmoor.

Any fighting for the defence of Plymouth would be on foot as the military commander thought the local terrain would be unsuitable for tank warfare. One problem was the shortage of defending forces. What forces were available would be concentrated at Yelverton, a suitable place from which to move to Dartmoor or to the east or west side of Plymouth. Defending Plymouth itself would be the Home Guard, and some naval and Marine personnel. Reinforcements, if they became available, would take ten days to arrive. The 48th Division charged with the task of defending Devon, would be barely sufficient to counterattack other than between Start Point and the River Teign.[59]

The watch on the seas was aided by HM Coastguards, in wartime known as the Auxiliary Coastguards and operated by the Admiralty using enrolled ex-servicemen. Dressed in khaki battledress with black shoulder badges and naval caps (the cap badge embellished with a CG monogram under the crown), these men watched for any suspicious vessels off the Devon coast, and any evidence of enemy mine-laying.

LDV members enjoy free hospitality while attending a parade near Lifton, West Devon, in August 1940.

Col. R. Bastard inspecting a parade of 400 members of the LDV near Lifton, August 1940.

With Britain on its own, even the Channel Islands had been occupied by the Germans, the British government in its adversity decided that the fight must be carried to the Germans as an indication that the will of the British to fight prevailed, even after the disaster of Dunkirk.

Churchill ordered that a number of Commando units should be formed and that a cross-Channel operation be carried out as quickly as possible. An appeal went out for officers to raise and command No. 3 Commando Unit. Four days were given to select men who were to report to Plymouth. Within a matter of days the Commandos began training for a raid against the Germans on enemy occupied Guernsey. The code name 'Ambassador' was given to the cross-Channel operations to be carried out by H troop of No. 3 Commando, acting as No. 11 Independent Commando Unit.

Few, if any of Dartmouth's wartime residents would have been aware of the reason the destroyers HMS *Scimitar* and HMS *Saladin*, with several RAF sea rescue launches, were anchored in the River Dart. The launches were to be used to take the Commandos ashore as there were no landing craft available. On the 14 July 1940 at 6pm this small force sailed out from Dartmouth to land on the Jerbourg Peninsula, Guernsey, at 00.50 hours the following morning. Two RAF launches assigned to No. 11 Unit developed engine trouble and returned to base. Another cause for concern was the noise of the RAF launch engines. This would not have come as a suprise to Dartmouthians who were familiar with the sound of these high-powered rescue launches echoing throughout the riverside town as they slid through the waters of the River Dart. The strong wash they produced splashed high up and over the Embankment.

Arriving off the Channel Islands, one Commando company became lost due to a faulty compass and landed on the island of Sark. Re-embarkation was difficult because of the heavy seas and three Commandos were left on the rocks and were captured by the Germans. Eventually the entire raiding force returned across the Channel to Dartmouth.[60]

Along with the presence of the Commandos and their secret operations, the River Dart was a base for other operations involving clandestine warfare. The Secret Intelligence Service (SIS) had been formed in 1938 to study the theory of sabotage, while the Special Operations Executive (SOE) was based on the River Helford near Falmouth (Cornwall) where SOE agents were trained in landing from dinghies, working alongside the Free French Navy. During 1940 an SIS flotilla was based on the River Dart. A Breton trawler had been acquired and registered as a French fighting vessel. Disguised as an ordinary fishing vessel, but armed and carrying the white ensign, she was crewed by servicemen who wore fishing smocks. The first operation from the River Dart was to collect the French Intelligence Officer 'Reny', Colonel Gilbert Renault-Routre. He with his agent, aide and family arrived safely from France with all their personal luggage.[61]

During this period four boats escaped to England from enemy-occupied Guernsey. One of the boats, with twenty-eight people on board, arrived in Plymouth, another made landfall at Start Point, near Slapton. Later in the war seven people arrived in Dartmouth in an 18 foot dinghy after a 14 hour voyage from Guernsey.

The fate of local men away at war was increasingly being reported; a death, casualty, or as a prisoner of war. On many occasions a wartime death of a person from a small community was a shared grief. An example of such a sad occasion was the loss of HMS *Campeador*, sunk by a mine off the coast of the Isle of Wight with the loss of all her crew. The death of Vernon McAndrew who went down with his boat ended a close association with Dartmouth. The motor yacht, the *Campeador V* was built and launched at Dartmouth in 1938 for Vernon McAndrew, a millionaire who had settled in the town taking up residence at 'Ravensbury' overlooking the waters of the Dart, at Warfleet Creek. Before the war, McAndrew had sailed his yacht to the Canary Islands to collect evidence regarding a German presence involved in establishing a naval base there.

At the outbreak of the Second World War, he offered his yacht to the Admiralty and it was then commissioned for naval service. HMS *Campeador* was commanded by an ex master of the Dartmoor Foxhounds, with McAndrew and two of his friends receiving RNVR commissions.[62]

Prior to the invasion of Holland, the Devon resorts were encouraged by the upturn in trade and holiday reservations; it was guarded optimism, but after the cold winter people were looking forward to the opportunity of a brief holiday away from what for so many people was a dreary wartime routine. At Torquay Sarah Churchill, the actress daughter of Winston Churchill, was in the cast of the play *Gaslight* at the Torquay Pavilion. The Spa Ballroom was having a midnight dance, with music played by the very popular Joe Loss and his band. The Harbour Lights Cafe, down the road at Paignton, offered delicious crab or lobster salads. An air of expectation pervaded the county, when came the news of the German

These two photographs show a mounted patrol made up from members of the Dartmoor Hunt, July 1940. Such daylight patrols covered remote moorland areas on the lookout for enemy parachutists. The women riders are unarmed.

A group of men on Plymouth Hoe, 1940, responding to the government plea to 'Dig for Victory'.

invasion of Holland. The British Government cancelled the official Whitsun Bank Holiday and people cancelled their holiday reservations. There was a dramatic fall in visitors to many towns, with the exception of Torquay, where crowds of people arrived determined to make the most of the delights on offer.

The bad news did not significantly change the domestic life of the county, although there were inconveniences and household disruptions as those men not in the regular forces had to report for Home Guard or Civil Defence duty at night, or at the weekends. More women were involved with voluntary work, making contributions on the Home Front and, for many, this meant being on duty during unsocial hours.

The anti-invasion measures, particularly the barbed-wire and tubular scaffolding that had been erected, provoked little response from the civilians; it was all seen as part of the war effort. The barbed-wire was up, but at many beaches one could still go walking on the sand.

One measure affected every Devon community, large or small. This was the total ban on bell ringing, imposed in the middle of June 1940. From now bells would only be rung as a signal of invasion. An exception to the ban on bell ringing was at Exeter, where the bells of the Cathedral clock were allowed to chime until the weights had run down.[63]

Of growing significance was the effect of food rationing, particularly the losses wrought on merchant shipping by U Boat attacks and subsequent food shortages. One reaction to this on the Home Front was the promotion of thrifty house-keeping and austere recipes to make the most of meagre supplies.

Dig for Victory was a government war cry and people responded by growing their own vegetables. All available ground was dug up for allotments: parks, land by railway lines, even parts of Plymouth Hoe were used for growing vegetables.

Salcombe became the first local authority in Devon to keep pigs under the wartime plan for increasing food production. Twelve pigs and a shed were purchased, and the pigs were fattened on swill collected from around the locality.

People were generally coping well with the food rationing. The tea ration meant that more cocoa or coffee, the latter from a bottle and made from chicory, was being consumed. For most it was frugal times. Many learnt to use their tea leaves twice over: after having a cup of tea, the leaves were taken out of the pot and laid out to dry. When the time came to make another pot of tea, the dried tea was added to an equal amount of unused tea.

Although food was rationed, this did not extend to hotels and restaurants where, assuming one could afford to eat out, the choice of food was wide and appetising. Menu favourites were Brown Windsor and Mock Turtle soup. To obtain something tasty and 'off ration' was a pursuit practised by most Devon housewives. At Tavistock on a Friday many would wait in a very long queue for the chance to buy some sausages from Sammy Friend's shop in West Street. Each customer was allowed 1 lb of his home-produced sausages, but supplies were restricted. For the lucky ones to have fried sausages on a Friday evening was a wartime treat.[64]

During the summer of 1940, at the height of the Battle of Britain, when London was being heavily bombed, there was another exodus of evacuees from London to Devon, although not to the extent that had occurred at the outbreak of war. Notices were given out that villages in the South Molton area and North Devon should be prepared to receive schoolchildren. Ilfracombe, already host to a thousand government evacuees was told to expect another twelve hundred children from Wimbledon, Mitcham, and Croydon. Notices were also served to Dawlish, Exmouth, Torquay and East Devon towns. Ilfracombe, having so many evacuees and servicemen to accommodate, was having problems attracting holidaymakers and one regular visitor for over fifty years wrote to the local newspaper regretting he would not be down this year (1940) as the town had no air raid shelters.

The black out regulations in the town were being enforced to the extent that the police would climb up through a window and remove an electric light bulb to effect a black out. One person up before the local magistrate believed in error that by using a coloured electric bulb there was no need to draw the curtains. Yet another Ilfracombe defendant described that the policeman accusing him of breaching the black out regulations could not find the correct end of his pencil to write down the defendants's name and address in his notebook because the room was so dark. At Totnes, one hotelier was fined for a black out offence, this after buying two and a half miles of material to double-cover 138 windows!

Two photographs of evacuees arriving at South Brent station from Bristol to be billetted in the Kingsbridge area. Up to late 1940 Bristol had served as an evacuation area for those escaping the London Blitz. Heavy raids on Bristol in November and December 1940 resulted in many travelling to the relative peace of Devon.

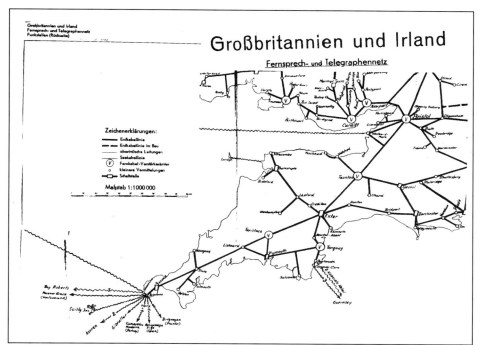

Still intent upon invasion, the German High Command planned their strategy with typical meticulous care, as this telecommunications map reveals.

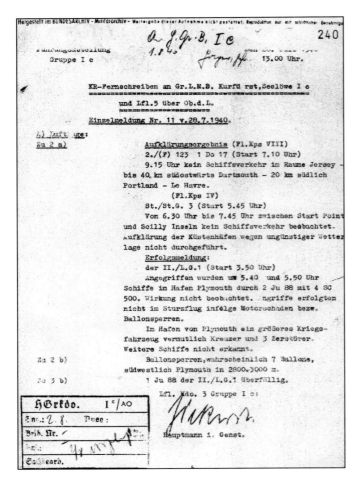

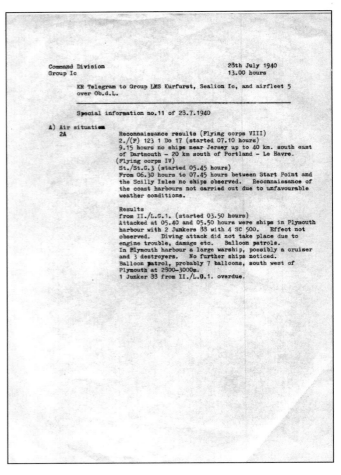

An original Luftwaffe report and its translation dated 28 July 1940. Such reports were completed following every mission and formed the basis of German intelligence on military and supply movements in the UK. The mention of barrage balloons reveals the importance to airmen of identifying the position of such static defences, especially when raiding at night.

After the defeat of France, the Germans assembled three large air fleets (Luftflottens) in their operational areas of France.

The United Kingdom has been assigned to Luftflotten 2 and 3 each with its own designated area of operation. The Luftflotte 3 area of operation included Devonshire, but when it came to flying sorties over the county there were occasions when Luftflotte 2 aircraft were also involved.

Luftflotte 3 was based at captured French airfields throughout North West France, with its headquarters in Paris. The commander of Luftflotte 3 was Feldmarschall Hugo Sperrle, described by Hitler as one of his most brutal-looking generals. The Feldmarschall had previously commanded the German Condor Legion in Spain during the Spanish Civil War. The Condor Legion was responsible for bombing the undefended Basque town of Guernica in 1937.

The threat of a German invasion of England continued to cause the gravest concern. A new fighter group (No. 10) was formed to operate in South West England. As the Channel coast of France was under enemy occupation, vital shipping lanes used by the merchant navy were exposed to enemy air, submarine and surface raiders. The government decided that the West Country ports should now harbour the Atlantic convoys.

The increased importance attached to these harbours meant they were obvious targets. Devon, with its two cities, towns, ports and smaller communities were only a short flying distance away from the Luftwaffe's air bases. Enemy occupied Alderney was just 80 miles away from the South Devon coast.

The German airforce quickly established a daily aerial reconnaissance of shipping in the English and Bristol channels, noting the position of any convoy and counting the number of vessels in the harbours.

As British Fighter Command came under increasing attack, 87 Squadron was sent to RAF Exeter to cover the defences of the Western Approaches. To further strengthen the West of England defences Spitfires of 152 Squadron were moved to the Middle Wallop sector of No. 10 Fighter Group, and a flight of Gloucester Gladiator biplanes of 247 Squadron was transferred from the Shetlands to RAF Roborough, Plymouth.[65]

During July 1940, the Luftwaffe increased its minelaying activities in British coastal waters. The technique of minelaying required extremely accurate

Gloucester Gladiator No 2306. On the 18 July 1940 a flight of these biplanes was transferred to RAF Roborough from their Shetland base. Outclassed by German fighters of the time and slower than some enemy bombers, they were a stop gap measure for the defence of Plymouth.

Hauptmann Hajo Hermann wearing his Iron Cross. On 22 July 1940 he flew into a barrage balloon over Plymouth and, despite a narrow escape from death, successfully laid mines in Plymouth Sound.

navigation, flying at low speed and low altitude. Plymouth was one of the ports the Luftwaffe attempted to seal off by the laying of mines.

On one occasion, on the night of 22 July 1940, four Ju88 aircraft, each carrying two magnetic mines, were flying towards Plymouth to lay mines at the breakwater in Plymouth Sound. As one of the planes came in on its descent path the aircraft flew into the top of a barrage balloon. On touching the balloon the Ju88 went out of control, flying upside down over Plymouth.

The stricken aircraft was caught and held by a searchlight as anti-aircraft guns fired on it. Somehow the aircraft's engines continued to run and, just as its pilot Hauptmann Hermann was about to order his crew to bail out, the aircraft righted itself. Now in control Hauptman Hermann decided to complete his mission of laying the magnetic mines in Plymouth Sound. This accomplished, his plane made height and returned to base.[66]

Along with their persistence in laying mines in Plymouth Sound, the Luftwaffe on one occasion took advantage of a gap in the balloon barrage defence between Eggbuckland and Plymouth Sound. Aircraft descended to 500 feet, dropping mines in the waters near to Devonport Dockyard.

Enemy magnetic mines, other than being dangerous, were a cause of considerable frustration for it meant that each morning naval minesweepers had to clear Plymouth Sound thus delaying the Sunderland flying boats of Coastal Command from becoming airborne.

The Luftwaffe were flying regularly over Devon by early July 1940. On Saturday morning 6 July 1940, a German aircraft dropped two high explosive (HE) bombs at Galmpton near Brixham. There were two casualties, superficial damage to property, and a very large crater. This may have been the first recorded air raid on Devon in World War Two. Later that same morning an enemy plane flew over Plymouth dropping three bombs on a row of houses in Devonport killing three people and injuring six others, the first fatalities from an air raid on the city.

No air raid warnings preceded the attack on Galmpton as permission to sound the warning sirens was refused.[67] Yet at Plymouth the same morning the public warning siren was given. This was a significant day in the history of wartime Devon as it marked the beginning of the Luftwaffe's attack on the county that in the coming years was to result in considerable destruction, trauma and casualties.

On the following day, a Sunday, a single enemy bomber appeared over Plymouth at teatime. Again the alert had been sounded before any bombs were dropped, but this did not prevent five people from being killed, and many houses sustained damage. On this same day an enemy aircraft appeared and dropped two bombs close to Teignmouth Pier. There were people on the pier and on the beach who immediately ran for cover but nine people, six of them children, were injured, and later one of them died.

These raids took place during the initial phase of the Battle of Britain, a time of epic air battles high in the summer skies over South East England. Each week of July 1940 Plymouth was attacked. Hawker Hurricane fighters based at RAF Exeter had their first major engagement in July during the Battle of Britain when they met up with a group of Ju88s and HeIIIs that arrived over Portland (Dorset) with an escort of fighters. That same afternoon there was a further formidable air attack. On the right flank a large formation of German fighters, flying ahead of the enemy bomber force, was intercepted off Portland by 213 Squadron of RAF

A collapsed barrage balloon settles on the roof of the Swarthmore Hotel in Plymouth, 3 May 1940

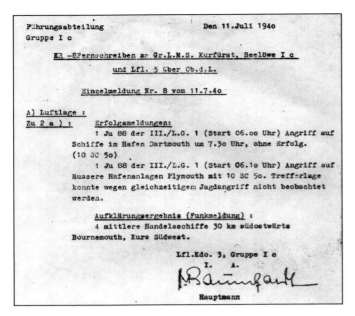

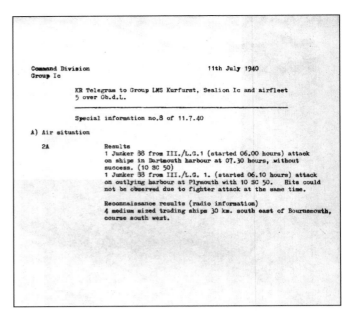

A Luftwaffe operational report and its translation referring to attacks on Dartmouth and Plymouth by Junker 88 aircraft. The report is interesting in so far as it was sent to the German Invasion Headquarters 'Sealion'.

Exeter and 152 Squadron of RAF Warmwell. The action that took place at 1600 hrs and the placement of 213 Squadron is shown on the map below.

The first air raid on Exeter was a minor event, when a single enemy aircraft flew over the city on the night of 20 August 1940 dropping bombs in the St Thomas area and causing slight damage to property. Also in August Brixham was bombed, followed two hours later, without any warning, by an attack on Torquay when eight bombs exploded damaging property and slightly injuring some people.

That same evening three enemy aircraft, flying in from the east, attacked Newton Abbot railway station with high explosive bombs and strafed the area with machine-gun fire. A passenger train bound for Plymouth had departed three minutes before the attack, but another Plymouth-bound train was waiting in the station.

Considerable damage occurred, fourteen people lost their lives and the total number of casualties was 75. Parts of the station were wrecked, 15 locomotives and 51 passenger carriages damaged, along with 22 goods wagons.[69]

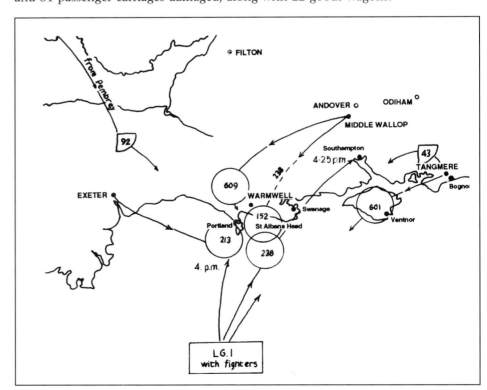

This map shows the involvement of 213 Squadron from RAF Exeter in attacking a large formation of German bombers off Portland Bill, 13 August 1940.

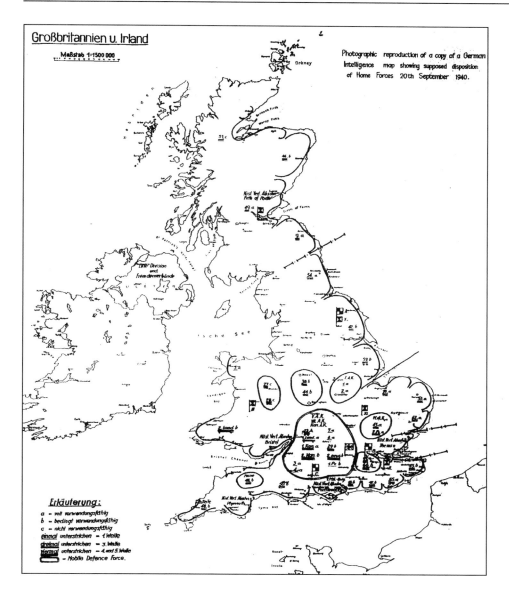

Großbritannien u. Irland

Maßstab 1:1500 000

Photographic reproduction of a copy of a German Intelligence map showing supposed disposition of Home Forces 20th September 1940.

Erläuterung:
a = voll verwendungsfähig
b = bedingt verwendungsfähig
c = nicht verwendungsfähig
einmal unterstrichen = 1. Welle
dreimal unterstrichen = 3. Welle
viermal unterstrichen = 4. und 5. Welle
☐ = Mobile Defence force.

A German Intelligence map dated 20 September 1940 showing the supposed disposition of British Home forces. It is interesting to note that they were correct in identifying the placement of the 48th Division in Devon.

The possibility of an invasion was still very much in the minds of the British military command. The German High Command cultivated a plan of deception regarding a possible landing in England, and continued with this even when great battles were being fought on the Russian Front and many of the German military units had been withdrawn from France. The expected time of the Germans attempting a landing was in September 1940, a period in Devon of false alarms. The Home Guard was called out early one morning to erect barbed-wire barriers across the road in the northern district of Plymouth. Five days later on 13 September 1940, the Home Guard manned the barricades at Ilfracombe. Identification cards were demanded to be shown, rumours spread of German agents, but the day ended in anti-climax.

Fears of fifth column activities and traitors among the population were all very much part of wartime Devon at this period. Unknown at the time, during the third week of September 1940, the French cutter *La Part Bleu* arrived in Plymouth carrying three German agents who had been recruited by the Abwehr, their mission probably sabotage.[70]
On the Home Front at Salcombe many housewives were, if not speechless, very angry, as there was no cheese to be found in the town. All the shops were completely empty, there was not a scrap to be had, and for some reason the main suppliers had used up all their stocks.
The talk of the town between Kingsbridge sportsmen was the result of a rugby match in which the local team beat an Army XV by 29–3. A local schoolboy playing in the team, aged thirteen, kicked three of the Kingsbridge goals.

More sophisticated preparations were in hand for training LDV (Home Guard) forces, although in 1940 it was largely a matter of using whatever local resources were available. This photograph, taken in May 1940, shows a makeshift rifle range in South Devon.

An impressive photograph of an RAAF Sunderland on the slipway outside the flying boat hangers at Mountbatten, Plymouth. These aircraft were used in Coastal Command duties and were a familiar sight taking off across the waters of Plymouth Sound. Now (1994) abandoned, the huge hangers can still be seen at the former base at Mountbatten.

The events of air battles over Britain made the Luftwaffe change its tactics. Reichsmarschall Goering called his Luftwaffe officers to the Hague to inform them of a major change in bombing policy. A strategic offensive was to begin with the intention of destroying England's industrial economic capacity and to terrorise and demoralise the British people. The Luftwaffe opened with a massive attack on the city of Coventry on 14 November 1940.

On 27 November 1940 Plymouth was attacked by a force of 112 enemy bombers over a period of eight hours. Bombs fell in many areas of the city. Over a hundred tons of high explosive bombs were dropped, together with 6000 incendiary bombs, and a number of flame bombs. These latter were large incendiary bombs containing an oil mixture together with an explosive.

The enemy force targetted RAF Mountbatten and set fire to one of the large aircraft hangers destroying two Sunderland flying boats of Coastal Command.

Near to RAF Mountbatten, in the vicinity of Turnchapel, one of the services' oil storage tanks was hit by a bomb and instantly burst into flames. The heat from the fire was so intense that water from the fireman's hosepipes evaporated before it reached the flames. Two days later the intense heat caused the other storage tanks to burn. One of these tanks exploded. The burning oil came pouring out over the wall into Hooe Lake catching two fireboats alight and killing two firemen. Other firemen swam ashore before the blazing oil completely covered the water, a few minutes later the two fireboats exploded.

The oil fires lasted five days, and high billowing clouds of smoke hung over the city. At night the fires illuminated Plymouth and people were fearful that this would encourage enemy bombers to return.

The aftermath of the air attack on RAF Mountbatten, Plymouth, November 1940. In the foreground is the ruined flying boat hanger while distant smoke rises from the oil tanks at Turnchapel.

As Plymouth was experiencing this fearsome air raid, three German destroyers were sailing off Prawle Point when they came across two British tugs, one of which was sunk, the other escaped. Further westward along the coast towards Falmouth, a cutter sailing from Plymouth was also sunk. As the three enemy destroyers were returning to Brest, a British Fifth Destroyer Flotilla was ordered to intercept the enemy force but in the ensuing engagement an enemy torpedo hit and destroyed the bows of HMS *Javelin*. A second torpedo then hit the stern of the vessel causing rapid flooding. The stricken HMS *Javelin* was towed into Plymouth on 30 November 1940. The attack killed forty-eight members of the crew and the destroyer was so severely damaged it took thirteen months at Devonport Dockyard to repair her.[71]

Two tiny figures gaze out on the ruins of their homes following the raid on Plymouth in November 1940. Smoke billows from the blazing Turnchapel oil tanks.

The second wartime Christmas in Devon was celebrated free from enemy attacks, but because of the wartime situation all Christmas leave for the home forces was cancelled. Many personal items were no longer in the shops to be purchased, but shops reported trading was very good. Christmas was quiet at Tavistock, with absent relatives and friends missed. Christmas breakfast at the Tavistock Public Institute was fried sausages, with roast beef and plum pudding for Christmas dinner.

An evacuee living at a farm in the village of Alverdiscott some six miles from Barnstaple remembers going with her foster parents to the local vicarage at Christmas and having goose for dinner, and then playing charades with the words taken from Christmas carols.

Christmas was also quiet at Sidmouth, the year ending with a Sidmouth fireman being called out to a fire only to find it was in his own house!

Chapter 3 — References
(PC = Personal Communication)

1. WO 166; 1252; *Southern Command Diaries*, PRO.
2. *Tavistock Times*, May 1940.
3. *Agatha Christie* (1984), Janet Morgan.
4. WO 166; 1252; *Southern Command Diaries*, PRO.
5. *The Little Ships of Dunkirk* (1989), Christian Avian.
6. *The Great Western in South Devon* (1990), Beck and Copsey.
7. *The Ships that Saved an Army* (1990), Russell Plummer.
8. PC: Mr P. Southcombe.
9. PC: Mr J. T. R. Snell.
10. WO 166; 1252; *Southern Command Diaries*, PRO.
11. *It Came To Our Door* (1945), P. Twyford.
12. PC: Mr P. Clare.
13. *Britannia at Dartmouth* (1966), S. W. C. Pack.
14. PC: Mr. P. Clare.
15. WO 166; 1252; *Southern Command Diaries*, PRO.
16. *The War in France and Flanders*, (1939–40), Major L. G. Ellis.
17. *The Royal Naval Medicine Service* Vol. 1. J. G. S. Coulter.
18. PC: Mr. P. Southcombe.
19. *The War in France and Flanders* (1939–40), Major L. G. Ellis.
20. *Chronicle of Major Rex* Ref: 87.31.1. IMW.
21. PC: Mr. P. Holland.
22. ADM 199; 807; ORP *Gdynia*, PRO.
23. ADM 199; 664; FS *Paris*, PRO.
24. ADM 199; 822; *Seizure of French Ships*, PRO.
25. *Who Sank Surcouf?* (1991), James Rusbridger.
26. *Express and Echo*, Exeter, June 1940.
27. *Pillboxes: A study of UK Defences 1940* (1985), Henry Wills.
28. *Somerset at War 1939–1945* (1988), Mac Hawkins.
29. *Invasion of England 1940* (1990), Peter Schewk.
30. *The Phoney War of the Home Front* (1961), E. S. Turner.
31. *It All Happened Before* (1945), John Rands.
32. PC: Mr P. Southcombe.
33. WO 166; 1275; *North Devon Defences*, PRO.
34. WO 192; 145; *Appledore Defences*, PRO.
35. WO 166; 1252; *Southern Command Diaries*, PRO.
36. WO 199; 605; *Armoured Trains*, PRO.
37. *Action Stations 5* (1982), C. Ashworth.
38. Air 41; *Royal Observer Corps*, PRO.
39. PC: Mr C. H. Martin.
40. AVIA 7; 463; *Radar*, PRO.
41. *Dartmouth Chronicle*, June 1940.
42. WO 192; 154; *Sidmouth Defences*, PRO.
43. WO 1252; *South West Defenses*, PRO.
44. PC: Mr L. Lownds-Pateman.
45. WO 192; 144; *Torquay Defences*, PRO.
46. *378 Battery Coast Artillery* (1989), R. Coleman.
47. WO 192; 141; *Brixham Defences*, PRO.
48. PC: Mr F. Park.
49. WO 192; 149; *Dartmouth Defences*, PRO.
50. *Dartmouth*, 1950, Percy Russell.
51. *Britannia at Dartmouth* (1966), S. W. C. Pack.
52. *Dartmouth*, 1950, Percy Russell.
53. 'Life in the South Hams in World War II' (1988), Neville C. Oswald,
    Rep. Trans Devon Assc. Advmnt Sci. 120.
54. WO 192; 142; *Salcombe Defences*, PRO.
55. PC: Mrs A. Warren.
56. PC: Mr P. Couzins.
57. PC: Mr Tony Porter.
58. *Citadel* (1987), F. W. Woodward.
59. WO 199; 1767; *Defence of SW England*, PRO.
60. *The Commandos 1940–1945* (1985), Charles Messenger.
61. *Clandestine Warfare* (1988), Ladd and Mellon.
62. *Dartmouth Chronicle*, June 1940.
63. *The Phoney War on the Home Front* (1961), E. S. Turner.
64. PC: Mr J. T. R. Snell.
65. AIR 50; 95; *Squadron 247 Roborough*, PRO.
66. *Battle over Britain*, 1969, Francis Mason.
67. *Torquay ARP*, Torquay Library.
68. *The Defence of the United Kingdom* (1957), B. Collier.
69. *The Bombing of Newton Abbot Station* (1991), A. R. Kingdom.
70. *British Intelligence in the Second World War*, Vol. 4, (1990), Hinsley and Simkins.
71. *German Destroyers of World War Two* (1991), M. J. Whitley.

THE GREAT FIRE RAIDS ON PLYMOUTH

Devon, together with the rest of the United Kingdom, spent the second wartime Christmas free from enemy air attack; it had in fact been an unofficial truce observed by both sides.[1]

Few people were present to see in the New Year (1941) at Bideford Longbridge compared with the large number of people who had attended the previous New Year's Eve celebrations. There were no church bells, it was still forbidden to ring them. Many Devon housewives still continued the tradition of brushing the Old Year out, with the front door opened to let in the New Year.

Wintery weather prevailed in North Devon with falls of snow causing deep drifts, and river levels high with fast flowing water. If there were no bells, at least music was heard in the streets of Bideford as the Home Guard had formed a silver band to help in recruiting new members. Over at Hatherleigh they had a Home Guard bugle band that made its first appearance early in January when it led its platoon to parade.

Four hundred people joined in the singing and dancing on New Year's Eve in the moorland town of Tavistock. Many attended the parish church and celebrated by prayer and meditation. At the town's civil defence report centre, two wardens toasted the New Year in with a cup of tea from a thermos flask.

New Year's Day at Sidmouth was quiet although there had been festive dinners held at hostels in the area. Roast pork, on ration, was served at one hostel, where a member of the food control committee was present. As she watched the amount of meat being served, she could not help worrying as to where all the pork had come from.

Sidmouth people complained, as did Tiverton people, about the reduction in gas pressure being made too early in the day, while others said it was impossible to read by gaslight as the light was so poor. At Plymouth some households had no supplies of gas at all due to the consequences of the air attacks on the city.

Many children, if they did not have a Christmas party, attended a festive party in the New Year. Among the many small communities in Devon the children in the villages of Chawleigh, Chittlehamholt, Chittlehampton, and Clannaborough relished eating the wartime sandwiches and cakes provided at their parties.

The Christmas 'truce' was short lived. Just three days after the holiday (1940), the German Luftwaffe bombed Plymouth using twenty-one aircraft. This particular air attack included three Pathfinder units each using its own specialised techniques of fire raising.[2] The city, having experienced its first air raid in July 1940, was now being subjected to increasing air attacks.

Even so, life went on in the city. Two dance bands supplied the non-stop dance music at the Victorian Pier Pavilion, to celebrate the New Year. All was then quiet until 9 January when the city had its 247th alert and an air raid.

January was the time when the new ration books were issued. There were 3000 unclaimed ration books at Plymouth's local food offices. Tramps were a problem for the city's food officers. Some men of the road still did not possess a government identity card and were suspected of each receiving two ration books.

The year started in an unfortunate way for two particular Devonians: at Exeter one person was fined ten shillings for having an unscreened oil-lamp on the front of his cycle as he was wheeling it along. In North Devon a lady was fined at an Ilfracombe court for using too much sugar at the local Methodist church canteen; the fine was paid by a Methodist minister.

Changes were taking place on the Devon Home Front: many more women were seen throughout the county taking on work and responsibilities that had been accepted previously as the domain of the male. Women now worked in industrial jobs; they toiled alongside the men at the shipyards, delivered the bread and milk and worked on the buses.

A Heinkel III crashed on Lundy Island early in March 1941 after attacking a merchant ship in the Bristol Channel, none of the crew were injured. News of the captured Luftwaffe aircrew reached Appledore, and when they landed they were given a hostile reception by a large crowd of people who had assembled on the quay.

Dartmouth had a new air raid siren in the market place, gas detector boards had been erected and placed in different parts of the town. Newly formed fire-fighting street squads were organised and sand heaps were placed in streets to extinguish any incendiary bombs that may be dropped in the vicinity.

The indigenous population of Dartmouth was 6729, with an additional estimated one thousand evacuees. The small riverside town had nineteen public houses and there were advantages to being part of a fishing community. On one day at this time the local people devoured six hundred oysters to raise money for charity.

A government order came into effect early in 1941 that made it a legal duty of occupiers of all business premises to notify the fire-fighting services as to the arrangements that had been made for fire watching. At Exeter, local builders were invited to contact the city's civil engineers and surveyors regarding the proposed construction of refuge centres and public air raid shelters.

At night, when most people were asleep in bed, men of the Royal Engineers company based at Ilfracombe would drive their vehicles and equipment on to Exmoor for night training exercises in chemical warfare; no gas was released, just a tracer powder. In the darkness of the night, often in rain and experiencing the most uncomfortable conditions, the Engineers would erect the steel projectors for throwing gas bombs into the blackness on to the high slopes of Exmoor near Martinhoe; thus large parts of Exmoor were pitted with holes caused by the Royal Engineers' nocturnal exercises.[3]

Sleepless nights were not uncommon, not only for those who had experienced air raids ever since the summer of 1940, but also by the various communities that were alerted by false alarms which compelled many people to get out of their beds to seek shelter. Many Devon communities that did not directly experience bombing, would hear the enemy aircraft flying overhead towards their target, perhaps in Devon, perhaps to a target in South Wales or the Midlands. Then at a later time the enemy bombers would be heard returning from their mission. This was the time of long winter nights listening for the enemy bomber, waiting for the break of dawn.

There were, after eighteen months of war, shortages of essential domestic supplies in Devon. Along with gas various households were on occasion without electricity, and to obtain a sack of coal was for some people impossible. The bombing had already affected the drinking water supplies of Plymouth resulting in water carts being sent out on to some streets in the city.

The increasing air attacks on Plymouth caused a growing concern for personal safety. Many more people were leaving the city, some on a permanent basis, others travelling away from Plymouth each evening. Spending the night in an air raid shelter was a firmly established routine. Plymouth had been actively building up its civil defence forces with a recruiting campaign for more civil defence workers. A compulsory Fire Waters Order had been implemented.

On 6 February 1941 War Directive Number 23 was published by the German Führer. Item 5 of the directive stated:

> Until the beginning of the regrouping of forces for Barbarossa (the code name for the Invasion of Russia) efforts will be made to intensify the effect of air and sea war, not only in order to inflict the heaviest possible losses on England, but also in order to give the impression that an invasion of the British Isles is planned this year.

Plymouth experienced a severe air raid during the second week of March. The city had already been bombed on thirty-one separate occasions. Physical changes in the appearance of the city were now obvious. As shop windows had been shattered so boarding had been put up to replace glass. The peacetime look had gone. Buildings that had been ruined by bombs, became bomb sites for weeds to grow and children to play on.

The Luftwaffe now attacked London and many provincial communities with night bombing raids using navigational aids to locate their targets. This system of radio beams was used to guide the enemy bombers for the devastating raid on Coventry in November 1940. British scientists subsequently achieved a solution (so they believed) in disrupting (bending) the German radio navigation beam.

This jamming of the beam had the effect of forcing the Germans to switch their air attacks from the industrial centres of England to coastal targets. They now used a radio beam signal laid across the English Channel from France and directed on south coast targets. The signal was so strong that British scientists could do nothing about it.[4]

'Knickebein', as the radio navigation system was known by the Luftwaffe, used two transmitters. The pilot using Knickebein flew along the approach beam and, when confident he was on course and approaching his target, he switched to the second beam. At the point of intersection the bomb load would be released manually. Using this method of bombing the accuracy when flying from Northern France to England was in order of one mile.

The German Pathfinder (fire raising) force, Kampfgruppe 100, was equipped with another beam system as an aid to target location referred to as the 'X Apparatus' (X-GERAT). This system had timing equipment that, with calculations taken from various factors during flight, led to the automatic release of the bomb load into the target area. A third, more refined system the Germans had developed, was the 'Y-Verfahren'. The III Gruppe of Kampfgeschwader 26 was at this time the only unit installed with the single approach beam. The aircraft would automatically signal it had intercepted the beam, receiving additional signals from a ground station. At a given time a signal would be communicated from a group controller for the aircraft's crew to release the bomb load.

Wartime Plymouth seemed to be grey all over as if someone had attempted to camouflage the city with battleship grey paint. One of the largest structures to be camouflaged was the tall grain elevator at Millbay Dock.

Still, for those with money, the city offered much by way of gaiety and comfort, particularly when it came to eating out. At one of the city's hotels the wartime breakfast menu had a choice of fourteen different dishes. There were also after-noon tea dances and splendid evening dinners requiring dinner dress, or dress uniform, to be worn.

Dancing on the Hoe in the weeks after the Plymouth Blitz. Here the dance band stands under the statue of Sir Francis Drake. To the left is the wartime 'hangar' cafe.

Plymouth came alive in the evening. The armed services and many Empire and Allied fighting units were stationed in or near to the city. The very size of the naval population meant that every serviceman seemed to be in naval uniform. Whatever the height or size of the sailor, they all had short back and sides haircuts, polished black naval issue shoes and well pressed uniforms, with horizontal creases in their bell bottom trousers.

But the shadow of war was never far away. Early in the year a member of the Ministry of Home Security visited Plymouth carrying an important government warning to the city that it must expect to be heavily attacked by the Luftwaffe in the near future.[5]

The last day of winter was a Thursday, early closing day in Plymouth. The weather was fine, visibility good. The surrounding countryside air was filled with the fragrance associated with springtime. Wild violets and yellow primroses were growing in the Devon hedgerows. The date 20 March 1941 was to be a special wartime day. A royal visit had secretly been arranged in response to an invitation sent to Buckingham Palace the previous year by Lord Astor.[6] Information that the King and Queen would be in Plymouth was announced at breakfast time by the local Rediffusion Broadcasting System. An estimated eight thousand Plymouth households were connected to the Rediffusion system that brought radio by cable to a simple loudspeaker broadcasting the BBC Home Service programmes. The advantage of this cable system was that whenever the BBC programmes were interrupted by an air raid using the normal radio receivers, the Rediffusion customers continued to receive their programmes direct from the BBC. The relay systems was also used in wartime Plymouth to broadcast local civil information, often requesting the listener to pass on any broadcast information to their friends and neighbours. These local announcements were made from a small studio situated in the basement of Plymouth's Guildhall next to the Plymouth ARP Control Centre.[7]

The royal train arrived at Millbay (Plymouth) station at 10.30am. After the official reception, the royal entourage were driven to Devonport Dockyard at the start of a very busy day of activities. The formalities over, the King and Queen had tea at Elliot Place, Plymouth Hoe, the local residence of Lord and Lady Astor. A brief visit was made to the YMCA before Their Majesties were driven to the royal train, departing from Plymouth at 5.45pm.

During the day Plymouth's defences had been alerted by a Home Office Security Intelligence Unit that an intensive air attack on Plymouth was probable that night. Senior members of the Civil Defence were instructed to stand by, with orders to underplay the situation, so not to cause undue alarm.[8]

On the morning of 20 March 1941 the city's main shopping area was crowded with people. Except for the royal visit, this was just another wartime day to contend with. Within the city there would be those who had received a telegram informing them that a relative had been killed or was missing on active service; other Plymouth families were coping with the grief of losing relatives and friends in the air raids. Mourning was mingled with the joy that the visit of the royal couple had brought to the city.

With a Sunderland flying boat in the foreground, the battleship HMS *Hood* leaves Plymouth Sound after repairs at Devonport Dockyard. Months later she was sunk with the loss of 1300 lives.

On the day of the Plymouth Blitz, 20 March 1941, the city was host to King George VI and Queen Elizabeth. Here they are greeted at the station by the official reception committee.

Throughout the day reception centres were being prepared, as they had been each day in the past, for those bombed out of their homes and in need of immediate shelter and rest.

By early evening the royal visitors had departed, the civic dignitaries had gone home, and the civil defences personnel who had been inspected by the King at the Guildhall Square reported back to their posts. For a short while the centre of Plymouth was quiet. Then the servicemen on their shore-leave appeared on the streets, as they did every night. Public houses, cinemas, music halls and dance venues in Plymouth and Devonport were soon filled with servicemen; custom was good.

The air raid siren sounded throughout greater Plymouth just after 8.30pm. The undulating whine of the warning signal soon gave way to the deafening noise of anti-aircraft fire. The German bomber crews had no problem in recognising Plymouth for on a clear moonlight night, with the broad silver estuary of the River Tamar gleaming below, the Devon city is easily identified from the air.

The attack on Plymouth began with Heinkel III aircraft of KG27 releasing their bomb loads on the city below. Then the Pathfinder force flew over the city dropping vivid coloured flares to identify selected target areas, followed by the release of thousands of incendiary bombs.

The enemy's plan of attack was to approach Plymouth flying in a single line with two to three minute intervals between each bomber. In all the raid lasted for over four hours.[10]

A Plymouth family, bombed out of their home, sit down to a meal in one of the city's reception centres.

A Heinkel III of Gruppe KG55 sets out from north-west France for a raid over England. It was this type of aircraft that took part in the Plymouth Blitz.

Fires soon took hold. Early reports received at Plymouth's control centre indicated the centre of the city was a major target. As the fires blazed, flames spread from shop to shop throughout the commercial heart of the city. The extent and ferocity of the fires resulted in urgent calls to other West Country fire brigades to immediately travel to assist Plymouth. Army and naval authorities responded in using pumps from their own establishments. As the infernos continued, further urgent calls were made to fire fighters from hundreds of miles away. Through the black out, along dimly lit roads, firemen travelled from Birmingham, Bristol, Swindon and Salisbury to the blazing city of Plymouth.

The timing of the air raid caught many people away from their homes, in cinemas, dance halls, and visiting friends. At the Palace (Variety) Theatre, the manager walked on to the stage to inform the audience that a major air raid was developing. As the Billy Cotton Band continued to entertain the audience of the first house, there was an enormous explosion extinguishing all the theatre lighting. People became frightened, some panicked, but calm was established as a trumpet player started to play. Then with some lighting established the audience was persuaded to stay at the theatre until 5.30am the following morning.

The morning after the raid the BBC's first morning news bulletin announced that a South West town had been raided and two churches, a cinema and many houses were damaged. Later that day, an official Ministry communique stated: 'Enemy activities last night were on a smaller scale than of late'. What in fact had

Plymouth, Derry's Cross, 20 March, 1941. Huge fires rage in the city centre.

Two photographs of the formidable Junkers 88. (Top) A Ju88 of KG54, the Death's Head Squadron, which participated in the Plymouth raids. (Bottom) A Ju88 in flight: the bomber was used in raids across Devon.

befallen Plymouth, was that 30 000 incendiary bombs and more than a hundred high explosive bombs of varying calibre had damaged or destroyed most of the city centre, civil buildings and the mother church of St Andrews. Furthermore, hundreds of homes were destroyed leaving thousands homeless.

Any elation the Plymouth people may have experienced on surviving the ordeal was quickly subdued by thoughts of those who had been killed or injured, and the dread of further raids. Their fears were confirmed on the following night, 21 March, when the Luftwaffe intensified their attack on the city. The evening was reasonably fine but with some heavy cloud. An ominously strong westerly wind was blowing through the city. The Palace Theatre was open, with Billy Cotton and his Band on stage to entertain; but when the curtain went up there were just eight people in the audience.[11]

The attack followed the pattern of that of the previous night. The German Pathfinders circled above the city for twenty minutes before releasing their flares. The target areas were adjacent to those of the previous night. The anti-aircraft defences again found it difficult to identify the type of aircraft the Germans were using to attack. The bombers were painted black, with exhaust cowlings shielded to hide their tell-tale pinpoints of flame. However, the approaching planes could be identified as belonging to the enemy by the characteristic drone of desynchronised airscrews that the Germans adopted to prevent the British sound detectors from identifying individual types of aircraft. Aircraft of KG51 (the Edelweiss Squadron) and Ju 88s of KG54 (the Death's Head Squadron) were among the units of the attacking force.

During this second successive aerial attack the enemy aircraft released 35 375 incendiary bombs, 6000 more than on the previous night. There was also a significant increase in the number of high explosive bombs that were dropped.[12] The prevailing south-west wind fanned the flames, spreading the fires with greater speed than on the previous evening.

Plymouth's control centre based in the Guildhall basement was hit and caught fire, compelling duty staff to be immediately evacuated to the Devonport report centre. The intensity of the air raid made it seem that everywhere in Plymouth

Plymouth, March 1941: the sad sight of personal belongings rescued from damaged houses and piled in the city streets. Such detritus of war proved dangerous, not only by restricting movement around the city, but in posing a possible fire hazard in the event of further raids.

was bombed or burning. Areas of Union Street, the haunt of the navy, were completely on fire. The Royal Marine and Naval Barracks were hit by bombs. To the east of the city fires were burning on the Barbican and two timberyards and a tar distillery were burning furiously.

What little remained of the city's centre was now destroyed with the exception of the *Western Morning News* offices and production department. On either side of the newspaper offices the buildings had caught fire and fire-fighters used water from a water-filled bomb crater to save the *Morning News* building.

The vicar of St Augustine Church, Plymouth wrote in the church diary. 'The second time a fire bomb fell through the roof of the Church, to see the Church brilliantly lit by that satanic light was a daunting sight'.[13]

The following morning not one person in Plymouth knew the extent of the destruction or the number of casualties that the city had suffered. The intensity of the air attack had resulted in a complete breakdown of communications throughout the city. Consequently, Plymouth Emergency Committee was unable to obtain a comprehensive situation report until later in the day. Conditions in certain areas of Plymouth were chaotic and desperate action had been taken to alleviate some of the acute problems. For example, an urgent request was sent to the army to send Royal Engineers to defuse eighty-five unexploded bombs. All approach roads to the city were closed by establishing road blocks manned by civil and military policemen.[14].

The harrowing and hard physical toil of searching for and rescuing trapped people under the heaps of rubble and collapsed buildings continued throughout

Plymouth, 1941: arrangements were made for Royal Naval personnel to remove salvaged furniture to stores away from the city centre.

Saturday and the following day. Plymouth Guildhall was a burnt out shell, the interior a charred mass of stone, brick and heavy oak beams. Everywhere scenes of destruction were desolate and macabre: steel skeletons rising from the pulverised brick of bomb fractured walls; pieces of roof clinging to distorted beams. A sickly odour pervaded the whole area.

Away from the ruined city centre, residential areas had also sustained fearful damage. Six thousand homes were in ruins, thousands of people were homeless. Thousands of others were unable to return to homes severely damaged and without light, heat and cooking facilities. Bomb craters were everywhere, with debris and rubbish heaped up in the streets preventing the passage of people and vehicles.

There had been many casualties, but initial estimates were grossly exaggerated, although excessive claims of dead and injured were easy to believe in the immediate aftermath. With emergency food supplies ruined by the bombing, and with thousands of people either homeless or denied cooking facilities, it soon became apparent there was an acute feeding problem. The timely intervention of the armed services in organising cooked meals prevented a serious situation from becoming a disaster.[15]

Many Devon communities had already reached saturation point in accommodating servicemen and civilian evacuees. This did not deter representatives of various Devon communities from travelling to Plymouth to discuss with the City Fathers what assistance they may be able to offer in accommodating the homeless. In the city no time was lost by the proprietors of the larger shops and small businesses in arranging alternative premises, however temporary, to continue trading as quickly as possible.

The Bishop of Plymouth conducts the burial service over the mass graves of victims of the March raids on Plymouth.

Three days after the air attacks a military funeral was held to bury the soldiers who had been killed by the bombing.

Most of the civilians who had lost their lives were buried in a communal grave. The funeral was a sombre occasion with civic leaders, military personnel and civilian mourners. The rows of coffins and Union Flag drapes said more than any reportage of the burials.

The weeks following, Plymouth carried on under a variety of difficulties and inconveniences against the background of grief and anger. In an attempt to carry out immediate essential repairs on the thousands of damaged properties an army of building workers was recruited from Cornwall and Devon and sent to Plymouth.

The wartime restrictions on news limited the amount of published information on the intensive fire raids on Plymouth. The news of the Plymouth Blitz however quickly spread throughout the West Country and people began to comprehend the magnitude of the bombing and destruction that had occurred. The experience of those dreadful raids on the city were but a prelude, for many people the worst was yet to come.

One month later, in April 1941, the Luftwaffe, using 120 bombers, attacked Plymouth in a raid lasting six hours. This was to be the first of several successive

Plymouth, April 1941: further raids on the city caused damage of almost unimaginable severity.

intensive air attacks that month. The Pathfinder force dropped 10 000 incendiary bombs within sixteen minutes of arriving over the city. The main target areas on the 21 April were the naval dockyard and the Devonport area. In terms of bomb loads, the attack was heavier than either of the March raids. The high explosive bombs that were dropped included thirty-one bombs of 1000kg calibre and nearly 36 000 incendiary bombs.

Any history of the Plymouth Blitz will record the 21 April as a night of disaster. One of the city's underground shelters (Portland Square) sustained a direct hit from a high explosive bomb killing seventy-two people — only two survived.

At Devonport no more than two miles away, within the confines of the naval base of HMS *Drake*, a tower of the Boscawen Block used for accommodating naval petty officers was set on fire. While still blazing a high explosive bomb crashed through to the basement and exploded where many of the petty officers were sheltering. Seventy-eight bodies were recovered and there remained, so it was thought, eighteen other dead bodies in the basement ruins. The following night a naval sentry heard what he thought sounded like a cry from the ruin, but his report was not believed. However, hearing noises again, the duty watch was turned out and a number of sailors were brought out alive.[16]

The Regional Commissioner for the South West area had travelled overnight from his Bristol Headquarters, arriving in Plymouth early in the morning. Walking through the city streets he had never before seen so many incendiary bomb canisters in any of the other blitzed cities he had previously visited.[17]

Plymouth was attacked again the following night with Devonport as the main target area. The south yard of the naval dockyard was damaged and various military establishments destroyed. The severity of the fires were such that an appeal was made to the London Fire Services to send men overnight by train to help.[18]

As air raid casualties were being received and treated at one Devonport hospital, a bomb exploded on the premises producing a scene likened to a battlefield clearing station.

There was to be no rest for the people of Plymouth, for the city was attacked for a third successive night. The civilian community of Devonport suffered yet again. Street after street of small terraced houses were set alight and destroyed. Huge stocks of petrol and diesel stored in tanks near to the dockyard were ignited and the raging fires were not extinguished until four days later.

The human toll in the Plymouth raids totalled 4500 civilian casualties of which 1174 were killed. This small boy with his head bandaged represents the horrors that the people of the city endured.

German propaganda services were quick to capitalise on the attacks on Plymouth and their newspapers published reports and headlined the air raids.[19]

The German radio news bulletins also included reports on the Plymouth raids. Aircrew and journalists who had flown over the city were interviewed as were the 'neutral' newspaper correspondents who had visited Plymouth and were invited to describe their experiences.[20]

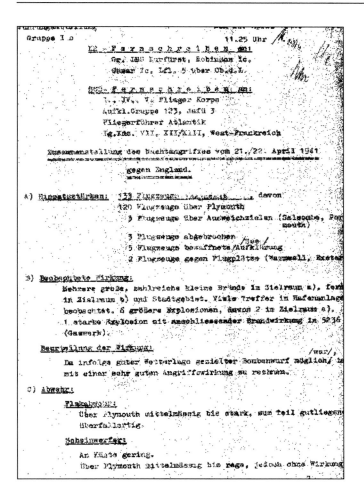
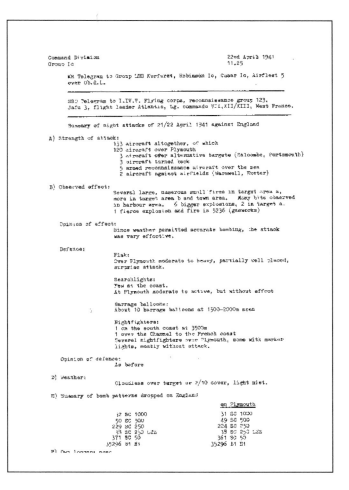

The scenes of destruction in Plymouth were horrific. People continued to go to work amid the desolation and dust-filled, polluted air. There was little absenteeism. People were tired and weary but under the circumstances cheerful and determined.

Five days had passed since the last intensive raid when the air raid warning sounded as enemy aircraft again approached the city. The Luftwaffe targeted the

A Luftwaffe operational report and translation of the raids on Plymouth of 21 and 22 April, 1941. It is interesting to note the large numbers of aircraft employed and the apparent absence of any losses.

Barton Avenue, Stoke, Plymouth, April 1941. Street after street was decimated by the bombing, with many becoming impassable. This hindered the fire fighters and swathes of the city were consumed in flame.

Marlborough Street, Devonport, April 1941. Residential areas close to the military installations such as Devonport Dockyard suffered terribly.

Plymouth, 1941: rubble has been cleared from streets in the city centre revealing a wasteland of ruined buildings, few of which have survived intact.

naval dockyard and the munition stores at Bull Point. On this occasion two huge SC1800kg (Satan) bombs were dropped and the whole of Devonport seemed to be on fire. The situation was so acute that the Chief Superintendent of the fire service flew overnight from the North East of England to RAF Roborough to assess the situation. One of the consequences of this urgent visit was for the London Fire Brigade to immediately send a further one hundred fire-fighters.

The nightmare was not over for Plymouth as the Germans attacked the city the following night. On this occasion, however, the opening of the enemy's attack was not successful and the Luftwaffe aircrew had difficulty in locating their targets. Many of the bombs that were released in the initial part of the raid fell on open country to the north and to the west side of Plymouth setting fire to woodland in the Mount Edgcumbe area.

At Devonport HMS *Trinidad* a cruiser class warship under construction at the dockyard received a direct hit (this was the warship that later in the war torpedoed itself).[21]

The eventual destruction in the city was considerable. Among the damage caused was the loss of some 80 000 books in Plymouth Central Library. The adjacent City Art Gallery containing the valuable Cottain Art Collection escaped damage. The collection was later taken out of the city for safekeeping for the rest of the war.[22]

The diary of St Augustine Church records on 29 April 1941: 'Swarms of people going past the Church into the country it almost seems as if we are present at the death of a city. Everytime there is a violent raid the desolation increases'.

The air attack on Plymouth during the night of 29 April was to be the last of the intensive fire raids on the city to occur on successive nights. From the time of

GB 15 35 b
Nur für den Dienstgebrauch
Bild Nr. F 83a/41/144 v
Aufnahme vom 24.4.41

Plymouth-Devonport
Marinefunkstelle Staddon Height
Länge (westl. Greenw.): 4° 07'   Nördl. Breite: 50° 21'
Zielhöhe über NN 91 m

Lfl. Kdo. 3 Dezember 1941

Karte 1:100000
GB/E Bl. 36 c

Maßstab etwa 1:25000

A Luftwaffe reconnaissance photograph taken over Plymouth Sound on 24 April 1941 at the time of the Plymouth Blitz.

the November raids of 1940 up to the end of April 1941 over 260 000 incendiary bombs had been released on to the city. There would however be more air raids, more destruction and casualties.

Joseph Goebbels, the German Minister for propaganda, recorded in his wartime diary details of the Plymouth Blitz. The entry in his diary written on 1 May 1941 summarises Plymouth as 'The image of horror'.[23]

The British air defences were unable to prevent the Plymouth Blitz. German aircrews had only to fly their aircraft along the radio beam laid from the Cherbourg peninsula across the Channel to Plymouth to reach their targets. There was nothing British scientific intelligence could do. Plymouth, like the other south coast ports of England, was powerless against attack by the Luftwaffe.[24]

Decoy fires were lit in an attempt to mislead enemy aircrews in identifying their targets, but the fires had no effect. In fact German aircrews reported sighting decoy fires when flying towards Plymouth. In another attempt to divert the enemy bombers away from Plymouth, Lord Louis Mountbatten sailed his flotilla of destroyers out from Devonport; when out in the English Channel he ordered the destroyers to shine their searchlights on to each other to attract the German aircraft to the illuminated flotilla.[25]

On 2 May, Winston Churchill visited the stricken naval city, two days after the last intensive air raid. The reception party greeting him on Plymouth station included two women Members of Parliament representing West Country constituents and both American by birth; a unique occasion.

The Prime Minister began his extensive tour of the naval dockyard, arriving by launch. He walked considerable distances along the dock quays, through workshops and inspected warships. After lunch he went to Admiralty House to sleep for a while as was his customary wartime routine. Later he toured some of the streets of Plymouth with his wife, in a large Daimler car. Churchill appeared deeply moved by the visit.

He left Plymouth and journeyed by train to Totnes where he was met and taken to Dartmouth Naval College. On returning to 'Chequers', the Prime Minister's

The Prime Minister and his wife with Lady Astor outside 3 Elliot Terrace, the Plymouth home of Lord and Lady Astor, May 1941. Such visits by the Premier did much to boost the morale of the civilian population throughout the war.

While on his visit in May 1941, Churchill surveys the destruction to the naval dockyard at Devonport.

'My Old Man said Follow the Van'. Lady Astor, Mayoress of Plymouth, rides on the back of a storage van. Helped by the armed services and local volunteers, hundreds of homeless people were moving out of the city, taking salvaged possessions with them.

country house, he was melancholic and kept repeating, with reference to Plymouth, 'I've never seen the like'.[26]

The weeks of May in the immediate aftermath of the air raids were a serious and potentially dangerous time for Plymouth. The needs of the homeless and the importance of bringing some order into civilian life was recognised. There was also a grave threat of the naval dockyard being destroyed due to its proximity to the streets of empty houses where great quantities of salvaged timber had been stacked. This now posed a serious fire hazard. At night this one-time residential area was now deserted. The exodus of people meant the property, indeed the entire area, was left completely unwatched. If, as was expected, there were further enemy air raids, the fires from the stacks of timber would provide a beacon for the enemy bomber crews.[27]

The day after the Prime Minister's visit the city experienced another air raid, and then from the 5 May, there were three successive but less intensive air attacks on Plymouth. That the city did not suffer further violent raids was due to the dramatic events that were developing in Europe. The impending German invasion of Russia resulted in many Luftwaffe units based in northern France being withdrawn and transferred to the Eastern European front. These events

The ruins of St Andrew's Church, Plymouth, April 1941. This is the church to which the citizens of Plymouth flocked to give thanks for their deliverance from the defeated Spanish Armada in 1588. The ruins became a symbol of the city's hope and courage, and remain today as a memorial to her suffering in the Second World War.

Plymouth April 1941: the face of despair. An elderly woman and her faithful dog sit among the remains of her bombed home.

Citizens walk single file amid the ruins of George Street, Plymouth, May 1941, once one of the busiest areas in the heart of the city.

Little Sisters of the Poor salvage belongings from the St Joseph's Home, Plymouth 1941. Over 150 old people were formerly housed here until its destruction in the April bombing.

A remarkable record from the Plymouth Blitz of the indiscriminate effects of bomb blast. While part of the house is totally destroyed, mirrors remain undamaged on the wall and bric a brac still stands on the mantlepiece unscathed. There are stories of individual people surviving when all around them had been killed: one young mother, nursing twins in her arms, was killed outright by bomb blast while both children survived untouched.

were the important factors that saved Plymouth from further destruction as, from May onwards, the German bombers were flown by largely inexperienced crews.

The city was still cordoned off from the outside world. An attempt was made to prevent inquisitive crowds travelling from areas outside the city to see the ruins that were once Plymouth.

The extent of the destruction so altered the city that the skyline of pre-war Plymouth no longer existed. The population was exhausted but the spirit was still high; contemporary official reports bear witness that the morale of the people had not broken.[28,29]

Gradually the daily domestic routine of the housewife, that had so often been disrupted by the air raids, was being re-established. For those women not engaged on war work, there was the drudgery of washing day, usually on a Monday. The wash was placed in a copper tub of boiling water and soap suds, then, after rinsing by hand, the washing was wrung slowly through a large wooden mangle. The mangle often stood in the kitchen or wash-house or out in the yard.

Attention could also be given to washing the front doorstep and cleaning the patterned-tile floor of the front porch. The brass plate of the doorstep and the door knocker were polished to a shine. Few families had their floors fitted with carpets, the floor cover was cut carpet, coconut-matting, patterned 'lino' or small rugs. The front room, if the family had a front room, was used only for special occasions.

Many front rooms had a piano with two brass candle-holders afixed above the ivory keyboard. In the corner of the room often stood a small wooden veneer cabinet with glass doors displaying the sherry glasses and a bottle of Empire Ruby Port. The cabinet might also reveal the fact that someone was or had been associated with the sea, a bright coloured oriental tea service taking pride of place. Framed photographs of the family and relatives stood in silver or dull metal frames, a serviceman in uniform usually placed in the centre.

For thousands of Plymouthians all these treasures of family life were now destroyed, or mouldering away in the ruins of their former home.

The townspeople who appeared in the streets, in what was once the centre of the city, looked in vain for the shops they had always patronised. Notices on bombsites and in the local newspapers informed the reader of what temporary accommodation the shopkeepers had been able to arrange. The destruction of civil and government offices and the relevant records and files caused considerable problems and inconveniences. Temporary offices that were established to deal with documents, coupons, permits and money allowances were now scattered all over the city area.

As each evening fell, followed by darkness, the streets of the city became deserted. This was not limited to the stark ruins of the city's centre, but extended to the areas of Stonehouse and Devonport. Public entertainment continued but people visiting the cinema, or going dancing, ensured they were able to catch the last bus home. People no longer tended to loiter in the streets. The naval dockyard damaged during the blitz continued its vital work of repairing and building the nation's warships.

The air attacks dramatically altered the social climate of the city. Many more people were leaving Plymouth. The local authorities urged families to move away, free railway tickets were offered to encourage people to go. Generous offers of accommodation came from communities in Cornwall and Devon, but these fell short of what was required to solve or significantly reduce the acute problems of accommodation and temporary shelter. Few people living in greater Plymouth had been immune from the air attacks. It was a small city with a large population. This was why, whenever there was an air raid on the city, everyone felt exposed to the bombers, and so many people were denied a restful night's sleep. Even the homes that had escaped any bomb damage had at some time been deprived of essential supplies, while many families were compulsorily evacuated because of the danger from an unexploded bomb in the vicinity.

The acute social problems of food and shelter resulted in many people becoming refugees in their own city. The suffering did not stop the moment the bombs had fallen. The ordeal of Plymouth became known to men serving away in the armed forces and servicemen were applying for compassionate leave after hearing the disturbing news of their city. Many returned to find their homes demolished and their families killed.[30]

Even before the Plymouth Blitz, people were beginning to trek out from the city to the surrounding countryside. The intensive air raids during March resulted in thousands of people joining the ranks of those who were already moving out

The evening trek out from Plymouth, April 1941. Long queues formed each evening with people hopeful of finding a lift into the countryside on buses or lorries.

each evening. This exodus was unorganised and made up of people from all social classes. Behind this movement was the belief that Plymouth was no longer a secure base.[31] Plymouth in World War Two had no suburban sprawl to offer temporary shelter for people who were homeless or who sought relief from the enemy air raids.

The trek out was like a tidal surge. Each evening people would move out of the city and then return to Plymouth early the following morning. Eventually there were families who settled more permanently in the countryside, camping out in tents and caravans.

In the late afternoons long queues of people began to form at bus stops in the city. These people were waiting to travel on the corporation buses routed to the Dartmoor communities. The buses were soon filled to capacity. Commercial and military vehicles also travelled out each evening to designated dispersal points, packed with people. Even with the strict petrol rationing, private cars would move out of Plymouth and park along the roadside and hedges. As the evening trek out gained momentum the vehicles would follow one another as though moving in convoy.

Other people would start to walk, sometimes alone, others in small family groups. Trekkers could often be identified by their luggage: a small case, carrier bag, or a blanket rolled up and slung over a shoulder. If a lorry slowed down people would move quickly towards it. The more agile would climb up into the back of the lorry and then assist others to scramble up. Each lorry would take thirty people or more.

Some trekkers took to the road each evening on their way out to the countryside, carrying with them their immediate possessions and blankets.

The trek out, March 1941: People clamber on to a lorry and van on their way out of the city. Someone has chalked 'Here we come Plymouth' on the side of the van, perhaps indicating that some transport came from outside the city to help with the daily exodus.

The trek out continued whatever the weather. Against the background of the ruined city, the cheery smiles from these women speaks of the high morale of the people of Plymouth - a feature recognised in official reports of the period. March 1941.

Many homeless people from the city set up makeshift camps in the surrounding countryside, away from the bombing of Plymouth.

Not far from Plymouth is the village of Plympton, the birthplace of Sir Joshua Reynolds. Here the grammar school was opened as a rest centre for trekkers. It was popular as a free supper and breakfast was supplied as well as a large blanket. The rest centre was always full, often overcrowded. The local medical officers believed it was a potential health hazard.

Other trekkers would travel on to Ivybridge where the rest centre was filled to capacity every evening. Lorries arrived loaded up with families, buses filled to capacity would quickly unload their passengers and drive away. The Wesleyan church hall served tea and sandwiches to the trekkers and, on occasions, over a thousand people arrived in the village, with three hundred sleeping in a small cinema with no toilet facilities. One Ivybridge rest centre was considered something of a black spot as it was the local public house, with mothers, sailors, girls and babies all in together.[32]

Strain showing through the smiles on some faces, these trekkers sit on the back of a lorry on their way out of the city clutching bundles and blankets.

Roborough village, on the edge of Dartmoor, had opened its small village hall as a rest centre, allowing women and children to stay the night. Other people camped out in their hundreds in fields by the village.[33] Further out, at the moorland village of Yelverton, trekkers sheltered in the hedgerows and camped out on Roborough Down, close to where RAF Harrowbeer was under construction. Here, with only a blanket to cover them, people slept out in the open. The WVS prepared 1500 beds for Plymouth trekkers at Paignton, but few people took up the offer as it was a long way from their place of work.[34]

As the March blitz subsided and April arrived, the number of people moving out from Plymouth each evening reduced and the rest centres began to close down. With the recurrence of the April raids the nightly exodus resumed. This time even more people joined the nightly exodus and more rest centres were called for. Premises of all sizes, many never having been blacked out, were opened and used as a shelter. Villagers in the moorland areas responded with great humanity, urgently organising such places to accommodate and feed the trekkers.

One lesson learnt from the March exodus was the importance of registering and controlling large numbers of people who congested the rest centres. Transport was made available to take people away from the overcrowded areas resulting in trekkers arriving in communities farther away from Plymouth. These included Kingsbridge, Modbury and Salcombe. The attempt to control the crowding did not prevent some dreadful situations occurring, for example Tavistock School, scheduled to shelter two hundred people, had accommodated six hundred on the night of 30 April 1941.

Not all the trekkers made their exodus across land. Many people ferried across the River Tamar to Cornwall, others chose to cross the waters of Plymouth Sound to the villages of Oreston and Turnchapel. The trekkers would then make their way up on to the clifftops overlooking the Sound where they were given a panoramic view of their city. During raids trekkers looked across at the daunting sight of the city in flames.

A contemporary report estimates that 30 000 people were involved in the exodus from Plymouth, for example on 24 April 1941 seven thousand people stayed in the Plympton area.[35] The official social history of World War Two states a figure of 50 000 people being involved in the Plymouth trek out.[36] What is also known is that many people, other than those sleeping out on the open moors, also sheltered in barns, lofts and haystacks.[37]

The intensive fire raids on greater Plymouth, as has been described, had changed the appearance of many areas within the city. But it was not just the shopping centre that had been destroyed. Residential areas, particularly at Devonport, suffered immense damage. Early in May 1941, the Government changed its policy and announced that part of Plymouth was an official evacuation area. Later this order was modified and greater Plymouth was now able to evacuate its school-children under the Government Sponsored Scheme. The first batch of Plymouth evacuees were sent to reception areas in Cornwall and Devon by the end of the month.

The huge task of effecting temporary repairs to thousands of damaged properties required a vast labour force. (There were many Plymouth properties that had been bombed on more than one occasion). The labour force was

After considerable controversy the government approved Plymouth to be an 'Evacuation Area'. This photograph shows the first batch of schoolchildren evacuees at the railway station on their way out of the city.

recruited from outside the city, in fact from outside the county, but accommodation required to house the labour repair force was itself a problem. For a considerable time these workers had to be transported each day from the Exeter and Torbay areas. Eventually Nissen huts and hostels were erected.[38] Plymouth for many years was not unlike a huge building site and a generation of Plymouthians were to grow up in an environment of temporary shops and bomb sites.

The Plymouth Blitz should be considered as the blitz of greater Plymouth for the destruction was widespread. Other than the changed appearances caused by the bombing, the 'workman's axe', used to make safe certain buildings, wrought its own changes. Many of the people who had lived all their lives in Plymouth became disorientated when attempting to find their way through the centre of the city. Years were to pass before the townspeople had a 'High Street' for shopping.

The movement of people, as distinct from the trekkers, was not always temporary, for many Plymouthians, moved from the city never to return. Meanwhile, many of the homeless were given temporary accommodation elsewhere in the city.

Communities throughout Devon were aware of Plymouth's distress. On the nights of the intensive air raids there were many friends and relatives from other parts of the county who were staying in the city and were among the casualties. Many such communities, often very small, organised collections of money through a variety of activities and sent it for the relief of the citizens of Plymouth. Shebbear, Buckland, Filleigh, Thornbury, Ashwater, Newton St Cyres were among the many communities that, by promoting whist drives, dances, social and other fund raising activities, showed their sympathy and support for the stricken city.

A bomb census of Plymouth (excluding Devonport) during the Second World War. The dots indicate where at least one high explosive bomb fell. It does not include the 260 000 or more incendiary bombs that were dropped on the city.

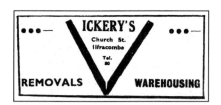
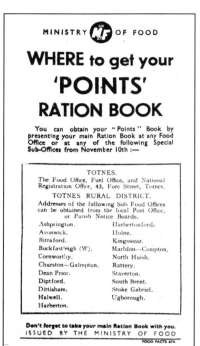

May 1941 was the month Rudolph Hess landed in Scotland, causing considerable national interest. Less well known was the fact that Rudolph Hess's father had married his first wife at Exmouth. On her death she was buried in the churchyard at Exmouth.[39] May also saw a serious raid on Brixham, with extensive damage to property.

At Tavistock, because of the vast number of people who had arrived in the small town at the time of the Plymouth Blitz, there was a proposal that Tavistock should become a closed town, with visitors to Tavistock being restricted to stay for no more than three days under the Lodger Restrictive Order.

Also at Tavistock, three JPs, including a vice admiral, a colonel, and a member of the clergy, were fined for obtaining meat in excess of the ration. Tavistockians at the time were annoyed as their milk delivery had been stopped, and there were no legal powers to enforce the milkmen to deliver. The threat of a German invasion also remained a concern at Tavistock and there was a debate as to whether or not the town's name should be obliterated from the war memorial.

The 'V' (Victory) sign, the symbol associated with the Morse code and used by the Resistance in occupied France, appeared throughout Devon on buildings, walls, vehicles and windows. Some Devon traders used the V sign in their advertisements in the local newspapers. The Mayoress of Exeter appeared at a meeting with an embroidered badge in red, with a V sign and three dots and a dash on her turquoise gown.

Evacuees continued to arrive in Devon. Not everyone welcomed this additional burden and in support of their misgivings was the 1940 report of the Devon Schools Medical Officer that stated, of the 19 233 schoolchildren who were examined, fifteen per cent were suffering from malnutrition. Comparative data showed that evacuee children were significantly better nourished than the Devon schoolchildren. Another report, of an entirely different kind and published by the RSPCA, stated that one thousand cats and dogs were treated due to the consequences of the Plymouth Blitz, along with many moorland ponies, cattle and sheep.

June came with the Whitsun holiday, and the introduction of the clothes ration with points assigned to various items of clothing. Trade was increasing in the temporary shops in Plymouth. People, not for the first time in the city's history, were dancing on the Hoe, often attracting large crowds. There was no dancing at the Victoria Pier Ballroom for this had been completely wrecked by incendiary bombs. An appeal was made by well known contemporary authors for people and institutions to donate gifts of books to replace those lost when the Plymouth Central Library stock was destroyed.

Make-do-and-mend was encouraged, with people not told but expected to use every part of their clothing. The government encouraged everything to be repaired, not only sock or stocking darned, but the toes of socks re-knitted. Re-knitting the heel was a particular problem for some who could not 'turn' the heel. There was an acute shortage of paper, reflected in the quality of wartime books and newspapers. Shopkeepers were not allowed to provide paper for wrapping or packaging.

Perhaps not obvious to the public at large, was the growing presence of the Royal Air Force in Devon. The summer of 1941 saw RAF Harrowbeer, built on the edge of Dartmoor with rubble from the Plymouth Blitz, become operational. The Yelverton airfield was a satellite of RAF Exeter, No. 10 Group fighter station. Operational activities varied, with many different units based at the moorland airfield. Here 276 Squadron for air sea rescue was based and Polish aircrew flew Spitfires for escorting convoys and ships, and provided cover for twin-engined Blenheim bombers. As the war years passed Belgian, Czech, French and Polish squadrons flew from RAF Harrowbeer, as did Empire units from Australia, Canada and New Zealand. A few days late, the small airfield at Haldon, some two miles from Teignmouth, was opened as a satellite station of Yelverton and used by target-towing aircraft.[40]

Although not unique, an RAF Station without any aircraft opened at Torquay in September 1941. This was RAF Torre Abbey where training wings for the RAF aircrew were established. Arriving at the station, cadets were medically examined, kitted out, and given some basic training before moving away to undergo further training at one of the RAF flying schools. Many of the local lads from Babbacombe ran a thriving business carrying the RAF men's kit to and from the station for those going home on leave. The presence of the RAF in Torquay was

The remains of a crashed German bomber on the slopes of Dartmoor, 1941. Throughout the war in excess of 200 Allied and enemy aircraft crashed on Devon soil, with many others falling into the sea around the coast.

obvious as so many of the large hotels were used to accommodate the airmen. Some 50 000 cadets passed through the initial training wings at Torbay.[41]

RAF Chivenor, located five miles west of Barnstaple, had re-opened as a wartime airfield on 1 October 1941, and was for a time used for training aircrew. On 26 November 1941, a Ju88, after searching in vain for shipping in the Irish Sea, decided to return to its base in North West France. Due to a navigational error the plane, when flying over Plymouth, thought it had reached the Bay of Biscay. The pilot turned north over Plymouth, supposing it to be the north coast of France, and now flew across Devon approaching Chivenor airfield. After an exchange of pyrotechnics with the ground control staff, the airfield lights were switched on and to everyone's amazement it was seen to be Ju88 with Luftwaffe markings making a descent. The German aircrew on landing realised their mistake, but a quick-thinking groundcrew member drove a lorry in its way to prevent it becoming airborne. The crew were captured and the aircraft was taken intact.[42]

Yet another RAF airfield opened in Devon a week before Christmas. This was RAF Bolt Head, not far from Salcombe. This dual-runway airfield had been constructed on the lofty heights of Bolt Head in an area of magnificent unspoilt beauty. The airfield runways that extended near to the cliff's edge must have seemed to the pilots of the aircraft as though they were taking off from an aircraft carrier. RAF Bolt Head came under the control of RAF Exeter and was destined to be involved both in important operations and associated with tragic events. Bolt Head was also of considerable importance as a Ground Control Interceptor Radar Station, constructed for the purpose of locating enemy aircraft and as an aid to navigation. Nearby, at Bolt Tail, a Chain Home Extra Low Radar Station was sited to identify low-flying aircraft and surface vessels.[43]

In December 1941, with the approach of the third wartime Christmas, dramatic events occurred that would have direct bearing on Devon and the people who were living there. On Sunday 7 December 1941, the Japanese Air Force attacked the US naval base at Pearl Harbor: America and Japan were at war. Four days later Germany and Italy formally declared war on the United States of America. A week after Pearl Harbor, the President of the United States, Franklin D. Roosevelt, extended the period of service for National Guardsmen. Americans were now drafted into the armed services from a period of two and a half years to a date six months after the end of the war. American forces could now, by the approval of both Houses of the American Congress, be deployed anywhere in the world.

As early as December 1941, the US Quartermaster Corps approached the British War Office concerning facilities for the burial and mortuary accommodation of American military personnel casualties. The outcome of this meeting was that thirteen burial sites, with a capacity for 230 000 graves, were reserved in the United Kingdom. Meanwhile President Roosevelt and the British Prime Minister met in Washington. Here the Europe First Strategy was agreed, with the initial official contingents of US troops arriving in the United Kingdom in January 1942.[44]

The spirit of Christmas prevailed in Devon during the third wartime festival despite food shortages and rationing. At Alphington, Christmas was a pleasant surprise for the village elders. Local men of sixty years of age and over who had resided in the village for five years were able to partake in drinking free beer and cider, the money coming from the proceeds of a will.

No extra official food rations were to be had. There were a few oranges for the children available in some areas, but compared with the previous Christmas supplies were more difficult to obtain. To find a duck or a turkey was almost impossible and meat rations for the individual was sixpence, with corned beef as part of the meat ration, one penny. The campaign to save fuel had been introduced; any person deciding to have a bath, even in the old zinc bath kept in the shed, was requested to have no more than a depth of five inches of water.

Everywhere, as on previous wartime Christmas holidays, children had their parties. At Torquay, 400 Belgian and French children were entertained. The shops were well-stocked with sweets and chocolates but it meant producing sweet coupons. Trade in terms of Christmas shopping for presents had been very good. The goodwill stopped at Tavistock for on Christmas Eve someone was prosecuted for selling unskinned rabbits in excess of the government's imposed maximum price.

Exeter readers of the *Western Times* newspaper may have felt a degree of satisfaction from the editor's Christmas message that ended 'Good fortune seems to have followed us throughout the last twelve months'.

Chapter 4 — References
(PC = Personal Communication)

1. *The Blitz Then and Now* (1988), Vol. 2, Winston G. Ramsey.
2. *The Blitz Then and Now* (1988), Vol. 2, Winston G. Ramsey.
3. PC: Mr D. Underdown.
4. PC: Professor R. V. Jones.
5. West Devon Record Office, Plymouth.
6. *The Astor Archives*, Reading University.
7. PC: Mr Harris.
8. West Devon Record Office, Plymouth.
9. *Bundesarchiv*, Frieberg.
10. *Bundesarchiv*, Frieberg.
11. PC: Mrs R. Durham.
12. *Bundesarchiv*, Frieberg.
13. West Devon Record Office, Plymouth.
14. West Devon Record Office, Plymouth.
15. Plymouth Emergency Committee: Minute No. 574, West Devon Record Office.
16. PC: Mr A. V. Godding.
17. HO 186; 625; *Raids on Plymouth April 41*, PRO.
18. London Fire Brigade Archives, Lambeth.
19. *Volkischer Beobachter Berliner*, March 1941.
20. *BBC Sound Archives*, Reading.
21. *British Sea War* (1989), John M. Young.
22. *It Came To Our Door* (1949), H. P. Twyford.
23. *The Göebbels Diaries 1939–1941* (1982), Fred Taylor.
24. PC: Professor R. V. Jones.
25. PC: Mr A. D. Saunders.
26. *The Fringes of Power* (1984), John Colville.
27. HO 199; 137; Plymouth, PRO.
28. INF 1; 292; Home Intelligent Reports Part 1. Plymouth, PRO.
29. HO 199; 137; Plymouth, PRO.
30. *It Came To Our Door* (1949), H. P. Twyford.
31. *Survey of Plymouth* (1941), Friends.
32. WRVS Archive, London.
33. PC: Mrs Dwyer.
34. WRVS Archive, London.
35. Survey of Plymouth (1941), Friends.
36. *Problems of Social Policy* (1950), R. M. Titmus.
37. *Survey of Plymouth* (1941), Friends.
38. *Plymouth Emergency Committee*, Issue No. 133, WDRO.
39. *Exmouth Chronicle*, May 1941.
40. *Action Stations 5* (1982), R. C. B. Ashworth.
41. *Torquay* (1992), John Pike.
42. *Action Stations 5* (1982), R. C. B. Ashworth.
43. *The Hope Cove Area during WW2* (1992), Arthur L. Clamp.
44. *Graves Registration Service: History of the Quartermaster Corps*, (USA).

5

EXETER, BAEDEKER, BOMBS AND BEAMS

During the second week of February 1942, the Luftwaffe resumed their attacks on Devon, after an absence of seven months, when enemy aircraft appeared simultaneously over Exmouth and Torquay. At Exmouth houses were destroyed and several people killed. These two raids of 12 February were the beginning of a long sequence of air raids on the county that would occur each month, sometimes several times a month, until the summer of 1943.

The library books of Devon County Council were wearing out. The black out and long winter nights had encouraged people to stay at home and to take up reading, consequently there had been a heavy demand for library books. Bideford Library was one of the many county libraries that had applied for an increase in grant money to purchase further stock and repair books.

News had been released that American troops had landed in the United Kingdom; the time would soon arrive when the first contingent of American servicemen would appear in Devon.

In 1942 there were thousands of Allied and British servicemen stationed throughout Devon. When off-duty, if they were not on the dance floor, some would be on the stage playing dance music. Service dance bands were popular and appeared at numerous public functions. Most of the musicians were professionals in civilian life and the music played was of a high standard.

At Tiverton, the local dancers could tango to the music of the Royal Artillery Dance Band or quickstep with the Royal Ordnance Band. Those who danced across the town's ballrooms were spoilt in this wartime period for the Czech Air Force also had a dance band that played at Tiverton, as did the RAF Silver Wings Band.

A tragedy occurred on 15 March 1942 when Spitfires of 317 Squadron, that had been escorting Boston bombers, were caught in a rolling mist during their descent at RAF Bolt Head. The British fighters, short of fuel, either forced landed on the clifftop airfield or the pilots bailed out. The commanding officer of the squadron was killed, five Spitfires were destroyed, and only two of the squadron's aircraft managed to land.[1]

Exeter at this period, when the war news was not encouraging, was very much involved in the industrial war effort. Among the city's manufacturers were those contracted to make parachutes, battledress, and aircraft components. The metal-working industries were very busy, especially vehicle engineering. A considerable number of people were also involved in working in government service establishments. Those people on war production were involved in working long shift periods.

If there was time to go out for a brief period of relaxation it could be to the cinema, or to one of the live shows at the Theatre Royal where productions varied from classic plays to music hall variety shows. Ballroom dancing was a glittering occasion for the young while a visit to Deller's Cafe for an evening out, meant the traumas of the war were temporarily forgotten.

The immediate threat of an enemy invasion had receded, but the British military were still concerned about the possibility of the Germans landing in England. That these anxieties persisted was due to the enemy successfully pursuing their policy of deception. The Civil Defence Corps had now been given additional responsibilities associated with anti-invasion precautions and, on occasions, they focused public attention on the assumed threat.

Exeter's Civil Defence conducted an exercise: everyone was expected to carry their gas mask; for the treatment of gas burns, anti-gas ointment could be

purchased in the city's shops at sixpence a pot. Sadness pervaded the city on 24 March when homage was paid at Exeter Cathedral to the sailors who were lost when HMS *Exeter* (of the Battle of the River Plate fame) was sunk by the Japanese Navy at the beginning of the month.

At the riverside village of Kingswear, motor launches of the 7th Flotilla, moored near the GWR ferry pontoon, would slip their moorings on late afternoons and head across the English Channel towards the enemy-occupied Channel Islands. The MLs would then stop midway in the Channel and wait until darkness before proceeding to sit offshore one of the Islands. These nocturnal patrols were in fact training exercises in preparation for the epic Commando raid on the French Atlantic port of Saint Nazaire.[2]

The main objective of the raid was to immobilise the large dry dock that was able to service the German battleship *Tirpitz*, and to deny the German Navy port facilities, including the use of the bomb-proof U Boat pens. A week prior to the raid, a night exercise code named 'Vivid' involving the British task force, was carried out against the defences of Devonport Dockyard as a final rehearsal for the raid.

The assembled force that departed from Falmouth on 26 March 1942 included men of No. 1 and No. 2 Commando units, a motor gun boat, sixteen motor launches, a motor torpedo boat, an adapted ex American First World War destroyer HMS *Campbeltown*, and an escort of two destroyers. The Saint Nazaire raid is well documented (see bibliography). Few people, however, are aware that four of the ML's that were involved in the attack were from the 7th Flotilla, Kingswear.

In the final run up to the caissons of the Saint Nazaire dock, the attacking force was led by the motor gun boat, with HMS *Campbeltown* following. The destroyer was ordered to ram the dock caissons at high speed with three tons of explosive, timed to ignite over two hours after impact. On either side, armed with torpedoes, were two of the Kingswear MLs launches ML160 and ML270. The other two MLs based on the River Dart, were ML156 and ML177. These followed at the rear of the force. Each launch carried a task force whose objective it was to destroy two enemy gunboats and to silence any enemy ships in dry dock. The Germans later admitted the raid was cleverly planned and boldly executed.

Only one of the four MLs that originally set out from the River Dart returned to base, this was ML160 commanded by Lieutenant Tom Boyd who was awarded the DSO. This motor launch has by chance been recorded for posterity by the war artist Charles Cundall whose oil painting 'Motor Launches Dartmouth' shows this gallant boat on the righthand side of the picture (see below).

ML156, lost on the raid, was commanded by Lieutenant Leslie Fenton a pre-war American film director associated with 'The Saint' films. He was seriously injured. The Commander of ML270, Lieutenant Irwin, survived the raid but his boat was scuttled as its steering mechanism was damaged. The young Commander, Sub-Lieutenant Mark Rodier of ML177, died during the course of the raid.[3] Following the Saint Nazaire raid thirty-one casualties were taken to the Royal Naval Hospital, Devonport.

Evacuees of all ages were well established in their new homes throughout the county, and many Devon communities were now billeting Plymouth evacuees. The Kingsbridge Rural District Council had organised an evacuee commune with a management that, through the appointment of directors, administered housing, health, social activities and gardens. Accommodation was obtained by requisition-

Motor launches at Dartmouth, 1940. This oil painting by Charles Cundall is of considerable historic interest as it records ML160, one of the four launches that took part in the epic raid on Saint Nazaire.

In strengthening the defences of Exeter in 1942, a squadron of Bristol Beaufighters moved into RAF Exeter. Used as night-fighters, these aircraft attacked and broke up enemy formations as they approached the Devon coast.

An airman paints a mural around the doorway of the officer's mess at RAF Exeter.

ing country houses, bungalows, cottages and any other property that was considered suitable.

Weekend cottages known as 'Love Nests' were available for visiting husbands home on leave from the forces. The radical lifestyle, described by a contemporary as a 'soviet' system, meant the evacuees worked together, entertained together, and collectively looked after the children who were reported to be the happiest evacuees in the country.[4]

The South West Civil Defence region held a fire-guard conference at Rougemont House, Exeter during March 1942. There is no known official ministry warning indicating the probability of an impending attack on the city, but the Mayor of Exeter during his conference speech made the statement 'don't be too sure that the old city of ours is not going to be blitzed!'

Anti-aircraft guns were moved to reinforce the city's defences, but their value was limited by the absence of a barrage balloon defence as the guns would be unable to deal with any low-flying aircraft. There were however night-fighter patrols that flew at differing heights above Exeter, although such protection gave only limited cover.

Signals had been received by British Intelligence that German bomber units based in France were becoming active again. The Germans had at first been sending out false radio messages with the intention of making the British believe the Luftwaffe was returning to bomb the United Kingdom. Later positive clues were obtained from the deciphering of the 'Enigma' codes. KG100 (Pathfinder Unit 5) was attempting to restore the performance of their X-System by imposing supersonic modulations on to their radio location beam system. Trials of the improved X-System, carried out early in March 1942, were so satisfactory that the radio location variant could be used for air operations.

British scientific intelligence having acquired this important information, proceeded to develop equipment to jam the enemy's modified beam. From this time Intelligence staff offered six weeks notice of any bombing threat to England.

The Americans, now at war with Germany, were at this stage developing their own air force capability. RAF Bomber Command was increasingly attacking targets in Germany, while the Russian armies were engaged in a furious onslaught against the Germans on the Eastern Front.

In the European theatre of war, the Germans had established a strong fighter defence system across northern Europe, designated by the British the Kamm Huber Line. RAF Bomber Command was attracted to attacking targets in the Baltic as it could route the bomber force round the north of the Kamm Huber Line, which did not extend into Denmark, where the enemy fighter defences were less effective.[5]

On the same day as the Saint Nazaire raid a force of RAF bombers attacked the Baltic port of Lubeck inflicting considerable damage and casualties. The attack on Lubeck caused a muted reaction within the German Nazi hierarchy. Hitler did not go to visit the stricken town, not that he ever visited any of the German communities that had been bombed. Goering stayed at his stately home engrossed in his art collection. It was left to Dr Goebbels the Minister of Propaganda to tour the bombed Baltic port. However, Hitler's later reaction to the raid was to have a far-reaching effect on the people of England and, in particular, those in Devon.

Early in April the British had learnt that the Germans had started to increase its bomber strength in North West Europe. Aircraft of 11/KG100 had been ordered back from the Eastern front, while bombers of IV/KG40 had been identified in Holland. The arrival of the bomber re-inforcements was interpreted by British Intelligence as being a precaution against a repetition of the raid on Saint Nazaire.

Seventeen days had passed since the Lubeck raid when Hitler ordered the Luftwaffe to attack civilian populations in England where the greatest possible effect could be expected. Five days after this directive was issued the RAF flew to the Baltic and attacked Rostock, where the Arado Flugzeugwerke Gmbh aircraft factory was situated. The German command responsible for the Luftwaffe bombing policy had already declared before Lubeck and Rostock had been attacked 'The distinction between industrial centres and dwelling settlements are insignificant'.[6]

To maximise the propaganda value of the intended 'reprisal' raids on Britain a press conference was held in Berlin for a group of journalists at which was revealed the Germans' intention of attacking those English towns listed in the *Baedeker Tourist Guide* marked with 'three stars'.

In fact Karl Baedeker's tourist publication never marked cities with a three-star status; the ratings were one or two stars. However, thereafter Luftwaffe attacks on English Cathedral towns were referred to as the 'Baedeker' raids.[7]

The first Baedeker raid, Exeter 1942: bomb damage at Okehampton Street after the blitz of 23 April, 1943.

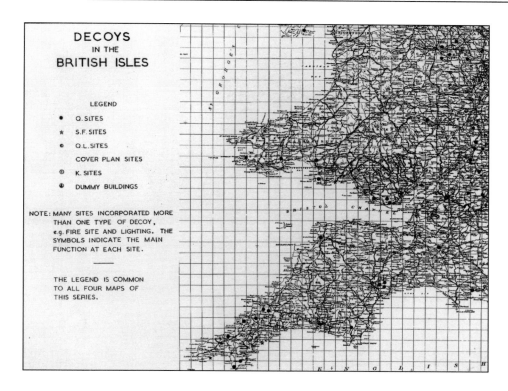

A contemporary chart showing decoy sites in Southern England and Wales. Such 'Q' sites were activated on the night of the first Baedeker raid on Exeter.

The Lubeck and Rostock raids seem to have made a deep impression on Hitler and spurred him to back the development of the V (terror) weapons that two years later would manifest their presence on the British public as the V1 Flying Bomb and the V2 Rocket. In the meantime, Hitler decided to attack English soft targets in preference to military targets, a decision based on emotion rather than reason.[8]

Exeter was well aware of the Luftwaffe. Apart from the minor raids that the city had so far experienced, the consequences of the devastating air attacks on Plymouth, only forty miles away, were known to every Exeter household. Exeter's Civil Defence had given their support to the naval city. The people of Exeter were also aware of the numerous air raids suffered by South Devon communities situated much closer to Exeter than Plymouth. The Department of Home Security had originally classed Exeter as being of 'Low Vulnerability' but the city had been uprated to a 'Class A' nodal point by the end of 1941.[9] Early in 1942 a government quota of six thousand Morrison indoor steel air raid shelters had been received by Exeter for distribution and applications were invited from the public to apply for a shelter.

It fell to Exeter to experience the first Baedeker raid on England. This occurred on 23/24 April 1942. A German bomber force flew to Devon but only one enemy aircraft arrived over the city, releasing bombs that fell in the Okehampton Street area. This brief raid killed five people and seventeen people were injured. On this same night other aircraft dropped bombs on the nearby communities of Bishopsteignton, Exminster and Totnes. As these three air raids were being carried out, three 'Q' decoy sites at Clyst St Mary, Aylesbeare and Woodbury were being activated.[10] Q sites were dummy airfields with landing lights used to mislead and entice enemy aircraft from their intended targets.

The first Baedeker raid on Exeter was not successful. The British defences were not even aware at the time of the significance of the raid, but the Germans returned the following night. Just after midnight a force of sixty bombers from the KG Pathfinder group arrived and circled over the city before releasing brilliantly coloured flares that hung above Exeter as enemy aircrews attempted to identify their target area. Most of the high explosive and incendiary bombs fell on residential property in the Pennsylvania district of the city, but other areas also suffered bomb damage.

During this attack two huge 1800kg (Satan) bombs, over nine feet in length, were released. One of these bombs dropped in the St Petrock's area.[11,12] Nearly a thousand properties were damaged and the casualties included seventy-three people killed.

A third successive raid occurred over Exeter on the morning of 26 April 1942. The air raid warning sounded again, by now a familiar signal for since the

Dornier Do217Es of Kampfgeschwader 2, one of the Luftwaffe units that participated in the Baedeker raids on Exeter. These bombers are painted in night camouflage.

beginning of April 1942 Exeter's air raid alert warning had been sounded on sixteen occasions. This air raid was carried out by a single enemy aircraft that released seven hundred incendiary bombs and one high explosive bomb. Three people were killed. This minor raid also damaged gas and water mains, and caused extensive fire damage to several properties.

High Street, Exeter, May 1942. Fire fighters damp down smouldering buildings in the aftermath of the May Baedeker raid. The destruction in the city centre, where buildings were densely packed, is apparent from this photograph.

Sunlight streams through the shattered walls of Exeter Cathedral following the May raid. The south aisle suffered considerably when hit by a high explosive bomb, but the building was mercifully saved from irreparable damage and much of the priceless fabric and stained glass had been removed for safekeeping at the outset of war.

The Germans were aware they had failed to inflict the havoc on Exeter that had been their intention. Other Baedeker raids on Bath and Norwich were both highly disruptive and a dreadful experience for both cities.

Visibility was six miles on the night of 4 May 1942 when the Luftwaffe again decided to attack Exeter. The attackers were to use stream tactics, a form of air attack considerably shorter in duration than the lengthy 'crocodile' tactics used against Plymouth the previous year. This method of attack also meant Exeter's defences could not engage all the enemy aircraft. The attack was concentrated both in time and area.

The absence of barrage balloons allowed the enemy bombers to descend to release their bomb loads, and numerous incendiary bombs could be released within a small area. The noise produced by the descent of the German bombs gave the sheltering population below the belief that they were being dive bombed. The intensity of the raid was extremely traumatic and one can only

(Bottom left) Exeter, May 1942. A view over rooftops towards the Cathedral provides an indication of how closely packed were the buildings in the city centre. Smoke rises from the gutted ruins.

(Bottom right) Exeter, May 1942. Ruined buildings hang precariously over the city centre streets. Hosepipes wind amid the rubble towards buildings that still smoulder in the morning air.

In Exeter's narrow medieval streets effective fire fighting was made almost impossible. Here, Catherine Street lies in utter ruin.

guess at the terror of those sheltering, or indeed those out in the open involved with their civil defence duties.

The fire-watchers, their role now fire-fighters, were out on the streets and in the city's commercial premises diligently attempting to douse the incendiary bombs. The low-flying enemy aircraft began to machine gun people, making them seek shelter. The very thought of being gunned down deterred some from coming out of their shelters to assist in the civil defence. The narrow city alleys, so quaint in peacetime, now presented difficulties of access making it almost impossible to reach the seat of many fires that were already raging.

The fire-fighters used water supplies from static tanks that had previously been erected throughout the city. The Exeter fire brigade had earlier recognised that Exeter's mains pressure was inadequately low and that the small diameter pipes were incapable of producing the required output of water sufficient for fire-fighting.

Urgent calls were received at Exmouth, Sidmouth, Torquay and Plymouth for their fire brigades to speed to Exeter; all responded to the call. The bombing had ignited an oil supply and a special request was made for a foam unit to travel from Plymouth.

Exeter's divisional fire-fighting reinforcements, usually so prompt to arrive, were held up on their way to Exeter because of the numerous fires that were burning in the hills and commons around the city. These compelled the reinforcements to make detours before arriving at their city rendezvous. One emergency fire-fighting

National Fire Services messengers of Exeter Fire Brigade, 1942. These men performed the difficult task of carrying messages co-ordinating the work of firemen during the air raids. Note the masked headlights used on all vehicles throughout the war.

A contemporary newspaper photograph of an army UXB unit outside Exeter's fire station. These men were responsible for making safe any unexploded bombs in the city, risking life and limb often under dangerous and difficult circumstances. The three small devices at the front of the group are French incendiary bombs as described in the text.

unit, formed to travel from town to town, were of limited assistance as the firemen were already exhausted; an echo of the Plymouth Blitz experience.

Exeter's streets and passages, other than being too narrow to allow approach to blazing buildings, were also too narrow to make fire breaks by which to control the conflagrations. On this fearful night, reports were received that the incendiary bombs were difficult to extinguish. Some were reported to jump around, even pop and explode. The 'new type' of incendiary bomb was in fact captured French stock adapted to fit German incendiary bomb containers. The bombs were marked 'INC' an abbreviation of the French word for incendiary and each had six small tail vanes. The use of these bombs on Exeter coincided with a German radio broadcast that the French Air Force had attacked targets in South West England in retaliation for recent RAF raids on Paris.[13]

An SC250kg bomb exploded and demolished three bays of the south choir aisle of Exeter Cathedral. This, with the nearby ruined St John's Chapel, gave the whole area a devastated look. The Cathedral had been afforded some protection by the construction of steel piping provided by the National Fire Service to convey water

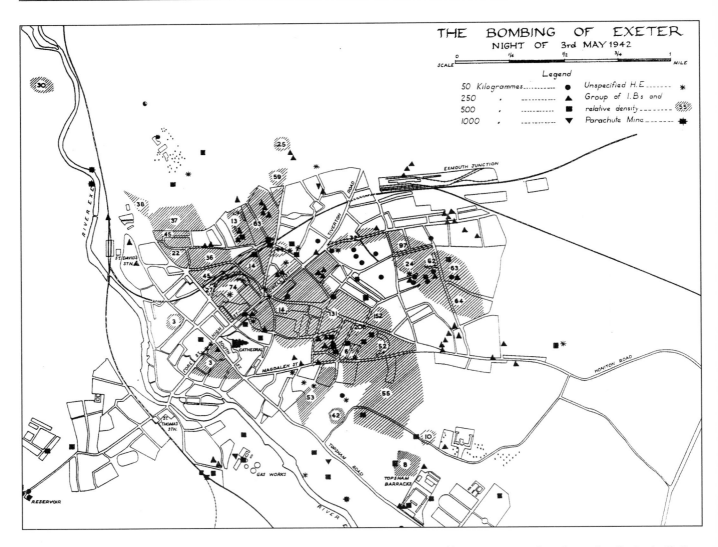

A bomb census relating to the raid on Exeter of 3 May 1942.

to the upper levels of the Cathedral.[14] The ancient glass from the Cathedral's East Window had previously been removed.

During the raid the Civil Defence control centre, situated in the basement of the city's library, was destroyed. The library, one of the finest municipal libraries in the country, was a total loss and a million books were destroyed. In that night of terror many important buildings were obliterated: churches, public houses, schools, historic property, together with retail shops and manufacturers premises. All lay in ruins, burnt down or bombed. Residential areas, many already suffering varying degrees of damage from the previous raids, were extensively hit.

The attack lasted for one hour. The enemy bombers returned to their base, with the exception of four aircraft that were shot down. A Ju88 of KG30 crashed on the cricket field at the Topsham Barracks, Exeter.

Rescue work continued throughout the night and the following day. Gallant council workers who had toiled throughout the night were required by the City Council to report for work at their normal time for the rest of the day.

Fires, although largely under control by the morning, would on occasion, start to blaze. One young girl out with her mother was passing the *Express and Echo* newspaper office when they observed a fireman fall through a burning roof. She recalls her mother saying 'I hope it is not your father'. It was. Badly burnt, with a severely damaged back, her father was very ill and away from work for a long time.[15]

The pattern of the bombing and the way in which the fires spread resulted in one half of Exeter being cut off from the other. The destruction also blocked many roads making it very difficult to travel through the city. Yet by a considerable physical effort vast quantities of rubble were soon cleared from the roads and a bus service was re-established. This was a great boost to the morale of the citizens.

Breakfast is served in the streets of Exeter on the morning after the May attack on the city. As always, the local voluntary services were quick to establish facilities for food and shelter for those whose homes had been destroyed.

The WVS were a key element in preserving morale and in ensuring the populace was kept fed and sheltered in the aftermath of the raids on Exeter. With the destruction of the city's bakeries these women were responsible for providing sandwiches from the huge stacks of bread behind them. The upturned box on the floor is labelled 'Ministry of Food - Vegetable Stew'.

The extensive damage to residential property resulted in thousands of people being homeless or at least without any facilities to cook. Consequently there was an urgent need to provide food. Mobile canteens quickly appeared, first offering breakfast on the morning following the raid and thereafter providing hot meals. This was another occasion when the WVS made a significant contribution in providing food and other social services to the people of Exeter.

Part of Exeter's High Street where many of the food shops were located had been destroyed by fire. Within hours 25 000 registered customers had lost their food retailer. Three of the city's largest bakeries were destroyed, but immediate arrangements were made to deliver bread supplies from Plymouth and Torquay bakers. The Ministry of Food released 60 000 eggs and large supplies of cooked ham. Except for milk, no concessions were made to civilians regarding rationed food. All the official records of the city's food rationing scheme were destroyed in the air raid, however some far thinking Exeter official had arranged for such records to be copied and these were sent and deposited at Honiton.

To help maintain morale the South West Regional Authority made arrangements for three million cigarettes and large quantities of tobacco to be sent immediately from Nottingham to Exeter.[16]

WVS members prepare food at an emergency feeding centre in Exeter. They are using field ovens, a familiar item in all blitzed towns, and renowned for their reliability and versatility, from preparing gallons of tea to boiled puddings.

A result of the earlier Baedeker raid was a trek out from the city. The local authorities were aware of this nocturnal exodus and allowed people to travel without exerting any pressure on them to stay at home. This policy changed after the air raid of 23 April when the number of trekkers significantly increased. Loudspeaker vans drove around the city streets appealing to people not to leave Exeter. Most of the trekkers had initially found accommodation in the rest centres that had been established within a seven-mile radius of the city. The people travelled in various ways. Open-back lorries packed with people drove out to the nearby areas of Redhills and Nadderwater. The weather being fine, hundreds of people slept in tents erected in fields and hills around the city. Others, wrapped in blankets, slept out in the open.[17] One family among many others travelled out to Ide and sheltered overnight in a barn.[18]

After the intensive raid of 4 May, when eleven of the twenty-seven rest centres had been bombed, a thousand people urgently needed shelter. Several hundred arrived at the reception centre at Whitestone that was scheduled to accommodate only a hundred people.

The trek out was causing official concern and, in an attempt to control this movement of people, a police cordon was established around the city. People were required to show their identity cards at the police checkpoints and those who could not give a satisfactory reason for having to travel outside the city's perimeter were refused leave of Exeter.

The number of trekkers declined with the end of the Baedeker raids on the city. At the peak of the nightly exodus an estimated 10 000 people were leaving Exeter each night.[19]

The Pathfinder unit aircraft that spearheaded the attack on Exeter were Heinkel IIIs of 1/KG100 (formerly KGr100). These aircraft were the Germans' first modern medium-range bomber, at the time a formidable offensive weapon. Also taking part in the raids were the Dornier Do217Es of Kampfgeschwader KG2. This aircraft's design was based on the Dornier 17, referred to as the 'Flying Pencil'. Junker Ju88 bombers also participated in the air attacks on Exeter. These aircraft flew to Exeter from airfields in Holland and Northern France.[20]

Temporary signs on Exeter's bomb sites let customers know where blitzed shops are now trading. The destruction of all else around it gives the Cathedral an air of desolate isolation.

The evening visit of the royal family five days after the May raid.

The accuracy of the enemy targeting their bomb loads within the city boundary on 4 May is shown on the contemporary chart of the distribution of HE bombs (see page 102).

Three areas in the city's centre suffered substantial damage; throughout Exeter four hundred shops were destroyed. Sadly there would be no more dancing at Deller's as the building was totally destroyed.

The bomb-blasted city buried its dead. Many were laid to rest on the Saturday morning following the raid, at the Higher Cemetery. A hundred soldiers were employed to help dig the graves as the task was too great for the Council grave diggers alone.

Exeter with its inner and outer areas was a small city with an estimated civilian population of 70 500 people living in 20 000 houses. The air attacks demolished 1700 houses and damaged 14 000 properties that needed some form of repair. When, in the immediate aftermath, temporary repair work was carried out, 'First Aid Repair' building material was used that had been purchased before the outbreak of war by some far-sighted Exeter Council official. This material was distributed at twenty-seven stores around Exeter, all of which had miraculously escaped damage by the bombing.[21]

The day after the intensive air raid on Exeter, a wedding was held in one of the city's blitzed churches. Nearly every guest was late as cars had to unload the wedding guests some distance away from the church because of all the rubble in the streets. The bridal bouquet was Lily-of-the-Valley picked from the bridegroom's garden, as a replacement for the bride's flowers.

Five days after the attack, the King and Queen on their West Country tour visited the bombed city. Loudspeaker vans toured Exeter during the day broadcasting the news that the royal couple would arrive in the early evening. The entourage arrived at St David's railway station and then travelled through many of the city's street in a large maroon-coloured Daimler saloon car, stopping along the route to inspect the bomb damage of Exeter Cathedral.

British Intelligence was disturbed by the number of enemy bombs that fell on target, and that while the Baedeker raids on Exeter (and Bath) had occurred, No. 80 Wing, a British listening station, was unable to detect the signals of the German radio beam. The results of an enquiry revealed a basic design fault in the British listening receivers manufactured to detect the enemy supersonic modulations. This mistake resulted in a greater tonnage of enemy bombs falling on target and a significantly higher casualty rate.[22]

Shortly following the raid of 4 May, the Inspector General of the Ministry of Home Security with his advisers visited the bombed community and eventually published a report. The Inspector General's report on Exeter's Baedeker raids comprised 39 pages. There are critical points and recommendations, but no evidence was found that the Exeter authorities or Civil Defence were negligent. Reference was made in the report to the magnificent work carried out by Exeter's

The Fire Guard Team, Exeter. A painting by William Clause, an Official War Artist.

Amid the city in ruins, life continues as normally as possible. The cheery landlord of The Dolphin in Burnthouse Lane draws a pint, Exeter 1942.

fire-guard organisation. The report stated that pre-raid planning had made efficient arrangements to deal with the situations caused by the heavy air attack. The value of such planning was evident in the efficient way everyone in the city carried out their work in circumstances of great difficulty. Throughout the raids and during the aftermath, the morale of the people had been excellent.[23,24]

Through the spring and summer of 1942 Exeter was occupied in clearing up the rubble and bomb damage. Unsafe buildings were demolished, and the destruction of so many shops meant temporary premises being set up far away from the traditional trading sites. Market traders moved, some to the Higher Market, since the Lower Market was destroyed. Schools that had been temporarily closed re-opened in the middle of May.

Repair work on bomb-damaged residential property started with a workforce of a hundred men and six lorries, working on one street at a time.

Regional and local civil defences reviewed and refined their policies, although anxieties continued regarding the possibility of the Luftwaffe returning. Two days

Inside the Lower Market, Exeter. Following the air raids many traders moved their business to the Higher Market which had escaped major damage.

later they did, but not over Exeter. It was the small fishing port of Brixham that was raided and an HE bomb sank a naval minelayer.

In Exeter's sister city open-air public dances on Plymouth Hoe recommenced on 13 June 1942, with dances on a Tuesday, Thursday and Saturday evening. Plymouthians responded to the government's request for people to have their 'Holidays at Home', not that many had much choice. Plymouth Corporation sold 91 000 deckchair tickets during the summer of 1942; at the Hoe Cafe 39 000 cups of tea were drunk, 9600 pasties eaten, besides the 24 000 buns that were consumed. Bathing in the Tinside open-air pool was a great attraction. During the summer of 1942 a total of 76 000 tickets were purchased to enter the swimming pool.

The British public were aware of the consequences of the Exeter and Plymouth Blitzes but there still persisted the belief that Devon was a safe haven. While Devon people stayed at home for their holidays, crowds of people arrived in the county for their summer vacation. Visitors had high expectations of the opportunity to relax, of a restful night's sleep, good food and a good time, away from the wail of air-raid sirens and enemy bombs. So they believed.

At Clovelly on the North Devon coast, this picturesque but remote village continued to attract people. There being no private car travel, visitors would arrive by bus, walking down the cobblestones to the water's edge, then back up the steep narrow street. On the South Devon coast there was another kind of beauty to behold, that of a Russian wedding, the first of its kind to be held at Thurlestone Church.

On the Home Front it was a time of increasing austerity. The clothing ration was cut from 66 coupons per year for each person to 45. 'Utility' wear was introduced governing the specification of clothes. The government's aim was that people would be able to obtain affordable clothing of a standard quality to meet minimum requirements. As clothing coupon allowance was being reduced, the cost of clothes was beginning to rise, with some items as much as 175 per cent of the pre-war level. Soap had been rationed since earlier in the year. Sweets and chocolates were rationed by the personal points system. Non-priority customers were allowed three pints of milk a week.

Farmers and certain other independent groups of people maintained a good food table. A farmer was able to slaughter a sheep and the occasional calf or pig, although this required a licence. This extra supply of meat meant that the farmer's family, his workers and friends were often able to eat well.

By various ways and means, extra dairy produce and eggs were obtained, and with jam and fruit to make pies and puddings, many Devon families sat down to an appetising meal. Fish and chips were usually available in the shops. Rabbit pie or stew was a popular supplement to the meagre meat ration. The abundance of rabbits in the countryside meant that even if one was not offered a rabbit, it was possible to go out and catch them.

Other people got by on their rationed food, and had few opportunities to supplement their larder. At times many went undernourished and those who remember the war from childhood days have an abiding memory of always being hungry.

During the summer of 1942 two dedicated walkers arrived at the remote Powder Mills, Dartmoor, for their holiday. The roadways of the moors were almost devoid of traffic. So few people during the war were seen on the moorland that its quiet loneliness was similar to the nineteenth century Dartmoor of William Crossing.

The two visitors had travelled to Plymouth by train, then on to their destination by branchline to Yelverton station, with a further change of trains for their journey to Princetown. Here they were met and conveyed by car to the farmhouse that was to be their holiday accommodation. After dinner and out for their first evening walk, the visitors were amazed to discover that their planned beloved moorland walks were now part of an expanded artillery range, the boundary markers of which had been erected near to the farm.

On occasion, the visitors would watch the Royal Artillery arriving, having hauled their guns from their Plymouth barracks along the roads to the moors, to practise on the firing range. Once the guns and accompanying paraphernalia had arrived, shooting practice would consist of firing from Powder Mills valley towards targets at White Ridge some three of four miles away. Practice completed, the gun battery would move off, leaving behind large muddy scars from the wheels or caterpillar tracks. On one occasion, walking to Bellever Tor, they observed a flight of fighter aircraft flying in the direction of Widecombe, then soon after a black column of smoke ascended in the still air. They later learnt that a plane had crashed on the ridge at Hameldon.[25]

A poster detailing registration for fire prevention duties among the people of Okehampton, 1942.

With America now at war with Germany, the supplies of iron, some 65 000 tons that were being shipped across the Atlantic to Britain to be used for arms, had stopped. Whether one accepted it as a patriotic duty or an unnecessary wartime effort, the Ministry of Supply issued orders in the spring of 1942 for the removal of all iron gates and railings from public and private properties. Calculations had been made that the railings from fifty houses sufficed for one army tank; 1 cwt of iron would make fifty rifle barrels, and 70 tons of iron would make a 6-inch naval gun.

Contractors under the order of the Ministry appeared throughout the county and, using heavy sledgehammers, biffed and banged to knock out the gates and railings. This was a sad sight. The government's attitude was that the people would freely donate their railings to the nation, although there was a system to claim for compensation based on the current price of scrap iron. Local authorities had no say in the matter, there were no apologies, no introductions. Damage was caused to walls and coping stones by the removal of the gates and rails. There were exceptions to all this destruction, railings around churches or tombstones in graveyards were exempt. However, many old and beautiful pieces of ironwork fell under the contractors' pickaxes and much of what was taken was totally unsuitable for armaments.

Individuals journeyed to Devon, unknown to the public, who through the realms of leadership, bravery or devotion to duty, made a significant contribution to the war. There was such a man who travelled one hot summer's day in July 1942 by train alongside the River Dart to Kingswear. This newly promoted naval Petty Officer took the ferry to Dartmouth and, travelling by boat up the river, eventually boarding a ship at anchor. This unknown sailor was eventually to become involved in one of the most heroic episodes of the Second World War.

Later, as Lieutenant Henty-Greer, he commanded the midget submarine X5 that together with X6 and X7 carried out the daring and dangerous operation in the attack on the German battleship *Tirpitz* during the autumn of 1943. Henty-Greer was recommended for the Victoria Cross along with the two other naval officers who participated in the attack, but because he was reported as missing, the award was never confirmed.

During the summer of 1942, Henty-Greer stayed for a month at Dartmouth on a boat anchored by the flotilla's temporary parent ship. His days were spent on daily manoeuvres sailing down the River Dart through the boom defence out to sea. Life for him at this time was also about swimming from the stern of his ship, sunbathing, and at night spending money in the town and visiting Torquay. There were visits travelling up the river to Totnes for Devonshire cream teas.

At the end of July, the flotilla's parent ship HMS *Prince Philip* arrived at Dartmouth. The flotilla launches went down in line to greet her arrival, and the following day the flotilla of eight craft, with their parent ship, set out from Dartmouth as a shake-down cruise. Out in the English Channel, while the crew were having lunch, the boats were attacked by two Me109s. Cannon shells holed the side of Henty-Greer's craft, although she was repaired and the flotilla continued on its way towards the Irish Sea.[26]

Ilfracombe was in holiday mood with crowds of visitors. An American soldier visiting the town who lost his wallet, rewarded the finder with £12. Soon the American servicemen would be a familiar sight in the area.

The wartime austerity did not interrupt all social activities that were taking place in Devon. Cricket matches and bowls were a familiar scene at Torrington and Bideford. Appledore, busy building boats, held a regatta with sailing, rowing and athletics. At Alphington near Exeter, the local WVS arranged facilities for its members to be able to can their plums, and for the women to go blackberrying for jam making.

Civil defence was still very much a concern. At the village of Germansweek, fire-guards patrolled the parish every night for a possible fall of incendiary bombs on the cornfields.

Not all heroes were human. There were in the county pigeon fanciers who bred and supplied birds as message carriers for the armed forces. These remarkable birds were involved in some amazing wartime escapades. During 1942 a Plymouth bred pigeon was released from a Sunderland flying boat in the Atlantic Ocean, 120 miles from its base at RAF Mountbatten. The bird flew home and delivered its message in 145 minutes. Another Plymouth pigeon was involved in fifty operational sorties associated with flying boats. A Paignton bred pigeon was dropped by parachute into German-occupied France with instructions to the finder to answer and return a questionnaire using the pigeon. Dropped in France on 28 July 1942, the pigeon returned to its base on the 23 August.[27]

A Messerschmidt Me109. This type of aircraft was used principally as a bomber escort but also engaged in hit and run raids over England.

Ever since enemy attacks on Devon had started in the summer of 1940, there had been many communities throughout the county that had bombs dropped on or near them. Some of these resulted from planned attacks by enemy aircraft or from bombs released at random due perhaps to an aborted raid elsewhere. These sporadic bombs, referred to as 'strays', even if recorded in an official War Diary, were usually of no interest other than to those who lived near to the scene of the incident. These isolated bombs may have killed a cow, damaged a barn, or simply made a crater in a field, but for the people who were nearby it could often be a stressful experience.

The depleted Luftwaffe bases in North West Europe continued their tip and run raids. Experiencing these lightening air strikes was traumatic and terrifying. Often referred to in official communiques as 'nuisance raids' they were minor terror raids. Such attacks would often happen without any prior public warning. Civilians would by chance be caught out in the open by the sudden appearance of enemy aircraft flying at low level, releasing their bombs and often gunning down the people in the streets. It required a quick reaction and presence of mind to seek shelter.

This form of enemy daylight attack became more effective from the latter part of July 1942 when the Luftwaffe introduced the Focke-Wulf 190 fighter bomber (FW190). This aircraft, with its air-cooled radial engine, was far less susceptible to combat damage than the liquid-cooled engine of the Messerschmidt Bf109. When introduced the FW190 with its improved performance had the respect of the RAF fighter pilots and, for a time, was capable of outperforming the Spitfire until the Mark XII Spitfires were built to counter the FW190 at low altitude.

The tip and run raids were carried out with small numbers of aircraft flying in low across the Channel waters to avoid detection by radar. Eventually a crash alarm system was introduced that gave the public a degree of warning of approaching enemy aircraft. The crash alarm system depended on the continuing vigilance of the members of the (Royal) Observer Corps who, on recognising a hostile aircraft, passed a signal to the control centre where duty operators immediately sounded the public air raid warning.[28] No effective system of alert was developed against the marauding fighter-bomber until the end of 1943, when low-looking radar was introduced.[29]

Throughout the summer of 1942, there were many tip and run raids on South Devon resorts, mostly in the Torbay area (see Appendix D).

The Sunday before the August Bank Holiday, two Messerschmidt Bf109 fighters attacked Teignmouth, the following day six FW190 aircraft bombed a residential area of Torquay, completely demolishing thirty-seven houses and damaging several hundred homes. Among the seventy casualties were seven civilian dead. Ten days later Teignmouth was attacked again by low flying FW190s, raking the streets with machine gun and cannon fire. Enemy bombs demolished Teignmouth town hall, fire station and ambulance station. The marketplace and an arcade were damaged, with the local gasworks set on fire. Again people were killed and injured.

Two FW190s flew in from the south-west on 24 August and attacked twenty-three flat-bottomed naval landing barges that were moored off Greenway Quay, nearby Agatha Christie's house, in the Dittisham area. The enemy planes, free of

These two snapshots show the damage caused to the Phillips & Sons shipyard at Noss in the air raid of 18 September 1942.

any anti-aircraft gunfire, dropped at least one SC500kg bomb; two barges were sunk, three naval seamen injured.

The Noss shipyard on the River Dart was bombed on 18 September, one enemy SC500kg bomb exploded killing twenty employees and causing considerable structural damage. Among those injured was a plater who was blinded; another employee lost an arm.

Phillips & Sons of Dartmouth, was a small, but important shipyard established in the nineteenth century. It had building yards at Sandquay near the upper chain ferry, and the Noss works upriver to the west of Dartmouth.

Here a completely non-magnetic vessel the *Research* was built and launched in April 1939 for British Admiralty work relating to the earth's magnetic field. The intervening war meant the *Research* was never fitted out and she was eventually broken up at Plymouth. The war enhanced the activities of Phillips, with the construction of many wooden vessels, including minesweepers and very powerful air sea rescue launches. Phillips also built steel ships: boom defence vessels, fleet water carriers, minelayers and naval armament boats. The Dartmouth Yard had docking facilities and undertook important repair work. The September air attack caused the company many problems and delayed their war production which was resumed early in 1943.

One month after the raid on the Noss works, an accidental fire broke out in the Sandquay yard damaging the patternmaking and fitting shops.[30]

At the time of the attack on the Noss works, a bomb fell on HMS *Brittania*, the Royal Naval College, killing a Wren. Fortunately the naval cadets were away from the college on leave. The consequences of this raid was the transfer of the naval cadets to a safer area, eventually to the Duke of Westminster's enormous house Eaton Hall, Cheshire, for the rest of the war. Yet, with the naval cadets moving out of the college, seven hundred Wrens moved into the Dartmouth area, some of them being accommodated at the Royal Naval College. Sandridge House, Hunters Lodge and Greenway House were all used to accommodate Wrens in the area.

At this period no South Devon community could feel immune from these lightning enemy raids. Yet whatever the apprehensions that may have been experienced by individuals and the civil defence, life went on and morale was high.

A week after the bombing of the Noss yard there occurred a disaster closely associated with RAF Bolt Head. The doomed fighter pilots of the tragedy were

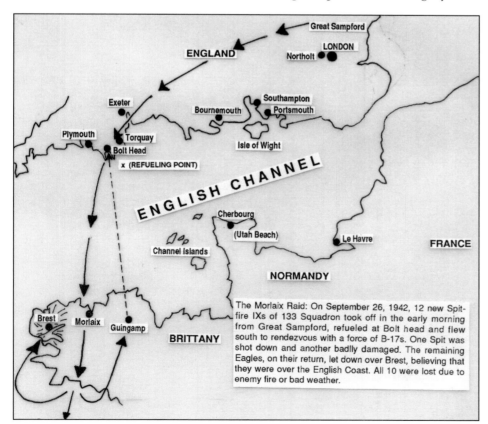

The Morlaix Raid: On September 26, 1942, 12 new Spitfire IXs of 133 Squadron took off in the early morning from Great Sampford, refueled at Bolt head and flew south to rendezvous with a force of B-17s. One Spit was shot down and another badly damaged. The remaining Eagles, on their return, let down over Brest, believing that they were over the English Coast. All 10 were lost due to enemy fire or bad weather.

The route taken by the ill-fated Eagle Squadron which lost twelve aircraft in the raid on Morlaix, 26 September 1942.

Abbey Sands, Torquay.
Smouldering wreckage of a FW190
shot down by anti-aircraft fire on 4
September 1942, the day on which
31 people were killed in an enemy
raid on Torbay.

Americans who had previously arrived in England as volunteers to fight with the
Allies against Nazi Germany. The pilots were members of the famed American
Eagle Squadron that operated under the command of the RAF. Now their country
was at war with Germany, the Eagle Squadron was transferred to the command of
the United States Air Force. The Eagle Squadron was based in South East England.

In late September 133 (Eagle) Squadron was ordered to fly their new Mk IX
Spitfires from Great Samford to RAF Bolt Head. Here, together with two Canadian
Spitfire squadrons they were to take part in an operation to escort eighteen US
B17 (Flying Fortress) bombers that were to attack a Focke-Wulf aircraft
maintenance plant at Morlaix and, as a secondary target, the U Boat pens at Brest.
RAF Exeter was the station handling the Morlaix operation.

At Bolt Head, one USAAF pilot and a British flight lieutenant, acting as the
Squadron Leader for the Eagle pilots, attended the briefing. The distance from
RAF Bolt Head to the target was less than 150 miles and the operation appeared
straightforward. However a serious error had been given in the weather briefing.
What had been forecast as a 35-knot headwind was in fact a 100-knot tailwind.
Radar coverage and radio communication was lost after fifteen minutes flying
time from the South Devon coast.

When the fighter squadrons reached the planned rendezvous the American B17
bombers were not to be seen. The fighter escort circled the area unaware the
Flying Fortresses had arrived twenty minutes earlier and had continued to fly
south. The Spitfires continued flying southwards oblivious to the tailwind and
meanwhile the bombers, that had been racing across the Bay of Biscay towards
Spain, decided to turn back. Here they met the Spitfires, now low on fuel. Two of
the Spitfires had already turned back, one due to engine trouble, the other aircraft
acting as its escort. These two fighters made their descent to land believing they
were over England. They were in fact over France; one fighter was shot down, the
other, out of fuel, crash-landed.

The remaining fighters had now decided to land, and began their descent. The
coastline in view was unfamiliar, but so for the American pilots was the Devon
coastline in the Bolt Head area. In fact the Spitfires were descending on the
Brittany peninsula and the city they saw below was not Plymouth, as they
thought, but Brest. As the descent continued the Americans came into the sights
of the German anti-aircraft guns, and were also attacked by FW190 fighters.

The eighteen Flying Fortresses all returned to their base. At RAF Bolt Head a
report was confirmed that a Spitfire had returned from Morlaix and crashed near
Bolt Head. Allied headquarters, London, announced the loss of some fighters and
pilots because of 'wing icing in adverse weather conditions'.

The American Eagle Squadron had lost the twelve Spitfires that had flown from
Bolt Head, five Eagle pilots were killed, seven were captured. On this tragic day
the raid on Morlaix caused the loss of twenty-two Spitfires out of a total of thirty-
six aircraft.[31]

The Trinity House lighthouses off the Devon Coast were on occasions attacked by
German aircraft. On 14 October 1942 an enemy plane fired cannon shells at Berry
Head (Brixham) lighthouse.

Close by at Torquay, the Palace Hotel had been requisitioned (in 1939) for use as an RAF hospital for officers. Among the officer aircrew patients were Flight Lieutenant Nicholson, the first RAF pilot to be awarded the Victoria Cross in the Second World War. It was while at Torquay that he first heard the news of his award. The Battle of Britain pilot Richard Hillary, author of the classic wartime book *The Last Enemy* was also at Torquay recuperating from his dreadful injuries. These were but two of many other heroic airmen who were patients at the Palace Hotel.[32]

To protect the hospital, a large red cross was painted on the hotel roof to conform to the requirements of the Geneva Convention. But to no avail; the Germans bombed the hospital on 25 October 1942 while strafing the vicinity with machine gun fire. The hospital was full of service patients at the time of the attack, nineteen people were killed, forty-five others were injured, and one person was reported as missing. During this air raid other areas of Torquay were also attacked and in the Hele area a gas-holder was set on fire. Two months later the Luftwaffe returned and repeated their attack on the RAF hospital, severely damaging the centre block of the premises.

Church bells were rung throughout Devon in November 1942 to celebrate the famous desert victory in Egypt. But despite better war news the fourth wartime Christmas was a more austere occasion in the county. Wine was scarce, there were few turkeys, chickens, ducks or geese in the shops, although the Devon housewife could still purchase hogs pudding. Canned food too was in short supply, and there were no supplies of nuts or oranges. The other great shortage of Christmas 1942 was children's toys. With the restrictions on manufacturing toys, it was left to the handyman to construct wooden toys for the children.

Chapter 5 — References
(PC = Personal Communication)

1. *Action Stations 5* (1982), Chris Ashworth.
2. PC: A. H. Lewis, RN.
3. PC: A. H. Lewis, RN.
4. *Illustrated News*, 1942.
5. *Most Secret War* (1978) R. V. Jones.
6. *The Luftwaffe* (1987), Karl Ries.
7. *The Blitz Then and Now* (1990), Vol. 3. Winston G. Ramsey.
8. PC: Professor R. V. Jones.
9. HO 192; 1652; Exeter: *Air Raid Assessment Report*, PRO.
10. HO 198; 57; *Region 7 Reports*, PRO.
11. HO 192; 868; *Exeter Regional Report*, PRO.
12. HO 192; 1652; *Exeter Air Raid Assessment Report*, PRO.
13. HO 189; 349; *New Type of Incendiary Bomb*, PRO.
14. *Fire Service Memories*, Sir Aylmer Firebrace.
15. PC: Mrs M. C. Smith.
16. HO 191; 183; *Exeter Inspector General's Report*, PRO.
17. PC: Mr T. Hallet.
18. PC: Mrs B. Laidlaw.
19. HO 199; 139; *Air Raids on Exeter*, PRO.
20. *The Blitz Then and Now* (1990), Vol 3. Winston G. Ramsey.
21. HO 186; 2957; *No. 7 SW Regional History*, PRO.
22. *Most Secret War* (1987), R. V. Jones.
23. HO 192; 1652; *Exeter Air Raid Assessment Report*, PRO.
24. HO 192; 1653; *Baedeker Towns, Exeter*, PRO.
25. *Days on Dartmoor* (1987), Kenneth Day.
26. *The Mystery of X5* (1988), F. Walker and P. Mellor.
27. *Pigeons in World War 2* (1950).
28. *Forewarned is Forearmed* (1948), T. E. Winslow.
29. *AVIA 12; 184; Radar War History*, PRO.
30. HO 191; 1351; *Dartmouth: Phillips & Sons*, PRO.
31. *The Eagle Squadrons* (1979), Vern Haugland.
32. *Torquay, The Place the People* (1992), John Pike.

FOCKE-WULF FURY

All seemed quiet on the Home Front in South Devon at the beginning of 1943. Exmouth council's meeting was almost a non-event with only nine councillors attending and with one person in the public gallery listening to the two questions that had been raised. The meeting was over in ten minutes. More attention was being given by the residents to the 'pea soup' coloured water they were obliged to use while repairs were being carried out to the mains supply.

Exmouth's Anglo-Russian Committee approached the District Council with concerns that Exmouth was not being represented at the Red Army Day celebrations organised in the West of England. Throughout Devon there were many fund-raising activities in support of the USSR. The Russians were at this time cast in the heroic mould. Just as cinema audiences would clap Winston Churchill whenever he appeared on the newsreels, Joseph Stalin and the soldiers of the Red Army would also be applauded.

Seaton and Sidmouth had experienced air raids in the late Autumn of 1942, and at the beginning of 1943 Budleigh Salterton was supplied with air raid shelters.

East of Sidmouth in the fields around Branscombe farmers grew their famous early potatoes. During the war an ammunition factory had been established at Branscombe village. A London factory owner who had secured a government contract moved the factory's machinery to the Nestlés factory in Branscombe Square. The production of shell fuses and aircraft components increased and at one time 114 people were employed on twelve-hour shiftwork. The shell fuses were loaded into a van and delivered to Seaton railway station.[1] At Beer, the stone quarries used for the building of many Devon churches and parts of Exeter Cathedral, were used as an ammunition store.

Dawlish, Exeter and Paignton were the last Devon towns to be bombed in 1942; the doubtful distinction of having the first enemy bombs dropped on a community in 1943 was given to Kingsbridge.

The current National Savings Campaign 'Wings for Victory' involved most of the communities participating in the event. One of Ilfracombe's exhibits in this particular campaign was the display of two large high explosive bombs on to which townspeople were invited to stick saving stamps. The Air Ministry had promised the townspeople that the bombs would be dropped on a target in

The Focke-Wulf 190 proved to be one of the most formidable of the Luftwaffe fighter-bombers. This was the type of aircraft involved in the attack on Teignmouth in January 1943, and in many subsequent raids over Devon in the months following.

Germany and the money spent on purchasing the saving stamps would be sent to the Chancellor of the Exchequer as a gift to the nation. When one of the bombs was removed from the exhibition some of the saving stamps were missing, resulting in two boys appearing before a local magistrate.

Life carried on in the South Devon communities despite the threat that sudden destruction and bloodshed could happen at any time. Yet there were also times of peace and tranquillity. A contemporary lady chronicler described a bus ride from Dartmouth to Torcross, enjoying the journey particularly after passing the cliff village of Stoke Fleming on the road to Slapton. Here are the most marvellous coastal views with undulating fields dipping gracefully towards the sea. The bus diverted to call at Slapton village then on to Torcross where this lady passenger alighted to take tea in a small hotel. Except for the barbed-wire defences along the seafront, for brief moments one could imagine there was no war.[2] Yet on this very day Torquay, some fifteen miles from Torcross, had been bombed, with five people killed, thirty others injured, and some eight hundred suburban properties damaged.

The day of 10 January 1943 was a Sunday and a very bad day for Teignmouth. This small holiday resort never became headline news on the BBC or in the national newspapers as a result of the destruction and casualties it experienced, despite suffering so cruelly under the aerial attacks that the Luftwaffe made on it.

Seven FW190s flew in very low over the town, dropping bombs mainly on residential property. People out on the streets were gunned down by the enemy machine guns. Twenty people were killed, their ages ranging from an elderly lady of eighty-two years to a one-year-old baby. One of the women killed had been widowed when her husband died during the Plymouth Blitz.[3]

Two weeks later at the small village of Aveton Gifford, situated near the River Avon that runs out to Bigbury Bay, a further surprise attack occurred. At 4pm on a winter's day the inhabitants of Aveton Gifford were surprised by glass being showered from the windows of their rooms and the noise of aircraft that seemed to be flying just above their rooftops. Above the din could be heard the rattle of machine guns. This was yet another tip and run raid; it was soon over but lasted long enough to cause considerable destruction. The village was shattered. One young girl aged five, an evacuee from the Plymouth Blitz was killed, twenty people were injured. Firemen, demolition workers, troops, the police and the WVS arrived at Aveton Gifford, but it was difficult to drive through the village streets littered with slates from the roofs of the houses, debris and masses of telephone wire. One hundred and fifty inhabitants, practically the whole community, sustained damage to their homes. Rescue work and searching continued throughout the evening by candlelight, for the bombs had destroyed the village electricity supply. At night the Home Guard patrolled the devastated church to guard valuables buried in the ruins. In the following two days the WVS served seven hundred meals to the villagers and civil defence workers. Many of the local householders had their china and cooking facilities destroyed.[4]

The village church of St Andrew's had been reduced to a ruin without form or design when a bomb exploded on the church. The thirteenth-century church

The ruined St Andrew's Church at Aveton Gifford. The building was struck by a bomb during a raid by five Focke-Wulf 190 aircraft on 26 January 1943.

An official 'secret' observer's report of the raid on Dartmouth, 13 February 1943. It shows the position of the sighting of the enemy aircraft (EA) and the route taken by the attackers.

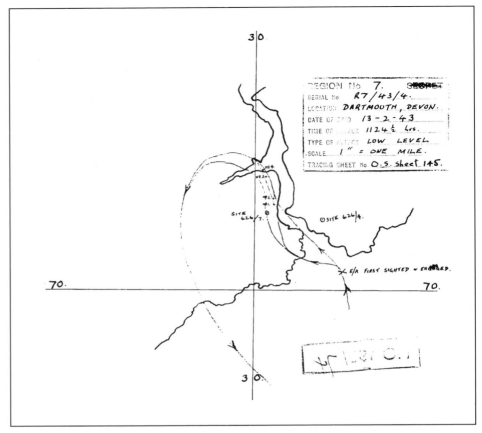

tower was devastated and the eight bells destroyed, as was the paraclose screen, the organ and furnishings. St Andrew's Church was the eighteenth church that had so far been destroyed in Devon by bombing.

Described as a minor raid, the attack was nonetheless a major disaster for this small undefended community. Twenty-seven years were to pass before the church tower was finally rebuilt.

The WVS introduced a pasty scheme early in 1943. This was different from their pie scheme that involved delivering pies to the Devon farmworkers in the fields. The Devon pasty scheme organised the baking of pasties that were delivered to various distribution points. Orders for pasties were written on cards placed in shop windows, indicating the numbers required for the next delivery. In North Devon for example the pasties would be baked at Bideford and distributed to the participating villages including Buckland Brewer, Bulkworthy and Horns Cross. During March 1943 the Bideford area villages ordered a total of 10 689 Devon pasties.[5]

The February night skies of South Devon were not always lit up by anti-aircraft gunfire but by the blinding flashes of lightning followed by colossal cracks of thunder. These were times of torrential rain and violent storms that would pass and give way to clear fine weather. It would seem as if the world was at peace again, but it was not to be.

On a beautiful morning of 13 February 1943, enemy aircraft were seen flying towards Dartmouth. One aircraft released two bombs in the area of Old Mill Creek near the Royal Naval College. The other two fighter-bombers flew directly over the town dropping one bomb in the vicinity of the old Butterwalk; another bomb was dropped on property away from the centre of the small town.

The bomb near the Butterwalk demolished buildings, trapping people beneath the debris. Rescue workers toiled ceaselessly endeavouring to locate the trapped. In failing light there emerged an incredible scene of shattered buildings floodlit with flares. A small army of soldiers dug and ambulances patiently waited while everywhere there was crumbling debris, bricks and plaster dust. Eventually after ten hours of toil a mother and her children, with four other people, were carried from the destruction, and all were dead. At 10pm there came a call for silence; everyone stood still as if in a floodlit tableaux, and people listened and tried to make contact with those buried in the demolished buildings. With the silence

came gunfire from the direction of Torquay, all the flares were extinguished at the scene of the rescue. Early on Sunday morning the flares were lit again and digging recommenced. At 4.30am the body of a woman was taken from the rubble.[6]

The anti-aircraft gunfire that interrupted rescue work at Dartmouth was responding to air raids over Torquay and Paignton. The attack at Torquay began before the local air raid warning had sounded. An intruder raider, following the course of returning British bombers, made it difficult for the British defences to detect an enemy presence.

The Germans used phosphorous incendiary bombs during this raid on Torquay. A fourth Devon target on the same night was at Plymouth, the city experiencing its first night attack for eighteen months. One of a number of bombs that were dropped outside a hotel where a dance was being held. The bomb blast caused considerable damage, but it was fortunate on this occasion only a few people were injured. In other areas of Plymouth several citizens were killed and injured.

One way to obtain a panoramic view of Dartmouth, which nestles in a steep valley, is to ferry across the River Dart and walk up one of the steep roads of Kingswear village. During the war if one walked further along this road, passing a white-painted farmhouse, crossing a field, then down a lane, passing a tower by the water's edge, one came to a forbidden area. Kingswear was the base for the 23rd MTB Flotilla of the Free French Naval Forces. An imposing house 'Brookhill' overlooking the River Dart, was the Flotilla's headquarters. Here and nearby 'Kingswear Court', a large gabled detached house, was where the French sailors were billeted. Operational command was exercised from HMS *Cicala*, the Royal Navy HQ based at the Royal Dart Hotel, Kingswear. The 23rd Flotilla's mother ship was the FS *Belfort* built at Lorient in 1919.

The Flotilla consisted of eight motor torpedo boats. One of them, No. 96, had been built at Morgan Giles Shipyard at Teignmouth. The boats were moored alongside the Kingswear jetty by the GWR pontoon. The torpedoes they carried were stored at Kingswear in a small Nissen hut.

Each evening MTBs of the 23rd Flotilla would sail out into the English Channel towards the French coast in search of enemy shipping. One of the Flotilla crew was Phillipe de Gaule, son of the President of France. The prey of the MTBs was enemy minesweepers, trawlers and E Boats.[7]

On Thursday evening 25 February, Lady Baden-Powell, the Chief Guide, visited Exmouth and met the local Girl Guides and Brownies. Many Exmouthians had, with their torches, ventured out to visit the cinema. The ever vigilant Exmouth Home Guard were drilling and participating in weapon training. The following morning people were out in the town shopping. A clear day, with good visibility on land, there were clouds in the sky and mist over the River Exe. At 12.15pm, as the sun was breaking through the clouds, eight FW190s appeared over Exmouth and proceeded to machine gun and bomb the town.

A contemporary photograph of the motor torpedo boat MTB96, of the Free French Flotilla based at Kingswear. The boat was one of a number constructed at the Morgan Giles Shipyard, Teignmouth.

A torpedo is loaded on to a Free French motor torpedo boat at Kingswear c. 1943. Powered by three Rolls Royce engines, these fast and well-armed boats posed an ever-present threat to German naval vessels operating out of ports in France.

The licensee of the Clarence Inn who was on his allotment at Albion Hill was killed by cannon fire; nearby a large gasholder was set on fire. Fortunately, the holder sank down and did not explode; a potential disaster was averted. Close to this incident a district nurses home was destroyed at Roddenstile Lane, and the wife of the President of Exmouth Rugby Football Club was killed when an enemy bomb exploded on her home.

Away to the north of the town, a bomb exploded on houses in Phillips Avenue and at the Fulham Road junction of Exeter Road. Two other bombs fell close to the GWR railway station and, to the south of the town, on Louise Terrace.

It was, however, in the town's shopping area where a remarkable but tragic incident occurred on this day. A 500kg bomb hit and penetrated a three-storey building without exploding. The bomb, on making its exit from the 'Happy Times' shop, continued its path across the Strand, hitting the paving and, with a slight change in direction, travelled across a lawn before just tipping the corner of a public air raid shelter. The bomb then crossed the Strand entering No. 19 The Strand (Mathews' shop), then into Hancocks' shop next door where it exploded.

Prior to the bomb exploding in the Strand many people out in the street, having heard the sound of machine gunning, had taken cover in the nearby shops and air raid shelters; others lay on the ground. Nearby a small 20-seater bus was waiting at a bus stop. Some of the bus passengers, hearing the machine gun fire, left the bus and also took shelter in the shops. The passengers who had remained in the bus crouched down behind the seats and were in this position when the bomb exploded in Hancocks' shop. All the passengers in the bus suffered shock and minor injuries, but escaped with their lives. The coachwork of the bus was severely damaged by falling debris; inside the bus were found three large pieces of concrete, slates and glass.

'Brookhill', Kingswear 1943. A Free French sailor is presented with a medal in the grounds of the Flotilla's headquarters.

A dramatic wartime photograph of Focke-Wulf 190 aircraft. These single-engined fighter-bombers were capable of carrying out swift terror raids from their French airfield bases.

The small block of shops where the bomb exploded was severely damaged. Hancocks' was completely demolished. Twenty people lost their lives in the Strand while four others were killed by the enemy in other areas of Exmouth.[8] The enemy aircraft flew away in a south-easterly direction leaving Exmouth to

The Strand incident, Exmouth, 26 February 1943. Taken a few hours after the bomb exploded inside Hancocks' shop.

The Strand incident, Exmouth in which twenty people were killed. A contemporary diagram plots the path of the bomb that fell on the 'Happy Times' shop before skidding into the premises of Mathews and then Hancocks, where it exploded.

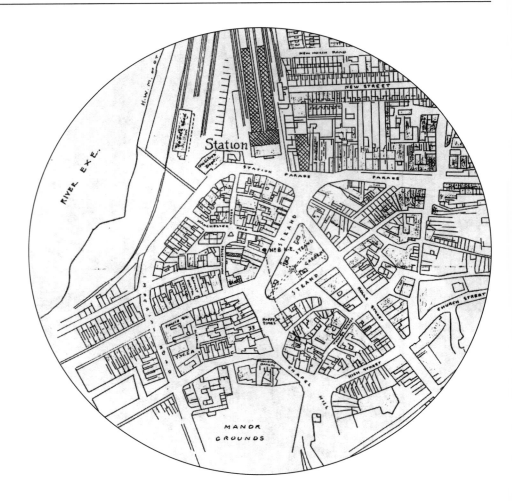

rescue the people trapped under the demolished shops and houses, to care for the numerous casualties and eventually bury its dead.

The day after the Strand incident at Exmouth, enemy E Boats attacked a convoy of ships sailing to Southampton near Start Point. The minesweeper, HMS *Harstad*, the anti-submarine vessel HMS *Lord Hailsham* were sunk, with the cargo vessel *Moldavia*. A trawler arrived at the ferry pontoon, Dartmouth, with survivors from this naval action. Arrangements had already been made to receive them, with lorries and other transport waiting on the Embankment. A crowd of half-naked figures in blankets moved up the sloping Dartmouth pontoon into the waiting lorries.

Three naval officers, wearing polo-neck sweaters and flannel trousers, were suffering the consequences of being in the sea for six hours. Two of the officers were immediately driven away through the quiet of the South Hams countryside to Devonport. Passing through the streets of Plymouth, alive with crowds of shoppers, was in striking contrast to the past turbulent hours for the naval men. Later that same day fourteen bodies from the E Boat action were landed at Dartmouth.[9]

Noel Coward came on tour to the Theatre Royal, Exeter, during February 1943, with one of his plays *This Happy Breed*. While at Exeter he developed jaundice and a temperature of 104° compelling him to cancel his stage appearance at the Palace Theatre, Plymouth. Coward remained in Devon to recuperate at the Imperial Hotel, Torquay.[10] The Manager of the Imperial Hotel discouraged long-stay guests during the war, based on the idea that the greatest number of people possible should enjoy a holiday as a relief from the strains and stresses of wartime. One exception was the permanent hotel resident, the American multi-millionaire Eugene Higgins who was cruising in the English Channel when war was declared and sailed to the nearest safe haven, that happened to be Torquay. Eugene Higgins, an eccentric, became a well known figure among the hotel guests. His entourage included his secretary M. Cousteau, whose son was to grow up to become the famous underwater explorer.[11]

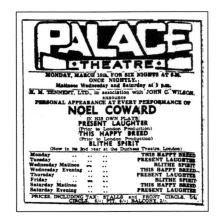

On 12 March 1943, a lady was preparing dinner at her home in Salcombe and was placing it on the Morrison shelter in the dining room, when she happened to turn towards the window and saw an object coming towards the house through the air. Instantly she dived into the shelter. At the same time the bomb exploded in an adjoining shop, a distance of fifteen feet away. The walls of the building came down on the Morrison shelter completely covering it. A hand bell was kept in the shelter 'just in case', and the trapped woman started to ring the bell, with no apparent result, for the Civil Defence rescue squad were busy extracting a sailor who had been buried in the rubble next door. One of the rescuers thought he heard the sound of a muffled bell and on searching they located and rescued the good lady and the bell![12]

Bomb battered Teignmouth was under attack again on the 17 May but no substantial damage occurred.

The American 29th Infantry Division moved into Devon and Cornwall by truck, or by marching along the roads and narrow lanes. Over 14 000 officers and men arrived in the South West. Units based in Devon during this period included the 121 Eng. Combat Battalion at Paignton, the 227 Field Artillery Battalion at Okehampton, the 116 RCT in the Plymouth area, and the 175 RCT at Torquay and Exeter. The Divisional Headquarters were at Tavistock. From this time on there was to be a significant change in the social climate of wartime Devon and an increase in military activities in the county.[13]

Morale of the civilian population throughout Devon had never been low, even when people were suffering the worst effects of the air attacks. Lack of sleep, tiredness and fatigue were not uncommon, but there was never any significant absenteeism from work. Now, in 1943, there were signs of optimism, with the military successes in North Africa and the Allied air offensive on Germany that was gathering momentum.

The presence of the American servicemen gave an indication to the local communities that something, sometime, somehow would be happening; the much referred to 'Second Front' now seemed more than a slogan. Whatever the optimistic response to the American 29th Infantry Division arriving during the merry month of May, the month ended in disaster and indescribable grief for many families in Torquay.

Fine warm weather was the greatest enticement to bring the Torquaians out on Sunday 30 May 1943, and people were out strolling, relaxing, or promenading along the seafronts. The air defences had been strengthened and alerted to an impending air attack when 21 FW190s of SKG10 flew in at low level, machine gunning and dropping bombs on the town. The air attack produced a heavy toll for both the enemy and Torquaians. The German Air Force lost five of their FW190s, one of them crashing into a terrace of houses at Teignmouth Road, Torquay.

The attack was widespread, one bomb released from a FW190 fell and exploded on the parish church of St Marychurch while children were assembling for Sunday school. The church was shattered by the exploding bomb, and people

Heavy damage following a raid on Union Street, Torquay, 30 May 1943. Note the shopkeeper is already beginning to sweep up ready for 'business as usual'.

The appalling scene following the direct hit on the parish church at St Marychurch, Torquay, 30 May 1943. Shirt-sleeved rescuers begin the search for survivors but tragically 21 children were killed, along with three Sunday school teachers.

hearing what had happened made their way to offer their assistance in rescuing the trapped children and Sunday school staff. The search went on throughout the night until the last body was found.

The Luftwaffe killed forty-five people on this Sunday afternoon, including twenty-one children and three of their Sunday school teachers. The injured numbered 150 people. A considerable number of properties including three hundred houses were destroyed or damaged.[14]

The Regional Commissioner for South West England visited Salcombe in 1943 to discuss civil defence for the district. Understandably people associated the new civil defence measures with the recent air raids in the area. Air raid shelters were made available for the Kingsbridge communities.

The threat of a German invasion of England was still a concern for those entrusted with the Defence of the Realm. The local invasion committees, set up since 1940, continued to meet and if necessary modify their plans. The Kingsbridge committee was still sensitive to the fact they were only seventy miles away from enemy occupied Guernsey. Concern was shown regarding the situation that existed at the village of Brownston a mile from Modbury. All was not well for the village was without any means of communication for no villager had a telephone or possessed a bicycle. The local WVS responded by undertaking the responsibility of providing the village with a bicycle if anyone could be found to use it.

The Allies recognised in their planning for the invasion of Europe that special training would be required for the assault troops. Few American soldiers had combat experience or had received amphibious training. Furthermore, none possessed the specialised skills required to assault heavily fortified coastal positions, for this was a new challenge in warfare. New doctrines were written to introduce new ideas, to learn new skills and then to practice what had been taught; thereafter to assess, modify and refine the training to perfection. For these reasons plans were made to train small combat teams of American assault troops and to acquire these essential skills an Assault Training Centre would be needed.

"I'm afraid the Regional Commissioner has roped us in for ANOTHER blasted exercise, so I want you all to be on your toes and show him how keen we are."

During the summer of 1943 US Naval bases were established at Appledore and Instow to provide facilities for training landing craft crew and to assist the US Army in acquainting soldiers with boat work. Further up the River Torridge, at Bideford, the Americans based their landing craft.

The old USS *President Warfield*, used to accommodate US naval personnel, was moored in the River Torridge between Instow and Bideford. The *President Warfield* was an old Chesapeake Bay steamer, built with a high superstructure and a high funnel, not unlike the design of the old Mississippi sternwheel paddlesteamers but without the giant paddle. In July 1942, the planners of the invasion of Europe (Operation Overlord) were short of cross-Channel personnel carriers and hospital ships. To resolve this problem the Ministry of War Transport chartered eleven American steamers, all originally built for inshore work or service primarily for holidaymakers.

Although the ships were modified, there remained a concern that the vessels would not have the speed and endurance for the rough Atlantic crossing.

RAF personnel man an Hispano anti-aircraft gun on Shaldon Bridge, Teignmouth, 27 March 1943. Note the anti-invasion obstacles in the water alongside the bridge.

The elderly American steamship SS *President Warfield* arrived from Newfoundland to accommodate US troops stationed in North Devon. Moored in the River Torridge throughout the war she was later used to carry Jews into Palestine.

Volunteer crews were recruited to cross the Atlantic but three boats developed technical problems that prevented them from sailing. The remaining eight boats set sail from St John's Newfoundland. Five days out at sea the convoy was attacked by a U Boat and two of the pleasure boats were sunk with the loss of their crew. The convoy was later attacked by another U Boat and the escort destroyer HMS *Veteran* and another boat was sunk. Somehow the SS *President Warfield* survived the crossing.[15]

After service with the US Navy, the *Warfield* was purchased and registered as a merchant ship, sailing under the name *Exodus 47*, and was used for transporting what were then called 'illegal immigrants' into Palestine. The boat was intercepted by the Royal Navy and at the time attracted considerable publicity.

At Ilfracombe, most of the hotel accommodation had been taken by American servicemen. Many of these troops then moved on to Braunton and Saunton to build camps that were to be associated with the Woolacombe Assault Training Centre (ATC). As more American troops arrived in the Ilfracombe district they constructed Quonset huts (a larger version of the Nissen hut). The construction of these huts continued through day and night with the noise of mobile generators and drills making it very difficult for anyone in the area to sleep at night. American troops were now to be seen marching through the town, very different in style to that which the townspeople had been used. Columns of US troops marched several times a day to the Quonsets, used by the American Army for cookhouses and mess-halls. Woolacombe Bay Hotel became the headquarters for the ATC.

Ilfracombe was full of US Army vehicles, many from units of the 156th Infantry Division who provided most of the ATC training staff. The old town hall was used as a US Post Office depot. A 'Doughnut Dugout' was opened by the American Red Cross, with other US forces' canteens and rest centres throughout the town. The American presence in North Devon was a familiar scene and Ilfracombe, for a few weeks at least, was one of the 'Little Americas' that were established throughout Devon.

In the South Devon town of Salcombe, this small community had experienced a second generation of 'Friendly Invaders', the first being the large number of civilian evacuees Salcombe had to contend with. Here, at this pleasant pre-war yachting resort, a place of memorable peacetime regattas, a US Naval Construction Battalion (CBs — Seebees) arrived in 1943 to set up an amphibious base. The Americans were to outnumber the depleted wartime population of Salcombe.

The Salcombe Hotel became the headquarters for the US Seebees Battalion. Above the town the Americans erected Quonsets and eventually requisitioned seventy civilian properties, converting the St Elmo hospital into a US naval hospital.

Down on the waterfront the Americans built a concrete slipway with a launching trolley and winches to enable them to haul the landing craft up from the water to repair and service them.[16]

The large numbers of vehicles and quantities of supplies that were having to be transported in and out of Salcombe along the narrow roads and country lanes resulted in severe traffic congestion. The presence of the American forces in this part of South Hams also considerably increased the volume of railway freight traffic. On occasion special trains loaded with equipment and stores would arrive at Kingsbridge railway station (there was no railway station at Salcombe).

Along the coast beyond Slapton Bay, Strete and Stoke Fleming, the US Navy established a school for amphibious training and gun support at HMS *Brittania*, Dartmouth. As the permanent accommodation of the Royal Naval College was inadequate to house the 3684 US naval personnel, numerous huts and tents were erected in the college grounds.

In Dartmouth, the Americans built hutted workshops on Coronation Park, by the side of the River Dart, as a facility to repair amphibious craft. A small US naval base was set up near the red cliffs of Teignmouth for the training and repairing of landing craft.[17]

The US Navy also went inland and established a small naval store at Tiverton. In contrast the US Navy established their largest store in the whole of the UK at Exeter. This vast depot required part of the city's golf course being taken over by the Americans. A purpose-built railway siding was constructed to bring the enormous quantities of essential supplies to the stores. The Exeter depot grew in size to cover ninety-five acres of land with 176 buildings and accommodating 2352 naval personnel. In addition, seventy-five acres of storage space was utilised in other parts of Exeter. From the depot a variety of spare parts for the US forces

The Southern Command Weapon Training School, Woolacombe, North Devon. This photograph was taken before the arrival of American servicemen and shows British troops training under fire.

British army amphibious training exercise, Appledore, May 1943. Early experiments in bringing heavy armour ashore stood the Allied armies in good stead when it came to D-Day.

were distributed. Later, at the time of the invasion of Normandy, the Exeter Depot prepared hot meals in containers that were supplied to the American and British landing craft carrying US combat troops across the English Channel.[18]

The remarkable events of 1943 were to reinforce the claim that Devon was the most militarily active county in the UK during the Second World War.

Southern (Army) Command had established a Weapon Training School at Woolacombe. At Appledore the Combined Operations Experimental Establishment (COXE) were involved in developing various projects that could be used for the proposed invasion, with service personnel from the navy at Instow, RAF Chivenor, and soldiers based at Westward Ho! Their work included building Bailey bridges, testing landing craft, demolition, and devising methods of destroying underwater obstacles. Here, as the experimental work progressed, the boffins would arrive to inspect their special projects. The Professors Bernal and Haldane would visit the establishment to discuss their specific projects regarding the use of explosives under water. Sir Malcolm Campbell, the famous racing driver associated with the record-breaking *Bluebird*, would arrive to discuss aspects of sand velocity.[19]

The Allies had learnt that the enemy beach defences along parts of the French coast comprised many obstacles and huge bastions of reinforced concrete. For the troops to land on the beaches and move inland the concrete forts would need to be demolished. To breach a concrete wall it was estimated that one ton of high explosive, placed at the base of the wall, would be required. The beaches, along with being mined, would also be swept with enemy gunfire.

It was vital to develop weapons to attack these enemy concrete defences and the challenge was taken up by the Royal Navy's Directorate of Miscellaneous Weapon Development (DMWD), a group of naval scientists affectionately known as the 'Wheezers and Dodgers'. A weapon to breach the enemy's coastal defences was sketched and the idea presented to a RNVR officer called Norway, better known as the author, Neville Shute.

This remarkable weapon of destruction comprised two enormous steel wheels, ten feet in diameter, with a one-foot tread connected by a drumlike axle containing high explosive. This monster would be propelled by large, slow-burning rockets fixed round the circumference of each wheel.

The plan was for the wheel weapon to be taken ashore by a tank landing craft. When the ramp of the landing craft went down the rockets would be ignited and

The 'Great Panjandrum' trials on Instow Beach, January 1944. Ten feet in diameter and driven by rockets, this early experimental monster, designed to break through coastal defences, was later abandoned.

the wheel would propel itself through shallow water up the beach to the concrete wall, moving and looking like a giant Catherine wheel. The weapon would reach a speed of sixty miles per hour by the time it struck the concrete defence. The wheels would then collapse and the drum would explode.

Approval was given to construct the weapon which was made in secrecy in a hut in East London. Neville Shute christened this giant wheel 'The Great Panjandrum' (because 'the gunpowder ran out from its heels'. Samuel Foote 1720–77). Later, in the summer of 1943, the wheel was loaded and transported with an escort overnight to North Devon, being locked up at every approved stopping place to prevent the wheel being seen by civilians. On arrival at Appledore security was abandoned; the Great Panjandrum was rolled off its transporter on to the beach where it was immediately surrounded by holidaymakers.

Eighteen rockets were fixed to the wheel that was launched for the first time at Westward Ho! There were problems as the monster wheel misbehaved. Another trial was held with the wheel being powered with more than seventy rockets. Trials continued well into 1944 but the wheel behaved in such an erratic manner (on one occasion it reached a speed of nearly one hundred miles per hour and sped out of control scaring the life out of the official observers attending the trial), the Great Panjandrum never made it to the invasion beaches.[20]

The Transportation Wing of COXE was involved in the laying of thirty miles of cable on the bed of the Bristol Channel to Combe Martin as part of the ingenious project of PLUTO (Pipe Line Under The Ocean).

The main Pluto network, one thousand miles of pipeline, distributed fuel oil from throughout the UK to supply fuel for the Allied armies on the Continent. The Swansea–Watermouth (near Ilfracombe) connection was an experimental pipeline, with thirty-five firemen of the NFS based on location, under the strictest security. Pumping started on 4 April 1943, with fourteen road-tankers allocated to take on 15 000 gallons of oil at Watermouth Castle. During the experimental period associated with the Bristol Channel pipeline a ship's anchor damaged the line four miles off Swansea with the loss of 130 462 gallons of fuel.[21]

In the summer of 1943 there was concern about the possibility of enemy retaliation raids taking place in response to the recent RAF Dambuster raids. In Devon consideration was given to the existing defences of Burrator Reservoir located on Dartmoor. Ever since August 1941, a boom and net had been installed in the south-west corner to protect the reservoir against aerial torpedo attacks. Because of the raids on the German dams there was a fear that the Heinkel 177, a larger enemy aircraft, would attack Burrator with a German version of the 'Upkeep' bouncing bomb. A request was submitted by the Plymouth authorities to install additional anti-mine nets some 15–20 feet upstream, near the face of the dam, as a counter-measure.[22]

Throughout Devon, celebrations mainly in the form of parades were being held to commemorate the third anniversary of the formation of the Home Guard. The Barnstaple 4th Battalion held a mass parade of 1300 men watched by crowds of local residents. At Bideford the Home Guard chose to hold a pageant depicting the development of the force from the beginning of the citizen's army. Summer trade at Barnstaple's pannier market was good; cooked beetroot cost 1 penny, turnips a halfpenny each, and parsnips twopence per pound.

These two photographs show Exeter's Home Guard on training exercises under the eye of Royal Marine instructors. Note the high standard of equipment and weaponry now (1943) available to home defence units.

(Above left) An artillery unit of the Home Guard practise live firing at the Okehampton range, Dartmoor, 1943.

(Above right) An armed motorcycle unit of Exeter's Home Guard with a Lewis gun mounted on the sidecar. Not all the Home Guard were 'old men' as this picture reveals.

The Bideford police force were extending their checks on people regarding identity cards and any person caught without their card was ordered to report to the local police station. Bideford traders considered a proposal that, as the local shops were so low in stock, shop staff should be released to work part time as agriculture workers. Later in the year the first of the 'shop girl harvesters' appeared at Eastleigh Barton helping in stooking in the barley fields.

Torrington Rural District Council wanted to get an increased allowance of cooking fat for their bakers so more pasties could be baked for the farmworkers. Five acres of Torrington golf course were ploughed up for agriculture. The ever-present problem of domestic water supplies was again attracting attention and in Torrington the concern was that some families had been without drinking water on several occasions. Tanked water was considered, but under the prevailing conditions there was little hope of improvement. In contrast at Bideford, there was too much water, as many areas of the town had been under flood.

Three years had passed since 1940 when Bideford had, within a period of three days, received 1500 schoolchildren evacuees. Now in the summer of 1943, a total of 607 evacuees remained.

Also in the late summer of 1943 the Woolacombe Assault Training Centre opened. The ATC embraced various beaches of golden sand including Saunton

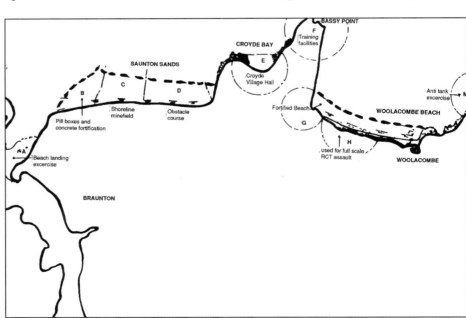

A map showing the main defences of the Woolacombe Assault Training Centre. Redrawn from a contemporary document.

Colonel Paul W. Thompson, Commanding Officer of the Assault Training Centre, Woolacombe. In the front of the jeep is Lt-General Jacob Devers.

US amphibious exercises on Woolacombe beach 1943, with Baggy Point in the background.

American troops are disgorged from the gaping bows of a landing craft during amphibious exercises on Woolacombe beach, 1943.

Concrete bunkers at Woolacombe ATC. Purpose-built replicas of German coastal defence installations were used by the Americans to practice and assess methods of assault.

A single concrete pillbox surrounded with barbed wire on Saunton Sands, used for training assault tactics at Woolacombe ATC. Obstacles such as these were identical to those facing the troops on the D-Day landings.

Sands, Croyde Bay, and Woolacombe Sands. Consideration had been given by the US forces to apply for the evacuation of Croyde, Georgeham and Woolacombe but this idea was abandoned.

After the official transfer of the training area had been completed, mines laid by the British Army in 1940 were cleared. The Americans, with considerable activity, went about constructing fortifications and obstacles on the North Devon shores, replicating concrete fortifications of the German coastal defences that had been photographed by Allied reconnaissance aircraft. The ATC exercise areas were organised in a way that certain beaches, or parts of them, were designated for particular types of training exercises.

Units of the 29th Infantry Division were the first to participate in the ATC training programme that commenced in September 1943. The Americans would arrive at Woolacombe to attend a two-to-three-week course on assault techniques and tactics. The troops would arrive at Braunton railway station and eventually be driven to one of the 'Tent Cities' at Braunton Burrows, Croyde Bay or Lincombe. Details of the ATC and the demanding training, in which many were killed and injured, are described by Bass [23] (also see Bibliography).

Throughout 1943, the number and size of Allied convoys sailing up the Bristol Channel increased. Often the convoys were no more than two miles off the North Devon coast. The American massed-produced Liberty Ships were a common sight, as were large tank landing ships carrying the small amphibious craft on their decks. These would dock at the port of Avonmouth. Troopships carrying either American or Canadian service personnel would also be seen sailing up the Bristol Channel. The ships would sometimes queue waiting for a vacant berth.[24]

In South Devon, before the establishment of the Woolacombe ATC and Slapton Battle Training Area, troops of the 175th Infantry Regiment would embark in amphibious craft at Dartmouth and, with the co-operation of the Royal Navy, sail out and around the coast to Slapton beach. These beach landings, almost demonstrations, were comparatively gentle compared to exercises that were to take place during 1944. The first landing exercises were held on 16 August 1943.[25] The landings were in fact tests to ascertain the suitability of the beach for the military exercises that had been planned.

The US troops, having completed their course at the Woolacombe ATC, would be required to participate in larger (Corps) exercises of embarkation, landing on enemy shores, assaulting and holding a beachhead for the landing of follow-up forces. To practice those exercises at Corps level a decision was made to establish an American Battle Training Area at Slapton, Devon.

This was the same beachhead area used by (Lord) Brigadier Bernard Montgomery for his amphibious military exercise in 1938. Slapton Sands was chosen for its similarity to features of the Normandy coastal area that the American forces were to assault (although this has now been disputed by Bass).[26] The pre-invasion training exercises at Corps level involved not only landing assault troops on to the beach, but battle exercises requiring troop movement into the hinterland. These exercises would on occasions be conducted using live ammunition fired by army and naval units participating in the exercises. The nature and extent of these exercises would require compulsory orders to be issued for the evacuation of the South Hams inhabitants, their animals and farm stock, together with all their personal possessions. Unconfirmed reports refer to the Americans originally requesting a much larger area of land to be evacuated than that which was finally agreed.

The long curved beach that stretches from Strete Gate to Torcross village is made up of shingle and pebbles; further along, past Strete Gate, is the finer shingle beach of Blackpool. Slapton beach is bounded by a raised road routed to Dartmouth and in the opposite, westward, direction to Plymouth. Alongside this raised coastal road is Slapton Ley, a freshwater lake fed by the River Gara and three small streams. The Ley, with its tall rushes, is a natural habitat for wildlife while the land directly behind is of undulating hills of rich agricultural soil. One mile from the beach inland is the village of Slapton.

The area is farmed by people living in scattered rural communities. Until the Compulsory Evacuation Order was served the inhabitants had lived a relatively peaceful wartime existence, but it would be naive to believe that the war had passed them by. Villagers were members of the Home Guard, or Civil Defence and were aware of the anti-invasion defences in the area. Out on the waters of Start Bay, merchant ships and warships had been engaged in action and sunk by enemy forces, and bombs had fallen at nearby Dartmouth and Salcombe.

The South West Regional Commissioner was first notified of the compulsory order to evacuate part of the South Hams area in September 1943. It was for the Regional Commissioner to serve the official notices of the evacuation to the villagers. The complicated legal transfer required the involvement of the Admiralty and other government ministries. The government order was a new experience for the Commissioner and his staff. Guidelines on how to organise the exodus were provided by the Eastern Region Commissioner who had previously

Lee Bay, North Devon, 13 December 1943. Cliff-scaling practice by US troops from Woolacombe ATC.

DUKWs (Amphibious Landing Craft) exercise on the sand dunes at Woolacombe ATC, 1943.

US assault troops at Woolacombe ATC exercise with a Bangalore Torpedo, a metal tube packed with explosives, used for blowing gaps in concertina wire defences.

This photograph reveals the formidably realistic defences set up in the area used for troop training exercises at Woolacombe ATC.

Assault troops take part in battle training exercises on Woolacombe beach, 8 November 1943.

Slapton beach, 16 August 1943. This famous photograph shows US troops, in co-operation with the Royal Navy (see LC A567), on an exercise to test the suitability of Slapton for future military training, as distinct from pre-invasion exercises that were later to take place here.

been involved with an order of compulsory evacuation of two areas of land in East Anglia during 1942, when all the civilians were evacuated. Two months were to elapse before the Commissioner was ordered to proceed with the evacuation order for South Hams.[27]

During the summer, the Kingsbridge WVS began to organise small teams of volunteers to cook and serve meals 'in case they were needed'. In August 1943 exercises were planned for these newly formed teams to try out their emergency service.

Although many inhabitants were surprised and shocked on hearing of the compulsory evacuation, there had been rumours circulating among the villagers that something was amiss. There were for example official looking men, not normally seen in the area, arriving at Blackawton village, calling at the school and church. The same men had been seen visiting Stokenham village near Torcross. Some locals recognised the visitors as members of Devon County Council and Kingsbridge Rural District Council. Current talk of a Second Front, and the recollection of the military exercises of 1938, and again in August 1943 all gave the villagers reason to believe the area may again be used for military purposes.[28]

Slapton beach was already out of bounds; areas of the beach had been mined and lengths of barbed-wire stretched for miles along the shore. Guns and pillboxes had been installed, all part of the anti-invasion defences. The Royal Sands Hotel (patronised by King Edward VII), built on the edge of Slapton beach, had closed down at the outbreak of war and had subsequently suffered damage by a mine detonated by a dog that had managed to get on to the beach.

The official evacuation order was carried out by the Admiralty Land Agent at Dittisham Court Hotel where representatives of the Regional Commissioner and staff of the government ministries were based. The order required the compulsory requisition of twenty-five square miles of South Hams countryside and the

US troops of the 29th Infantry Division on exercises near the Okehampton training camp, Dartmoor, 1 September 1943.

A contemporary map showing the extent of the Slapton Battle Area, South Devon.

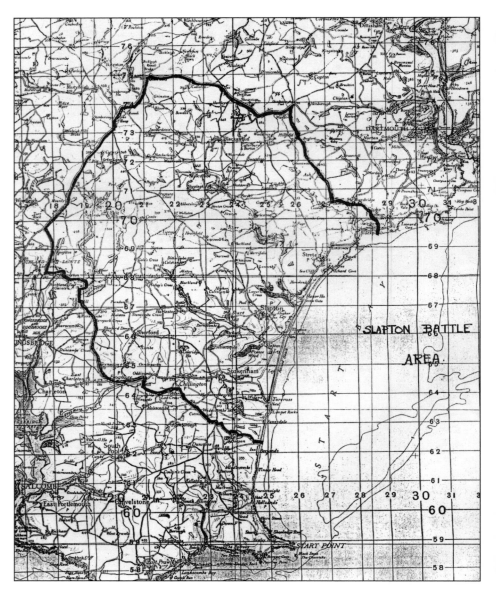

evacuation of all the inhabitants from six parishes. This meant three thousand people from seven hundred and fifty households were required to go. No official scheme had been planned to offer accommodation to the people who were to be evicted from their homes. The order also required that six thousand cattle and twelve thousand sheep were to be removed, together with ten thousand tons of root crops and all farming implements and machinery.

The evacuation was required to be completed within six weeks. To initiate the exodus, arrangements were made to organise meetings. The first meeting was attended by members of the local council and voluntary groups at Stokenham Victory Hall, where the plans were explained and details of the timing of events were given.

The second meeting was with the clergy from the various churches in the areas to be evacuated. The clergy were given details of the government's financial arrangements towards the cost of temporary accommodation and the arrangements for the payment of rents and storage of furniture during the enforced absence. The clergy were also told that their churches came under the compulsory order.

Printed public notices were displayed informing local people of the important public meetings they should attend. Two meetings were to be held, with two similar meetings on the following day.

The Lord Lieutenant of Devon, Earl Fortescue, chaired the morning meeting at East Allington church where the arms of the Fortescue family are carved on the oak screen. He explained to the people the need for the US military forces to use the area to enable the troops to practice assault landings. The explanation to the

An official poster advises citizens of public meetings prior to the evacuation of the South Hams.

Poster text:

IMPORTANT MEETINGS

The area described below is to be REQUISITIONED urgently for military purposes, and must be cleared of its inhabitants by DECEMBER 20th, 1943.

Arrangements have been made to help the people in their moves, to settle them elsewhere, and to advise and assist them in the many problems with which they will be faced. To explain these arrangements

PUBLIC MEETINGS

will be held as follows:

FRIDAY Nov. 12th
11 a.m.
EAST ALLINGTON CHURCH
2-30 p.m.
STOKENHAM CHURCH

Earl Fortescue, M.C., The Lord Lieutenant
in the Chair.

SATURDAY Nov. 13th
11 a.m.
BLACKAWTON CHURCH
2-30 p.m.
SLAPTON VILLAGE HALL

Sir John Daw, J.P., Chairman Devon County Council
in the Chair.

These general meetings will be immediately followed by special meetings to discuss the problems of farmers, who are requested to remain behind for them.
IT IS VITALLY IMPORTANT to every householder that he should arrange to attend whichever of these meetings is nearest to his home, and where necessary employers of labour are requested to give their work-people time off for this purpose.

THE AREA AFFECTED

ALL LAND AND BUILDINGS lying within the line from the sea at the east end of Blackpool Bay in Stoke Fleming parish to Bowden; thence northward along the road to the Sportsman's Arms; thence west along the Dittisham-Halwell road to the cross-roads ¼-mile east of Halwell village; from this cross-road along the Kingsbridge road to the Woodleigh-Buckland cross-roads; thence along the road Buckland, Frogmore, Chillington, Beeson and Beesands to the sea, but excluding the villages of Frogmore, Beeson and Beesands. The roads forming the boundary are outside the area.
The parishes involved are the whole, or almost the whole, of Blackawton, East Allington, Sherford, Slapton and Strete, most of Stokenham, and parts of Stoke Fleming, Buckland-tout-Saints and Halwell.

villagers had to be carefully given in order not to alert the enemy to the Allied invasion plans. For this reason each village had to have its own information centre.

Whatever rumours had been previously circulated, many of the villagers were deeply shocked and bewildered. For many it made no sense that they had to give up their homes and move away from the rich earth they had worked to produce the essential food demanded by the Ministry of Agriculture. The knowledge they were to be out of their homes by 20 December 1943 was dramatic and traumatic. They had been given just six weeks to pack up, find other accommodation, other work, and move out.

The compulsory evacuation of the old and the sick aroused considerable concern in the rest of Devon for, with the official announcements made public, the events were now being reported in the local newspapers. One Parish Council sent a protest to the Rural District Council and to the local Member of Parliament; several protest meetings were arranged but later abandoned.

Information leaflets were delivered to each household, information centres were opened at Blackawton and Stokenham to assist people with their problems. Soon after, centres were set up in other villages.

The WVS were given the responsibility for transporting people to their new homes. Many villagers found accommodation at Dartmouth, other people travelled farther afield. One lady moved to Scotland. Others went to Cornwall.

This contemporary document is the form that each household was required to complete prior to the evacuation of the South Hams. It is interesting to note that the form was printed in October 1943 in anticipation of the eventual clearance.

Form A   FORM OF ENQUIRY

Please fill in this form at once. It will be called for after four days, and the officer fetching it will advise you about any entry about which you may be in doubt.

Parish _____ Name of householder _____ Requisition no. _____

Address _____

1 Particulars of household Name	2 Age	3 Sex	4 M. or S.	5 Occupation	6 Employer and place of work
Householder					
Wife					
Children					
Other members of household and lodgers					

Note. If Children are attending school enter in col. 6 the school they are attending.

Can you find new accommodation outside the area for yourself and your family? _____

If so, give address _____

Do you want the authorities to find you billets? _____ For how many? _____

Do you want transport for your furniture? _____

If so, how many furnished rooms have you? _____

About what date will you be ready to move? _____
   (In your own interest, make this as early as possible).

Are there in your house any:
       Infirm or old people _____
       Invalids _____
       Expectant mothers _____
       Pensioners _____

Do you want work found   (a) Farm work _____
for you or members of
your family?   (b) Other work _____

State here any personal problems, special circumstances, or matters on which you need assistance or advice _____

_____

_____

_____

Householder's signature _____ Date _____

If you need more room, use the back of the form.

D.B.6896-2 1,700 D/d 191 10/43 R.P.

This was the largest single task undertaken during the war by the WVS volunteer car pool in which 4300 gallons of petrol were used. The heavy demand on local resources produced shortages at the local petrol stations, many of them using up all their supplies. This meant the WVS drivers having to drive miles out of the area to refill their petrol tanks.

A considerable number of people were required to staff the two main information centres at Blackawton and Stokenham. Fifty WVS were required to offer assistance to the villagers. Packing household possessions was a real problem. As so few of the inhabitants had ever moved in their lives, they did not possess cases or suitable containers for removal purposes. The problem was resolved by an urgent nationwide appeal to WVS depots which provided a

WVS workers help prepare meals during the evacuation of villagers at Strete, November 1943.

Workers in a temporary kitchen set up by the Ministry of Food to supply villagers and helpers concerned in the evacuation of the South Hams, November 1943.

thousand cases. Brewers and cider makers supplied barrels to be used for packing household items.

Although the WVS had the major role in the administration and transport arrangements, they were assisted by a contingent of British sailors and American troops who help to load the household items into the lorries. The American army made an important contribution in providing fifty trucks.

Mobile canteens arrived to supply meals to the helpers; hot cooked meals were also received from Brixham's British Restaurant. At the village of Strete, the Ministry of Food arrived with a mobile kitchen but it was not very popular due to the unappetising meals. Meat dishes were costed on a halfpennyworth of meat for one meal for one person.

As the evacuation proceeded, local resources diminished as village stores closed down. Emergency bread and milk deliveries were organised to supply the evacuated villagers and the other nearby communities that had until now relied on the services and deliveries of the village tradesmen. Notices were put up informing the villages of the date and time of van deliveries in their area.

From the time the evacuation started it rained continuously. The narrow Devon lanes, so beautiful in the dry summer weather, turned into rivers of mud. Lorries loaded with furniture would sink in the quagmire and would have to be dragged

Part of a monthly WVS report from the Kingsbridge area, December 1943. It records the strangeness of the silent village of East Allington, deserted following the evacuation.

MONTHLY NARRATIVE REPORT

CENTRE Kingsbridge Rural

COUNTY Devon.   MONTH December 1943

This report should describe the activities of the W.V.S. Centre during the month. Where W.V.S. members are assisting in activities outside the work of the Local Authority, the Authority or organisation responsible for such activities should be stated. Subjects should be dealt with in the same order as on the new statistics return. Training, and Registration questions should be included under Organisation. Any new activities should be entered at the end.

Evacuation.   Total number of evacuees   750
                Unaccompanied children   117
                Mothers & children   647

Salvage   During the month 7½ tons of paper, and 1ton, 7cwt. of
                rags were collected, but as the lorries were often needed
                on more urgent jobs, some of the villages are still
                awaiting transport.   Jam jar washing will be resumed
                next week, and there are some hundreds waiting to be
                cleaned.

Welfare for
The Troops   Net weaving   The Organiser Mrs Galt reports that some 60
                nets were despatched during the month, a few villages
                have, of course dropped out now.
                Vegetables for Minesweepers.
                By permission of the Admiralty, we were allowed to collect
                vegetables in the allotment at East Allington, and some
                very fine sprouts, leeks, and turnips were despatched to
                the 'little' ships. This allotment with empty houses all
                round, and the church like a sentinel on the hill, seemed
                almost uncanny. for with the exception of a tractor in a
                near by field, there was no sign of life and one felt an
                air of unreality about everything. It was almost a
                relief to get back on to the main road and to habitation.
                     At Xmas we were able to send 1½ cwt. of apples
                besides vegetables, through donations, and gifts of
                apples, while the baskets were decorated with Xmas
                Greetings.   During the month 30 baskets weighing 1 ton
                have been sent.

An Evacuation
Drive in the Black-out
                Returning home after a long day, the driver was looking
                forward to a belated cup of tea, when the telephone rang.
                Two grown ups and a child were stranded, and no large car

                Signed _____
                                    (Centre Organiser)

Two young boys help with the removal of household items during the evacuation of Blackawton village, December 1943.

Farm workers clear agricultural equipment prior to the evacuation of the South Hams. Higher Heathfield, East Allington, December 1943.

The main village street Blackawton, the George Inn on the right, during the final stages of evacuation, December 1943.

out by a tractor. There was a fleet of two hundred cars in the area, but driving became a nightmare as, with all the signposts removed and houses emptied, it became difficult to locate villages and individual property.

Considerable effort was made to find suitable homes for the expelled people, but by their own efforts 75 per cent of the evacuees arranged their own accommodation. The national shortage of agricultural workers eased the situation for some men to obtain further employment. Household pets were offered homes by people who lived in areas adjacent to the battleground. If no accommodation could be found the pets were put down by the RSPCA.

The removal of agricultural machinery was often troublesome as the machines had to be driven or towed away from the area. Neighbouring farmers were very co-operative by either storing or arranging to loan the machinery. Cattle sales were held at Kingsbridge market but it soon became apparent that few of the cattle would sell. Certain farmers believed that if stock was moved from their

The last round at the King's Arms, Strete, before final closure, December 1943.

The last family to leave East Allington. Sergeant Burgoyne of the Home Guard with his wife and daughter.

farms, the cattle would die. Then there was the need to transport vast quantities of root crops to be sold. It was a daunting task.

The villages involved in this exodus including Blackawton, Chillington, East Allington, Slapton, Stokenham, Strete and Torcross, along with other, smaller communities.

Arrangements were made for the six parish churches to have their contents, sometimes valuable, often of historical importance, listed and removed for safekeeping. Blackawton church had an irreplaceable rood screen that through the centuries retained its ancient colours of vermilion and blue. The Tudor screen was carefully dismantled and sent to Exeter Cathedral for safekeeping. The pulpit, dated 1547, and the carved oak screen of the parish church of East Allington were also sent away to safety.

As the evacuation moved into its final stages the villages grew silent and deserted. The church treasures had been removed; items that were to remain were protected with sandbags, or boxed and locked up. The last church services were held, the great locks secured. Each church had a notice fastened to its gate:

To our Allies of the USA

This church has stood here for several hundred years. Around it has grown a community, which has lived in these houses and tilled these fields ever since there was a church. This church, this churchyard in which their loved ones lie at rest, these homes these fields are as dear to those who have left them as are the homes and graves and fields which you, our Allies, have left behind you. They hope to return one day, as you hope to yours, to find them waiting to welcome them home. They entrust them to your care meanwhile, and pray that God's blessing may rest upon us all.

Charles,
Bishop of Exeter

As the evacuation proceeded so more transport arrived in the villages. Blackawton became blocked with every type of vehicle. The villagers had never seen anything like it before and it was all happening in a sea of mud. The inns and public houses served their last drinks and then closed. The evacuation was completed on the 20 December 1943. The people had gone, the villages were empty and all that remained was a number of voluntary workers who left on Christmas Eve 1943.[29,30]

The battle area was formally handed over to the American Army. Their first act was to erect barriers across the relevant roads; one of the main barrier posts for example was sited just outside the village of Chillington, on the approach to Frogmore village. The length of the boundary of the battle area was defined by miles of barbed-wire patrolled from the inside by American security troops, and on the outside patrolled by the Home Guard.

Vacated houses within the perimeter were soon occupied with bunks installed to accommodate the armed guards.

US troops move bunk beds into a recently occupied house at Slapton, January 1944.

US troops set up a machine gun post in the Chancellery at Slapton, January 1944.

With the evacuation completed, Captain Buckley of the US Navy arrived on Slapton beach to survey the gradients of the shores and to confirm its suitability as a training combat area for Overlord. He was quickly recalled to report back to his base at Falmouth (Cornwall) for his own safety when it was discovered, and no one had told him, the beach area he had started to survey was mined.[31]

In November 1943, as the South Hams evacuation was underway, the US Naval Advanced Amphibious base was commissioned at Plymouth. Two US Navy construction battalions were engaged on extensive building operations for the maintenance and repair of a wide range of amphibious craft located at Queen Anne's Battery. Across the waters at Calstock and Saltash (Cornwall) other US repair bases were established to service small craft. Many of the units of the US 29th Infantry Division were now moved into Cornwall, with some troops remaining in the Plymouth area.

The Luftwaffe had not been very active over Devon during the latter part of 1943. In the summer the enemy raided Plymouth injuring several US troops of the 29th Infantry Division. Then, in the dawn light of 16 November, an enemy force arrived over Plymouth dropping bombs over a wide area of the city. These included incendiary, phosphorus and oil bombs, but it was the high explosive bombs that caused extensive damage to over two thousand houses, as well as killing and injuring many people.

Against the background of tragedy and upheaval, Christmas was celebrated in Devon with traditional parties for the children and hot meals for many of the old folk. A paper shortage meant there were no Christmas decorations to be purchased in the shops, and people made do with their old flags and bunting and used holly and evergreens as decorations. There was no apparent shortage of food, but the bread was no longer white, by government decree. For many people the Christmas fruit bowl consisted only of apples. But despite these deprivations people went carol singing, churches were decorated, and sufficient coal and wood was found to enjoy a relatively austere Christmas in warmth.

Rather too hot for comfort was the news that troops had accidentally burnt down the great house of Clovelly Court on 29 December 1943.[32] This was the second time in its history the building had been in flames.

On the last day of the year, the US 29th Infantry Division were at Slapton taking part in Exercise Duck, a three day amphibious exercise. This was the first of seven exercises conducted at Corps level, one aim of which was to judge the lessons learnt by the assault troops who had attended the Woolacombe ATC.

Such landing exercises were held under considerable secrecy but the Germans were monitoring with interest the military operations between Plymouth and Portsmouth throughout December 1943.[33]

Chapter 6 — References
(PC = Personal Communication)

1. *Around Seaton and Sidmouth* (1991), Ted Goslin.
2. *Moyra G. Charlton Diaries*, I.W.M.
3. PC: Mr C. Rushworth.
4. WRVS Archives, London.
5. WRVS Archives, London.
6. *Moyra G. Charlton Diaries*, I.W.M.
7. ADM 199; 1036; *Coastal Craft in Action*, PRO.
8. HO 192; 907; *Exmouth*, PRO.
9. *Moyra G. Charlton Diaries*, I.W.M.
10. *A Talent to Amuse* (1969), Sheridan Morley.
11. *The Story of the Imperial* (1982), Garbor Denes.
12. HO 192; 909; *Salcombe*, PRO.
13. PC: Richard T. Bass.
14. HO 192; 910; *Torquay*, PRO.
15. *Sea Breezes*, (c. 1990).
16. *The American Forces at Salcombe and Slapton WW2* (1984), Muriel and David Murch.
17. *History of US Naval Operations in WW2* (1962), Morison Samuel Eliot.
18. *A History of the US Naval Bases in the UK* (1947).
19. PC: Mr J. Thorburn.
20. *The Secret War 1939–1945* (1956), Gerald Prawle.
21. POWE 45; 50; *Pluto*, PRO.
22. ADM 1; 1209; *Burrator Reservoir Boom Net Defence*, PRO.
23. *Spirit of the Sands* (1992), Richard T. Bass.
24. PC: Mr P. Southcombe.
25. *The American Forces at Salcombe and Slapton WW2* (1984), Muriel and David Murch.
26. *Spirit of the Sands* (1992), Richard T. Bass.
27. HO 186; 2957; *History of No. 7 S.W. Region*, PRO.
28. *The Land That Changed Its Face* (1973), Grace Bradbeer.
29. *Women in Green* (1945), Charles Graves.
30. WRVS Archives, London.
31. *The Atlantic War Remembered* (1990), John T. Mason.
32. *The Country House at War* (1989), John Martin Robinson.
33. *British Intelligence in the Second World War*, Vol. 3 part 2.

THE IVY BOYS IN DEVON

The year 1944 arrived with the early blossoming of wild White Violets and flowering Primroses on the banks of the River Dart near Dittisham. The war had yet to be won but a mood of optimism prevailed in Devon stimulating many of the local civil authorities to publish their post-war dreams and schemes for their respective communities. The Beveridge Report, the eagerly awaited social charter for the benefit of the citizens of the country, had been published. Public meetings were organised throughout the county to discuss the implications of the report.

Totnes Council's plan, which they wished to implement after the war, proposed that every village in the area be connected by a good roadway. Road traffic at this time was a problem in the town as both civilian and military drivers ignored the recently introduced one-way traffic system in the Station Road area. There were also plans for a new swimming pool and for new houses to be built. Nor were the Council's ambitions limited to houses or roads, for they also thought that Totnes should have its own airport, sited at the top of Kingston Hill. All this was for the future, the current concern of Totnes was that their cinema had been burnt down.

Early in 1944 there was cause for some people to celebrate when the Mid Devon Branch of the Devon Guild of Bellringers held its first wartime meeting since the government had lifted the ban on ringing bells.

Torquay's ambitious post-war plans included the development of the town's amenities as a yachting centre. One councillor suggested that after the war all the municipal railings, public noticeboards, buses, even the Torbay Express, should be painted in the same standard colour-scheme.

Devon families, as were those in the rest of the country, were deprived of supplies of imported fruit. The younger children, with few exceptions, had never seen or tasted a banana; oranges were a rare wartime treat, even lemons had long disappeared from the greengrocer's shop.

Many Devon women were unhappy with their wooden-soled shoes. This item of wartime fashion footwear had been introduced by the government due to shortage of leather. However, after wearing the shoes for only a few days they were having to be returned to the shop for repair.

The war had changed many people's lifestyle and attitudes but not everyone believed change was for the good. Barnstaple for example was still debating the opening of cinemas on Sunday, which proposal was defeated. The North Devon town, like many other communities, had been involved in a 'book drive', the objective of which was for the town to collect 30 000 books for distribution to service units. Within a period of two weeks, the small town had managed to collect 60 000 books. Such generosity was characteristic of people throughout the county during the war.

Plymouth had announced that it had received 35 000 books resulting from an appeal made by many well known writers and academics. These books were to replace the huge loss of library stocks that occurred during the Plymouth Blitz in April 1941. Since the time of those terrible raids, the city had continued to re-establish its civil life amidst the burnt-out bomb-blasted buildings and bomb sites. The subsequent demolition and clearance of hazardous shattered buildings meant there were some very large open spaces in the city. Few shops were able to be immediately repaired and, as time went by, plans were made to erect Nissen huts for the traders. A generation of children was to grow up in a Plymouth of temporary shops and bomb sites, and many years would pass before the naval city had a purpose-built shopping centre. One of the problems facing post-blitz Plymouth was the public transport service. Many corporation buses had been

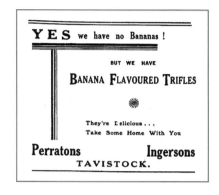

destroyed by the bombing and it was not possible to get replacements. This loss gave a reprieve to a few of the old Plymouth trams. The blitz had destroyed a considerable amount of the tram track, but some had survived and a limited tram service was introduced to the delight of the enthusiasts.

Plymouth Barbican's fish market was handling record catches of fish in 1944 yet because of the method of wartime distribution the Plymouth housewife was required to queue for many hours to buy fish. The problem was so bad that the City Council was called upon to investigate.

At the beginning of 1944 there was a total of 3564 Plymouth schoolchildren remaining in government reception areas in South West England from an original 12 997 evacuated from the city in May 1941.

A serious situation for ale drinkers occurred during the springtime of 1944 when Plymouth and other areas of Devon experienced one of the severest beer shortages of the war. One licensee closed his public house and put up a notice:

No Beer • No Stout

Fed Up • Gone out

News that a supply of beer had been delivered was greeted by a rush of people eager to buy, with long queues forming at off-licences. Supplies of Devon cider were always available and the American servicemen enjoyed the drink they referred to as 'Invasion Juice'.

Bicycles were also in short supply. With the American servicemen being keen cyclists there was a huge demand; at one shop there was a waiting list of two hundred people.

Professor Abercombie of the University College London presented his plan for the rebuilding of Plymouth to the City Council. Disputes and disagreements over the Abercrombie plan grew between the local politicians, but the plan went forward with keen interest and anticipation shown by Plymouthians.

Early in 1944 the US 4th Infantry Division arrived in Devon and were to make a significant impact on so many of the county's communities. The Division was reformed at Fort Benning, GA., USA at the time of Dunkirk (1940) and during the summer of that year they were selected as an experimental unit to develop blitzkrieg methods similar to those used by the German army. Later, with America at war with Germany, the 4th Infantry Division had been alerted on several occasions to move overseas. While awaiting specific orders the Division travelled

"They won't let on who the camp is for."

to the shores of Mexico for amphibious training using a variety of assault landing craft in anticipation of invading Europe.

The Division sailed from New York on 18 January 1944, arriving at Liverpool eleven days later. On disembarkation the Americans immediately travelled by train to Devon. This troop movement was all part of the massive build-up of US soldiers in the South of England.

The men of the US 4th Infantry were known as the 'Ivy Boys', from the Division's Roman-numerical designation IV, subsequently pronounced 'Ivy'. To symbolise this name four ivy leaves were entwined to produce the divisional shoulder patches, with the words 'Steadfast and Loyal' adopted as the divisional motto (taken from the traditional significance of the ivy plant).

On the arrival of the Ivy Boys in Devon, 'little Americas' were set up throughout the county. The Divisional Headquarters were established at Collipriest, Tiverton, and here they stayed until their departure for the invasion of France. Before leaving they presented Tiverton with a silver plaque embossed with ivy leaves.

The 42nd Field Artillery Battalion was based at Broomhill Camp, Honiton, while later in January, the 44th Field Artillery arrived and was based at Denbury Camp (a one-time hospital site) near Newton Abbot. Immediately on arrival in the UK, the 44th Field Artillery lost its Commander in a fatal accident.

At the By-Pass Camp, Exeter, the 4th Quartermaster Company and the 704th Ordnance Company were accommodated, and at Tiverton, the Divisional Signals and Cavalry Reconnaissance troops were encamped.[1] The arrival of American troops was a momentous occasion and the presence of these youthful and exuberant servicemen lives on today in the memories of many Devonians.

The presence of the US 4th Division, and a continuous flow of American soldiers arriving in North Devon to participate in exercises at the Woolacombe Assault Training Centre resulted in the streets, the shops, pubs, cinemas, and cafes being full of American servicemen.

Concern about the presence of black American troops in the United Kingdom had been discussed at government level. The policy of the Americans was to segregate black servicemen from those of other races. Each group had its own camp, but there were occasions when fighting would break out between them. For this reason, when socialising, arrangements were made, as they were at Newton Abbot, where it was 'one night black, the other night white'.[2] There was at this time a very different social climate; heads would turn and tongues would wag if a white girl was seen out with a black American servicemen, although troops of all races were befriended by Devon families.

If the American accents seemed strange to Devonians the soft dialects of Devon were equally puzzling to Americans. Even so, the British 'reserve' was quickly broken by the uninhibited friendliness of the Americans who readily related to the local people. Invited home, American servicemen would bring presents of chocolates, cigarettes, cakes, even turkey legs. Local girls were invited to the American camp dances. A truck would be sent to the offices of the Gaumont British News at Crediton to take a bevy of girls back to an officers' dance at the US naval stores base Exeter. Here would be drink and food, the like of which few people had seen in wartime Britain.[3] This was the age of big bands and swing music, when the waltz gave way to the jitterbug.

Girls would date the Americans, and nylon stockings, often a gift, sometimes a bait, were eagerly accepted. Whatever the frequency of dating, some relationships became firmly established and many Devon women eventually became 'GI Brides'. The conduct of the American troops covered all known aspects of social behaviour: friendship, affection, love, immorality and more serious offences in wartime Devon. This was not, however, unique to the county or to the American servicemen.

The planned Allied invasion for the liberation of Europe (Overlord) involved a massive build up of equipment, troops and stores referred to under the code 'Bolero'. The name was chosen for, like Ravel's musical masterpiece, it would build up gradually towards a climax. The logistics of the vast operation were expected to be put into place within a period of three months. Many British companies were contracted to supply the American armed forces, but most of the needs of their gigantic war machine were imported from America.

In the South West and South Wales, and in particular Devon, ports and harbours were chosen for the eventual embarkation and departure of the Allied forces for the cross-channel attack on the German coastal defences in Normandy. The Devon departure points were, in alphabetical order: Brixham, Dartmouth, Plymouth, Salcombe and Torquay. These harbours also served the Allies for pre-

"DON'T DESPAIR, GERTRUDE ! I HEAR THERE'S ANOTHER THOUSAND COMING IN NEXT WEEK".

An aerial view over Dartmouth. The 'hards' by the upper chain ferry are clearly visible sloping into the water on the bank of the river above the buildings in the foreground. To the right of these hards is the US naval base for the repair of amphibious craft where a number of Nissen huts can be seen. Two smaller hards were sited on the Dartmouth Embankment above the gantry.

invasion training and for servicing the amphibious landing craft which were to carry 25 000 troops and 2750 military vehicles.[4]

At selected departure points sloping hards were constructed. These hards were concrete slipways built from the high-water line to an approach road. This enabled the front-loading amphibious craft to moor in a position allowing troops and transports to load up. An enemy invasion, the ever-present concern of the Allied High Command, resulted in some of the hards being designed to include demolition charges.

The hards used by the Americans on their departure for D-Day at Torquay and Brixham can still to be seen and are now used by local boat owners. The Dartmouth hards, built on both sides of the Dart by the upper chain ferry, have been destroyed, as have those that were constructed alongside the Dartmouth Embankment. There are surviving hards located in the upper reaches of the Dart near Dittisham.

At Plymouth, invasion hards were built in the Hamoaze estuary of the River Tamar, at Queen Anne's Battery, and by the waterside village of Turnchapel to the east of the city near to what was once RAF Mountbatten.

The increase in military traffic required new roads to be built. Near Plymouth, for example, roads were laid at the Kitley Estate in the grounds of Saltram House, and at Hooe.[5] Road construction work was often carried out by the Americans, but on other occasions, for example, the extension of the Totnes by-pass, was undertaken by private contractors.

Whatever the beauty of the Devon hills, the steep inclines, narrow lanes and roads that led down to the newly-built hards and training areas made it almost

A view across Queen Anne's Battery in the Cattewater, Plymouth. The Americans occupied this area prior to D-Day and this picture, taken in 1944, shows an amphibious craft lying on a hard. The same hard can be seen today in the recently built marina.

impossible for military traffic to make its way through the tortuous thoroughfares. The worst area for congestion was at Dartmouth where huge transporters carrying tanks or troops slowly made their way from the marshalling areas down narrow descents to the water. Obstructions such as walls would be knocked down and repaired at a later date. On one occasion a convoy approaching the Slapton battle area was brought to a standstill by a small private car driving towards the convoy. The lady driver refused to move. It happened that near the front of the military convoy was a mobile crane. The Americans fastened chains around the car and, with the lady driver still inside, lifted the car over a hedge into a field, leaving it there while the convoy proceeded on its way. Similar problems of traffic congestion were experienced in the steep narrow roads of Salcombe.

Security was always uppermost in the minds of the military who were anxious to ensure the enemy was deprived of news of the vast number of troops and increasing loads of military equipment that continued to arrive in Devon. The logistics of the build-up also caused headaches and frequent meetings were held in an attempt to ensure that the American's requirements were being met. US military leaders were reluctant to meet with all the separate civil defence authorities within the county. Eventually agreements were made for the South West Civil Defence regional organisation to work within the structure of the American Armed Forces' committees to provide adequate civil defence measures.

The massive concentration of US troops and equipment in South Devon gave concern not only to the safety of the military personnel but also the civilian population. The situation evoked the possibility of a German super-blitz. Ever since September 1942, the areas that were later to be specified as assembly ports had been supplied with Morrison indoor shelters. Now increased shelter facilities were offered to the communities of Bideford, Dartmouth, Kingsbridge, Plymouth, Salcombe, Teignmouth and Torquay. One type of public air raid shelter built at Torquay was erected from two or more Anderson (outdoor) shelters pushed end to end and covered with concrete.[6] Large numbers of Civil Defence and National Fire Service personnel were drafted into the assembly port areas, further straining existing resources locally.

There was also a real concern that the Germans would use gas attacks on those areas being used for the preparation of the invasion. Additional precautions were provided to counter any gas warfare.

At each assembly port in Devon additional supplies of water were provided for fire-fighters by installing 6-inch steel lines and fixed piping. Large circular steel tanks, designed by a Bristol engineer, were erected in those areas of Devon considered vulnerable to air attacks, particularly those involved with invasion preparations. A total of six hundred such static water tanks were supplied within the South Western Civil Defence region. The largest artificial water storage supply in Devon was at Stonehouse Creek near Devonport. Here a dam was constructed for a storage lake measuring half a mile in length and two hundred yards wide, with a capacity of thirty million gallons of water. This huge store of water was on standby at all states of the tide and covered one of the high-risk areas of the city, namely the Royal Naval Dockyard and naval base.[7]

An important consideration was the potential problem of civilian refugees. The social problems of the consequences of enemy attacks were well known, but lessons had been learnt concerning the movement of people in the aftermath. The government recognised that the south-west of Devon was a high risk area and that it may be necessary to evacuate civilians from Paignton, Torquay and Plymouth, sending them to reception areas in the Midlands, North of England and Wales.[8,9]

The increasing military presence in Devon made it clear to the local communities that the size and form of the preparations they were seeing could only be for the implementation of the 'Second Front'. At Salcombe for example the US naval community outnumbered the indigenous population. The construction of the marine facilities and the concentration of amphibious craft in the harbour, and those moored further upriver towards Kingsbridge, was ample evidence to the Salcombe people that the Americans were contemplating massive military action.

In the other ports of departure a variety of strange-looking craft loaded with troops and equipment could be seen sailing out from the harbours on exercises, then later returning. The concrete hards were places of intense activity; troops would assemble, embark on a craft, then perhaps disembark, this being repeated several times before they sailed away. These and other activities were all components of training. The amphibious activities became part of a familiar daily scene and most local people eventually accepted them with an air of nonchalance.

A 'Most Secret' document dated 3 March 1944 reveals the security problems surrounding the preparations for Operation Overlord. Eighty per cent of private correspondence opened by the censor made mention of the proposed invasion.

THIS DOCUMENT IS THE PROPERTY OF HIS BRITANNIC MAJESTY'S GOVERNMENT

The circulation of this paper has been strictly limited.

It is issued for the personal use of...

MOST SECRET.   Copy No. 20

O.P.(S)(M)(44) 17

3RD MARCH, 1944

WAR CABINET

COMMITTEE ON "OVERLORD" PREPARATIONS

SUB-COMMITTEE ON "OVERLORD" SECURITY

Note by the Secretary

The attached note by the Secretary of the Inter-Services Security Board is circulated for the information of the Committee.

(Signed)   W.S. MURRIE

Offices of the War Cabinet,
S.W.1.

3RD MARCH, 1944

SECURITY OF OPERATION "OVERLORD"

Our attention has been drawn by G.H.Q. Home Forces to the results of a recent snap censorship in the areas Torquay, Dartmouth, Brixham and Totnes.   The total number of letters examined was between 22,000 and 24,000.   The majority were from civilians.   Of the civilian mail, no less than 80 per cent. of all the letters examined required excision of references to preparations for invasion.

You will recall that we have already recommended that the most effective method of improving general security would be for the Prime Minister to include a statement on this subject in his next broadcast.

In view of the above, you may care to consider whether a further approach could be made to the Prime Minister in this matter.

(Signed)   E. GOUDIE

Secretary,
Inter-Services Security Board

War Office.

An important feature of British wartime propaganda was to encourage people not to gossip or spread rumours. Poster displays and government films were based on the theme 'keep mum', but not all the people kept their own counsel. Evidence as to the extent of the 'invasion preparations' being referred to in letters was revealed in a wartime census taken in South Devon. From a sample of some

20 000 letters intercepted eighty per cent of them referred to the preparations for the invasion.[10]

Whatever the fears of a massive German blitz on South Devon, the actual danger was severely restricted, not only by the limitations of the number of operational aircraft available to the Luftwaffe for missions, but by the strength of the combined Allied airforce. Advances in radar technology made it increasingly difficult for the Germans to fly across the English Channel and penetrate inland. Nevertheless the Luftwaffe was active, with day and night air reconnaisance between Dover and Land's End increasing from the middle of April 1944 until the second week of May 1944.

German surveillance over the western parts of the English Channel between Plymouth, Dartmouth, Sidmouth and Southampton was curtailed with the introduction of Spitfire patrols that were flown along the whole of the south coast of England. The Messerschmidt 410, introduced for reconnaissance, ceased most of its offshore sorties. No enemy aircraft were penetrating inland. The Germans were not however totally ignorant of what was happening. One German pilot reported large concentrations of assault craft and warships in Plymouth Sound, other enemy pilots reported the evidence of assault shipping.[11]

The size of the concentration of troops in the UK during the spring of 1944 made it impossible for deception to be implemented on the level of a grand strategy. All that could be done was to attempt to deceive the Germans as to the time, place, and strength of the Allied invasion force. A plan of visual deception (Operation

An official map showing the placement of decoy sites around the south coast. Sites 6 and 7 were for the protection of hards at Dartmouth.

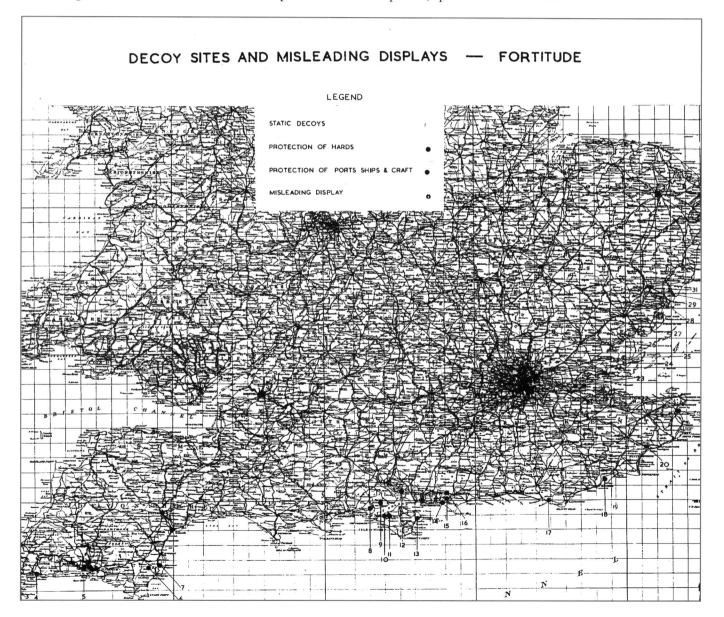

DECOY SITES AND MISLEADING DISPLAYS — FORTITUDE

LEGEND

STATIC DECOYS

PROTECTION OF HARDS

PROTECTION OF PORTS SHIPS & CRAFT

MISLEADING DISPLAY

An official wartime map details the assembly areas and camps in the area west of the Tamar.

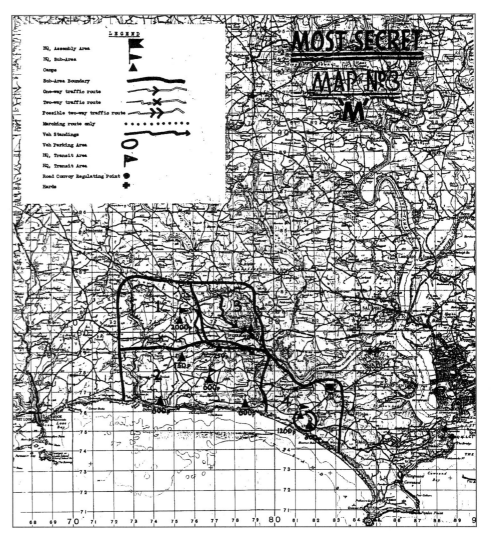

Fortitude) was introduced to mislead the enemy as to the direction of the Allied attack on France and to protect, using decoys, the hards and ports of embarkation.

The deception plan was intended to make the German High Command believe that the main assault and the follow-up would be to the east of the Pas de Calais so as to encourage the Germans to maintain or increase the strength of their forces in this part of France at the expense of other areas. It was also planned that when the main Allied assault had struck, the largest possible number of German forces in the east of the Pas de Calais would remain there for at least fourteen days in the belief that a secondary landing would take place.

Among the many subterfuges was the use of decoys and misleading displays of military activity set up in Devon. To protect the South Devon hards, Fortitude decoy sites were introduced; for example at East Cornworthy decoy lighting was erected to draw attention away from the Dartmouth hards. Similar decoys were used at Churston for the protection of the Brixham hards.[12]

The size of the American military presence in Devon was bewildering. It sometimes looked as if there was going to be insufficient space, and every available building was occupied by American troops, including historic country houses. Bowden House, near Totnes, became a camp for some two thousand troops. The 4th Infantry Division troops were stationed at Seaton in south-east Devon, and across the county to the north-west, in the remote area of Holsworthy, yet more American troops were camped. In many Devon lanes, for example in the Torrington area, small wooden huts were erected in the hedgerows for the storage of artillery shells. If the Americans were not in camp, they were moving all over the countryside as part of their exercises. They marched, walked and often slept on the boggy soil of Dartmoor, amongst the heather and bracken, as part of the toughening-up exercises.

MAP Nº 2 'L'

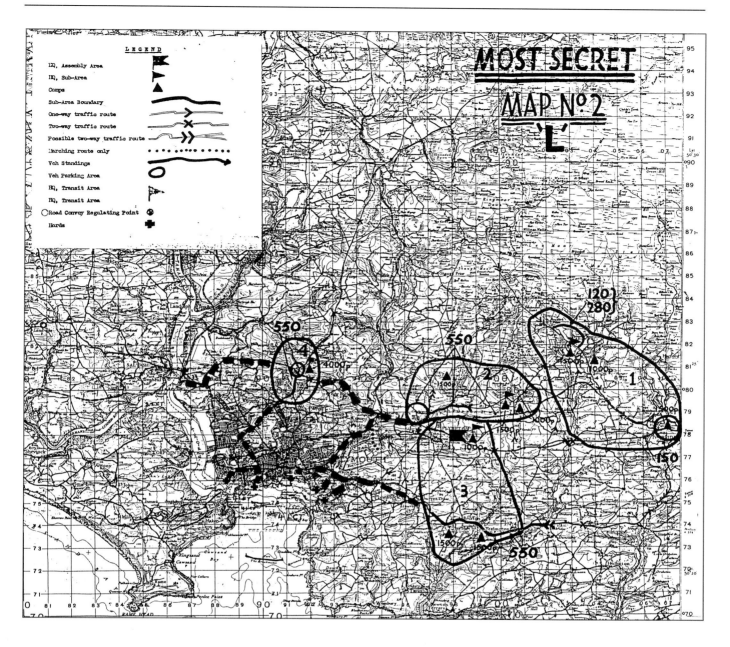

ASSEMBLY AREA 'L' – EAST PLYMOUTH					
HQ LOCATION – PLYMPTON 258775		COPY.			MOST SECRET.
		Ref Map 1" to 1 mile Sheet No.144			APPENDIX 'B'.
		Maximum tide capacity 4,000 personnel.			
		550 vehicles.			
Sub-Area	Camps	Map Ref	Distance from Embarkation Points.	Capacity.	Remarks.
Reception L1	CORNWOOD	033815		1,000	Tented
	DELAMORE HOUSE	029819		1,500	Tented
	IVYBRIDGE	0778		1,500	Hutted
Marshalling L2	HEMERDON	003795	10½ miles	1,500	Tented
	BEECHWOOD	005797	11 miles	1,000	Tented
	NEWNHAM DEER PARK	974807	9 miles	1,500	Tented
Marshalling L3	CHADDLEWOOD	985778	9 miles	1,000	Tented
	KITLEY EAST CAMP	989735	9 miles	1,500	Tented
	KITLEY WEST CAMP	977735	8½ miles	1,500	Tented
Spare L4	CROWNHILL BARRACKS	9180	8 miles		Barracks.

A 'Most Secret' map of the site designated 'L' - outlining the assembly areas and movements for US troops in the area east of the Tamar. The accompanying table provides details of the numbers of troops in each area. Dotted lines indicate the routes taken to the hards.

In Devon large marshalling areas were created in which to assemble troops. The contemporary jargon for these areas was 'sausages' and 'goose-eggs' for, with some imagination, the general plan of these security encampments were shaped not unlike these objects. The 'sausages' were coded: in Devon the marshalling areas were designated L and K, with M sited to the west of Plymouth in Cornwall. Each security area was divided into sub sections; for example the K 'sausage' (Torbay) had sections K1 (reception), K2 (marshalling), K3 (marshalling), K4 (spare). Assembly areas L and K are shown on pages 151 and 163, with their associated camps. Close examination of these maps, the originals in colour, indicate the routes that the American convoys would take from leaving the marshalling area to embark at the hards. The vast assembly areas were sited along stretches of main roads, and were closed to all traffic with the exception of those vehicles permitted to enter by the military security forces. The marshalling areas were guarded and protected by wire fencing. At Site L (East Plymouth), the 'sausage' was guarded by two thousand members of the American Counter Intelligence Corps.[13] The size and location of these marshalling areas meant that many civilian families were living in their homes within a 'sausage'. The routine of daily life could be very difficult with the strict security that was enforced forbidding civilian residents to be in personal contact with the American troops. Likewise the American servicemen were forbidden to talk to the civilians.

A civilian could be out in the front garden of a cottage with American soldiers on the other side of the gate, but no communication however informal was

The view from a cottage window inside a marshalling area in South Devon, May 1944. This home, like many others, was inside the marshalling area, where strict security prevented any communication between civilians and military personnel.

allowed. This posed real problems with the children, who would continue to persist hanging around the army's cookhouses.

Special arrangements were made for the delivery of food supplies, letters, newspapers and service calls to civilians. To reduce the difficulties caused by the closure of considerable stretches of important roads, certain entry points were agreed at which civilian traffic could pass through the 'sausage' under strict security control.[14]

At any given time the marshalling areas could contain infantry, signals, artillery, engineers and other units that had been ordered to report from bases throughout Devon and from other areas. Here in the 'sausage' troops were briefed, and issued with supplies, petrol and oil. The vital function of waterproofing vehicles and equipment was also carried out.

Departure from the 'sausage' and the move towards embarkation points was in accordance with a strict timetable. All the military personnel involved with the embarkation would be at a complete state of readiness. Each vehicle displayed a label indicating which hard it would report to, and the type and serial number of the specific amphibious craft. Each hard had a commander responsible for overseeing the operations.

The military convoy en route passed through a road convoy regulation point. Every such checkpoint had an official number, and each pass it issued to the convoy had, in addition to its service unit, the number of the issuing control post, made out with carbon copies. These copies formed a record of each vehicle's movement on its way to the appropriate embarkation point.[15]

Military personnel travelling from 'sausage' K moved south to embark in the Torbay area which included the hards at Brixham, Dartmouth, or Torquay (and on occasions Plymouth). Convoys from 'sausage' L were routed to embark on the Plymouth hards, or from Salcombe. This description is a simplification as some amphibious craft would partially load at one hard and sail to another harbour to complete their loading.

The lessons and skills learnt at the Woolacombe Assault Training Centre, together with other training exercises, were now to be tested on a much larger scale.

Most but not all of the American troops stationed in Devon after the first week of January 1944 belonged to units of the 4th Infantry Division. However the first major training exercise, conducted at the Slapton Battle Training Area, (Operation Duck), involved men of the US V Corps, part of the US 1st Army that on D-Day was to assault the Omaha Beach at Normandy. The exercises included the landing of troops and equipment on Slapton Beach and then advances inland. They were carried out under conditions that were sometimes too close to the actuality of the real landings. Warships out in Slapton Bay participating in the exercise would, at stated ranges, bombard the troops with shellfire.

Following on from Operation Duck and the assessment of the exercise, Operations Fox, Muskrat and Beaver were further exercises known to have been carried out by American units. In simple terms these training exercises would involve the loading of the amphibious craft at the hards and their assemblage out towards Slapton Bay. Exercises in the bay in battle formation preceded a simulated assault on the Slapton Beach. Inland, units such as paratroopers would play the part of enemy forces attempting to repel the invaders, or would themselves practise invasion techniques.

One of the final dress-rehearsals for the US VII Corps, that included the 4th Infantry Division, was ordered to take place between the 26–29 April 1944 (see Appendix). This was to be the largest of the pre-invasion landing exercises so far organised and would proceed under the code-name Tiger. Among the military observers at Slapton was General Montgomery.[16]

The Tiger exercise required all the American marshalling headquarters to be fully manned and from 20 April security restrictions were imposed. Early in April a ban had been imposed on all visitors to designated coastal areas of Southern England and Wales. Anyone who had arrived in a prohibited area without permission was escorted back to their transport by the police. Train passengers' credentials were checked to confirm if they were allowed to continue their journey. A father who had travelled from London to visit his evacuated son at Brixham was at first refused permission to leave Paignton railway station. Explaining the reason for the visit, he was eventually allowed to continue to Brixham to meet his son, on condition he returned to London later the same day.[17]

The restriction of movement meant that many civilian employees in the prohibited areas were issued with special permits allowing them to travel.

US troops waiting on the hard at Dartmouth having travelled from the Torbay marshalling area to take part in Operation Duck. Taken in January 1944, the photograph shows the hard situated on the Kingswear side of the upper chain ferry.

An aerial view of the pre-invasion exercise, Operation Duck, on Slapton beach near Strete Gate, January 1944.

Pre-invasion exercises at Slapton. The photograph was taken before the destruction of the Royal Sands Hotel which can be seen on the extreme right, above the tank. Operation 'Trousers', carried out by the 3rd Canadian Infantry between 12-15 April 1944, was one of the last pre-invasion exercises to be held in the Slapton Battle Area.

Pre-invasion exercises at Slapton (spring 1944). A Sherman tank, equipped with exhaust breathers for amphibious landing, emerges from an LCT (Landing Craft, Tank). Much of the equipment used in South Devon exercises had been developed through the North Devon training area.

A lull during a pre-invasion exercise at Slapton in the spring of 1944. The quality and quantity of military equipment available at this time is clearly evident from the photograph.

Throughout this sensitive period many civilians were having to make compulsory detours from their normal route to work.

The Tiger exercise was planned to simulate operational conditions as closely as possible, and included a secondary 'follow-up' convoy that, on the date of the actual invasion of Normandy, would shadow the initial assault boats.

Simulated assault landings on Slapton beach were carried out as scheduled on 27 April 1944. On this same morning five LSTs part of the follow up convoy (T4), sailed out from Plymouth escorted by the destroyer HMS *Azalea*. Another destroyer, detailed to act as an escort for T4 had not sailed, for HMS *Scimitar* had been damaged during the night and ordered to return to base. No immediate replacement escort was provided for T4. As the convoy sailed past Start Point to Torbay, three LSTs from Brixham joined the slow-moving exercise force, and the eight vessels continued in an easterly direction to Lyme Bay. The reason for this was the requirement for T4 to be at sea for the same period of time that it would take a follow-up convoy to travel across the English Channel to the Normandy beaches.

The lack of signals and the misunderstanding by the naval authorities regarding the damaged HMS *Scimitar* eventually resulted in a replacement escort HMS *Saladin* sailing out to catch up with T4. There were other naval ships in the English Channel to protect the convoy and three British motor torpedo boats were stationed off Cherbourg to watch and intercept any German E Boats.

A facsimile of a travel pass issued just two days before D-Day. Security at this time was exceptionally tight and this pass allowed a Wren to travel only within specified areas of South Devon.

ANNEXURE I

RANGE RULES

SLAPTON ASSAULT TRAINING AREA

1. The Range Boundry is marked by signs which read, "ADMIRALTY, DANGER, KEEP OUT, BATTLE RANGE" and by 20 large red range flags. These flags will be flown only when an Exercise in which live ammunition will be used is scheduled.

2. The impact area for guns ashore, all calibres, including small arms, is marked by signs which read, "NO FIRING INTO THIS AREA". These signs face toward the inside of the area and are on white painted posts. This line is also marked by white flags.

3. The impact area for guns afloat is marked on the shore so as to be visable from the sea. Each flank is marked by two navy markers and three army markers all on the same line. The navy markers are triangles, painted with black and white horizontal stripes, mounted on steel frames about fifteen feet above the ground with the point of the triangle down. The army markers are plain white triangles set up on the ground with the point of the triangle up.

4. No building will be used for a target and care will be exercised in selecting locations for targets so that the danger of missiles striking buildings will be reduced to a minimum.

5. Historical Monuments in the impact area are marked by white strips, either paint or cloth, 36 feet long and 36 inches wide across the top of them. These can be seen from the air or ground. In addition "OUT OF BOUNDS" signs have been posted around them.

6. No buildings will be entered or used except for official purposes. Any question as to what constitutes "OFFICIAL PURPOSES" will be referred by the Range Commandant to the Commanding General First Army for decision. No building will be used as a billet, except by permanent range personnel, unless authorized by C.G., First Army. The responsibility for preventing acts of wanton destruction, such as breaking into houses or using parts of buildings or fences for fuel rests with Unit Commanders.

7. The Unit conducting the exercises will maintain a liaison officer at range headquarters at least twelve hours prior to the beginning of the exercise, during the exercise and during the time the area is occupied by troops. He will be provided with the means of contacting Headquarters of the Unit from the time the first shot is fired in order that over or wild shots can be reported and stopped at once. This is essential. In a recent exercise some shots fell as much as one thousand yards outside of the range boundry endangering lives and property. A radio will be required prior to the landing and either radio or wire after landing.

8. Units will not make bivouacs or establish dumps outside of the area unless arrangements are made with the district engineers office prior to entry to the premises.

9. Units which move into the area prior to the opening of the exercise and who are to participate in the exercise will arrange with the Range Commandants Office for bivouac areas along and just inside the range perimeter.

10. Unit Commanders will exercise care in placing guards around bivouac areas so as not to include perimeter or other outside roads in their posts and thereby stopping all traffic on these roads.

11. In compliance with Para2, Part II "ORDERS FOR SLAPTON ASSAULT TRAINING AREA" a weekly program will be submitted to the Range Commandant and in addition, at least five days prior to the opening of an exercise a statement showing, quote:

'Range Rules' covering the Slapton Assault Training Area, 1944.

A British intelligence signal had been received indicating nine E Boats were to leave Cherbourg at 22.00 hrs on 27 April 1944, but the signal was not deciphered until late on 28 April.[18]

Early on the morning of 28 April the convoy T4 was attacked by E Boats that had sailed from Cherbourg, successfully avoiding the British MTB patrol. The sudden enemy attack resulted in two of the American LSTs being torpedoed and sunk; LST 289 was hit by a torpedo in the stern of the ship and severely damaged, this craft managed to make Dartmouth harbour with its casualties.

This incident was a wartime disaster of the first magnitude, with 749 US servicemen known to have died or reported as missing. The Allied High Command were for a time tortured with the fear that the Germans may have obtained information regarding their most secret plans for the invasion of Normandy.

Amongst those sailing on convoy T4 were special intelligence officers (BIGOTS) who possessed information relating to the Overlord plans, and other BIGOTS were on the LSTs that were torpedoed. In the immediate aftermath of this disaster there were questions and investigations as to the possibility that the German E Boat crews may have captured some BIGOTS by taking them from the sea. Eventually all the BIGOTS that had sailed on the LSTs during the exercise were accounted for, to the considerable relief of the Allied commanders responsible for Overlord. German naval records however reveal that American servicemen of Convoy T4 *were* taken from the waters of the English Channel on this fateful occasion.[19]

The Tiger disaster was shrouded in secrecy, with survivors and medical personnel who cared for the casualties sworn to secrecy about the incident in order to maintain security regarding the forthcoming invasion.

Subsequent enquiries and reports directed the blame at certain naval officers, although in reality it was a dreadful accident of war. The Tiger incident resulted in the first casualties suffered by the US 4th Division by enemy action. (The 4th Division's first prisoner of war was captured when a German aircraft flew over the assembly area and was shot down by an American anti-aircraft gun).[20]

With the passing years the events surrounding the Tiger incident have been the subject of much speculation and intrigue, particularly regarding the true number of casualties, where and how they were found and buried. Although the incident occurred off the Dorset Coast, in Lyme Bay, perhaps because of the association of the US 4th Division with Devon, and with the T4 convoy sailing from the Devon harbours, the impression remains in the public mind that the fateful events occurred off Slapton Beach. The whole incident is well documented.[21,22,23]

Within the Slapton Battle Area at the time of the Tiger exercise, engineer troops of the 9th USAAF laid out a temporary airstrip for observation and liaison aircraft, while the USAAF 36th Fighter Group flew single-engined fighters. The official history of the Group records the flying of P47 Thunderbolts from this airstrip.

The air raid warning sounded over Plymouth two days after the Tiger incident. The city had not been attacked since the latter part of 1943 and this raid was of

Exercise Tiger, April 1944. Until recently little was known of this ill-fated exercise although much has been written in the past two decades which confirms the scale of the tragedy. Estimates of fatalities vary from around 450 to well over 1000, most of whom died at sea during a night attack by E Boats. This photograph, possibly staged, shows a paratrooper injured during the land-based part of the exercise being taken into a field hospital, April 1944.

Loading the USS *Bayfield* in preparation for Exercise Tiger at the Hamoaze, Plymouth, 25 April 1944. The two Torpoint ferries can be seen moored in the background.

LST 283 sails out from Dartmouth to take part in Exercise Tiger, April 1944. Designated Landing Ship, Tanks, these shallow-draughted vessels were cheaply constructed and designed to carry the maximum number of men and equipment on to the invasion beaches. They were known to some as 'Large Stranded Targets'. To the left of the photograph can be seen three Free French MTBs, to the right is the Dartmouth harbour boom defence.

A pre-invasion armada sails across Start Bay, April 1944.

A German Schnellboot (E Boat). Sleek, capable of speeds up to 35 knots, and armed with torpedoes, such vessels were responsible for inflicting heavy casualties during the ill-fated Exercise Tiger operations in Lyme Bay.

particular interest as it was the first and last time the Luftwaffe released radio-guided bombs against targets in the United Kingdom. Twelve Dornier 217 bomber aircraft, it is believed, each carrying a Fritz-X guided armour piercing-bomb, arrived to attack warships anchored in Plymouth. The prime target was the battleship HMS *King George V*. The Fritz-X guided bomb was a huge 3100-pound armour-piercing weapon, released from a high altitude and whose trajectory could be corrected during its fall to earth. The enemy attack did not succeed as the naval harbour-defence smoke screen had been activated in time, making it difficult for the enemy bomb aimers.[24] Enemy aircraft also attacked the waterside village of Oreston to the east of Plymouth, by the historic anchorage of the

The damaged LST 289 limps past the Embankment, Dartmouth, following Exercise Tiger.

A P47 Thunderbolt fighter of the US 78th Fighter Group. This type of aircraft was used during Exercise Tiger, flying from a temporary airstrip at Slapton.

Cattewater. This was close to the area of some Plymouth hards. One of the bombs fell on a public air raid shelter killing nine people, another exploded on an Anderson shelter killing the six people who were taking refuge. The raid on Plymouth lasted twenty minutes, causing widespread damage that included considerable destruction to the Western National bus depot at Prince Rock.

Two of the attacking Dornier 217 bombers were shot down by RAF Mosquito fighters, one of the enemy bombers crashing into the sea off the Plymouth Breakwater, the other near East Allington in the vicinity of the Slapton Battle Training Area.

The burnt-out remains of buses at the Western National depot, Prince Rock, Plymouth, destroyed in the Luftwaffe raid of 30 April 1944.

The final exercise before D-Day, Exercise Fabius, early May 1944. This involved the US 1st Army Infantry Division that was later to land at Omaha Beach.

Countdown to invasion, Salcombe 1944. Air sea rescue launch 3504 passes a group of US amphibious craft moored in the harbour.

LSTs anchored in Plymouth Sound, April 1944, as part of the invasion build up along the south-west coast.

'Somewhere in East Devon'. A camouflaged US column waits out the days and hours in the countdown to D-Day, May 1944.

As May arrived it was becoming increasingly obvious to the people of Devon that something was to happen in the very near future, but conjecture prevailed.

The final full-scale rehearsal for the invasion was carried out between 3–8 May 1944 under the code name Fabius. This also involved marshalling exercises for the US troops. Boats of all shapes and sizes were arriving and anchoring in the South Devon harbours. Plymouth was packed with invasion craft and warships. Indeed, there was insufficient accommodation for all the American warships that were arriving, resulting in a number being transferred to bases in Northern Ireland. The scene of large numbers of craft and warships was also to be found at Dartmouth, Salcombe and Torbay.

Amid the paraphernalia of war, US troops line up for food inside the Torbay marshalling area, May 1944.

The Devon countryside seemed alive with military convoys, and more were continually arriving from different areas of the UK. Along many Devon roads and lanes, long lines of jeeps, trucks and transporters, all identified with the white star insignia, were parked, many shrouded with camouflage netting. This was all part of the initial stages in assembling the attacking force for the assault on the Normandy beaches.

When the US military units were called forward from their camps to prepare for embarkation, each proceeded to its designated marshalling area. As the process of marshalling broke up unit administration, a complete catering service for the troops was provided in the security area. The men who had been called would stay within the 'sausage' perimeters for anything between six and thirty-six hours according to shipping arrangements.

The marshalling areas were sealed for the final briefings on the D-Day landings on 26 May 1944.[25] Stories of how some GIs spent their last hours before joining their assault team in riotous or romantic revelry should be discounted, unless they were deserters, as all US combatant troops were under strict security guard.

US troops enter a tent for final briefing, May 1944.

US assault troops passing a control post in Torquay on their way to embarkation for D-Day, June 1994.

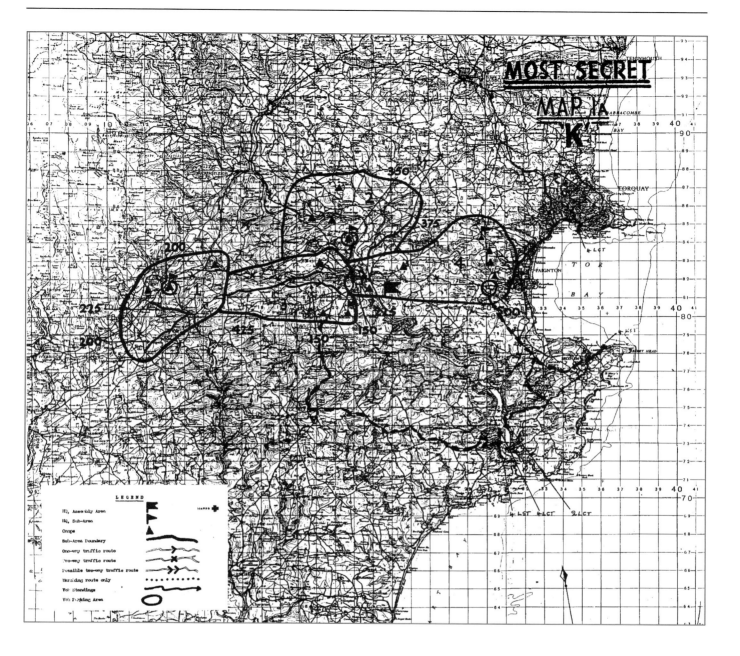

ASSEMBLY AREA K - TORQUAY TP LOCATION: TOTNES 2431		COPY. Ref Map 1" to 1 mile Sheet No.145 Maximum Tide capacity 5000 personnel 725 vehicles.				MOST SECRET. APPENDIX 'E'.
Sub-Area	Camps	Map Ref	Distance from Embarkation Points.	Capacity.	REMARKS.	
Reception K1 SOUTH BRENT.	SOUTH BRENT 'A'	132817		1,500	Hutted	
	SOUTH BRENT 'B'	123815		2,000	Tented	
	SICH ABBEY	154826		1,500	Tented	
Marshalling K2 DARTINGTON	DARTINGTON	227843	11 miles	600	Tented	
	STAVERTON BRIDGE	218852		1,900	Tented	
	HOOD MANOR	203852	13 miles	1,000	Tented	
	KINGSTON HOUSE	224872	13 miles	1,500	Tented	
Marshalling K3	BOWDEN HOUSE	227802		1,000	Requisitioned and Tented	
	BROCKWOOD	215830	12½ miles	2,000	Tented	
	DUNBRIDGE HOUSE	212801	11 miles	2,000	Tented	
Spare K4 TOTNES	TOTNES	238815	12 miles	1,500	Requisitioned	
	BERRY POMEROY	258827		500	Requisitioned and tented.	
	PAIGNTON			500	Requisitioned	
	DIXON'S CAMP	See map.		1,330	Requisitioned	
	S. DEVON CAMP			1,020	Requisitioned	
	THE NEST			150	Requisitioned	

A 'Most Secret' map showing the Torbay marshalling areas (within solid lines) and the routes to be taken to the hards (dotted lines) from where the American 'Utah' force sailed for Normandy, June 1944. The table opposite shows troop capacities within each of the designated areas.

A column of US troops approach a control post on their way to their embarkation point at the Torquay hards, June 1944. Note the three large concrete civilian air raid shelters in the centre of the road (see page 147).

Brixham hard, June 1944. American troops and equipment embark en route to Utah Beach, Normandy.

A contemporary document details the daily loading capacities of the hards and ports along the south-west coast. Such detail was typical of the meticulous planning that followed all aspects of the preparations for D-Day.

STATEMENT SHOWING CAPACITY OF HARDS AND CAPACITY REQUIRED FOR ASSEMBLY AREAS

MOST SECRET
Appx 'A' to S.C. Z/15695/2(O)
Dated 24 Jun 43

Sector	Ports or Hards	Personnel		Vehicles		1 Reception Sub-area each for approx	3 Marshalling Sub-areas each for approx	Total accn required in Assembly Areas(1 Reception, 3 Marshalling Sub-areas) approx	Assembly Area	Remarks
		Daily capacity approx	Each flight ½ daily capacity approx	Daily capacity approx	Each flight ½ daily capacity approx					
(a)	(b)	(c)	(d)	(e)	(f)	(g)	(h)	(j)	(k)	(l)
TORQUAY	TORQUAY	3080	1540	300	150	5000	5000	20,000	K	
	BRIXHAM	1080	540	450	225					
	DARTMOUTH	1680	840	700	350					
	BRIXHAM or DARTMOUTH	4000	2000	-	-					
		9840	4920	1450	725					
PLYMOUTH	VICTORIA WHARF) TURNCHAPEL) CATTEDOWN) SUTTON HARBOUR) ST BUDEAUX) OCEAN QUAY) MILL BAY)	8000	4000	1000	500	4000	4000	16,000	L	
PLYMOUTH	BARNPOOL) JUPITER POINT)	4,000	2000	600	300	2000	2000	8,000	M	
PENZANCE	POLGERRAN WOOD) TURNAWARE POINT)	2000	1000	750	375	1000	1000	4,000	N	
PENZANCE	FALMOUTH TOWN) POLGWIDDEN COVE)	7000	3500	550	275	3500	3500	14,000	O	
	TOTALS	30840	15420	4350	2175	15500	15500	62,000		

The point of no return. Such notices were placed close to the approaches to the hards advising troops to rid themselves of all non-essential items of equipment.

The obvious absence of the Americans from the streets and their favourite haunts alerted the locals that something special was about to happen.

After their briefing the troops were issued with arms, equipment and supplies. Army vehicles had to be waterproofed before the port would open for vehicle embarkation. Waterproofing prevented the adverse effects of seawater on vehicles that would be disgorged from landing craft into the waves on the shores of the Normandy coast. As the military preparations were being made on land, flotillas of MTBs, including those based at Kingswear, were out each night patrolling the English Channel in search of German E Boats.

The American assault force 'U' was to land on the Utah beachhead at Normandy after departing from the designated South Devon ports. Strict security extended to all Allied service units in Devon close to the planned points of departure. Service people were forbidden to talk to civilians or to receive or make private telephone calls or telegraph messages. All naval personnel were confined to their quarters or to their place of duty. The American military war machine in Devon, part of the huge Allied invasion force, was on the move.

To allow the military convoys to pass unhindered along the departure routes from the 'sausages' to the hards, the routes were patrolled by hundreds of police and security officers. All other traffic was excluded from these routes. Most of the American troops were transported in trucks to the hards, while others marched through the streets to their embarkation points.

Torbay was a marvellous sight, the bay full of ships: troop carrying amphibious craft, corvettes, destroyers and minesweepers. The River Dart too was packed with boats loaded with troops and equipment. Above the sounds of the Dart, jazz music could be heard coming from one of the troop-laden vessels. One Wren, stationed at HMS *Cicala* was ordered to deliver Admiralty orders and spent a considerable time sailing up and down the River Dart looking for specific boats. Climbing aboard to deliver an operational bag she was given last letters to post and requests to mail and register money.[26]

Between the hours of 15.45 and 20.58 on 3 June 1944, assault convoys of Force U2 sailed from specific departure ports in Devon. The last sailings from Dartmouth included 86 LSTs.

While out in the English Channel, the order came for the postponement of D-Day and the instruction that convoys should back-track to use up the extra day. Two hundred and fifty landing craft and gunfire support vessels of U Force sought temporary shelter in Weymouth Bay and Portland harbour before being ordered to continue their cross-Channel journey. Other convoys had also returned to port under the most atrocious weather conditions. The American convoys that sailed from Plymouth returned to port to find no suitable anchorage and were ordered to 'hold' outside the Plymouth Breakwater which, because of the terrible weather, caused many casualties. On D-Day minus 1, the invasion convoy again set sail.[27]

(Right) Phoning Stateside: US Navy airmen from Fleet Air Wing 7 based at Dunkeswell airfield, September 1944. (Inset) The same scene fifty years on.

Below: A US Navy Liberator at Dunkeswell airfield, September 1944. Perhaps the most distinguished personality at the base was Lt. Joseph Kennedy Jnr, eldest brother of John F. Kennedy, later President of the United States. Joseph was killed in August 1944 whilst flying an experimental aircraft out of Dunkeswell to attack the V1 sites in France.

Bottom left: A Liberator at Upottery/Smeatharpe airfield. Designated PBY4-1, these were the anti-submarine variant of the aircraft and were flown by a number of US squadrons out of West Country bases.

Bottom right: US Navy airmen meet some of the Dunkeswell residents, September 1944.

Admiral Alan Kirk, responsible for the American participation in the cross-Channel assault, together with Lt-General Omar Bradley, Chief of the 1st Army Group, were invited on Sunday 4 June 1944 to a reception at Elliot Terrace, the Plymouth home of Lord and Lady Astor. The following Sunday Lady Astor had promised to attend a Girl Guide rally and had invited her two distinguished American guests, who were based at Plymouth, to accompany her. The invitation was accepted by both Americans, knowing they could not be there.[28]

In the planning of Overlord, Task Force U, departing from South Devon, had further to sail than the other Allied assault forces. Force U comprised twelve separate convoys made up from 865 vessels.

The first assault force to land on Utah Beach under enemy fire on 6 June 1944 had embarked at Dartmouth on 2 June 1944. The total number of casualties of the American 4th Infantry Division sustained on the Normandy beachhead on D-Day was less than the number of deaths that occurred during the ill-fated Tiger incident. However, it must be stated that through a navigational error Force U landed in the wrong sector, which fortunately was not so heavily defended by the enemy.

In East Devon, high on a plateau four miles from Honiton is the village of Dunkeswell, set in magnificent rural countryside. Here during the Second World War was the base of the only United States Naval Air Station in the United Kingdom. From this elevated East Devon airfield the US Navy flew PBY-5A and B24 Liberator aircraft on anti-submarine patrols. At the time of the Allied invasion of Normandy these aircraft were active in searching for German U Boats. (It was one of the Dunkeswell Liberators that first identified operational U boats using a snorkel tube. This was an important discovery as the snorkel allowed submarines to sail submerged, if necessary, for a period of one month).

The American servicemen developed close ties of friendship with the villagers, drinking with them in the local inn, and together experienced the grief of a Liberator crashing near the village, with the loss of all the aircrew.

The continuous vibration caused by the huge aircraft resulted in the tower of Dunkeswell Church becoming unsafe and having to be rebuilt.

Four miles to the East of Dunkeswell, near the border of Somerset, US Air Force Station 462 was opened at Upottery, close to the tiny village of Smeatharpe. The Americans, who took over the airfield from the RAF, used Upottery as a base for the 439th Troop-Carrying Group. Here training was carried out using Horsa and Hadrian gliders. On the eve of D-Day the Troop-Carrying Group flew men of the 101st Airborne Division to Normandy in eighty-one sky trains. Following were glider missions flown across the Channel from Upottery. American paratroopers were dropped over Normandy from Dakota (C-47) aircraft based in Devon.

RAF Exeter, became USAAF Station 463 in April 1944. Hadrian gliders that were to be used on D-Day arrived at Exeter and training exercises began. The Americans also flew C-47 aircraft used for transporting paratroopers. As the Allied invasion developed, an ambulance service was operated from Exeter to fly in wounded servicemen from the battlefields.

The presence of German U Boats in the English Channel resulted in an extensive aerial search being maintained throughout the period of the invasion and these patrols were undertaken by Wellington Squadrons flying from RAF Chivenor, North Devon. Meanwhile from the moors near Yelverton the new Supermarine Spitfire Mk XIVs and the rocket-firing Typhoon fighters were flying from RAF Harrowbeer to attack enemy radar sites and enemy shipping. At RAF Bolt Head, the most southerly airfield in wartime Devon, the new, more powerful Spitfires were used to attack pre-invasion targets. Allied airforce units in Devon made a vital contribution to the invasion of Europe.[29]

A US Navy Liberator at Dunkeswell. September 1944. Such aircraft were also used by both the USAAF and RAF Coastal Command for anti-submarine patrols.

Chapter 7 — References

(PC = Personal Communication)

1. *History of the US 4th Infantry Division*, IWM.
2. *The GI's* (1975), Norman Longmate.
3. PC: Mrs N. Minting.
4. WO 199; 2322; *US Forces, Exercise Tiger* PRO.
5. WO 199; 2227; *Summary of Overlord Planning*, PRO.
6. HO 207; 1164; *History of Region 7*, PRO.
7. HO 207; 1164; *History of Region 7*, PRO.
8. HO 186; 2249; *Overlord Evacuation Plan*, PRO.
9. HO 186; 2268; *Evacuation Overlord*, PRO.
10. *War Cabinet Papers* Op (5) (m) (44) 17, PRO.
11. *British Intelligence in the 2nd WW*, Vol. 3 Part 2.
12. AIR 41; 3; *Fortitude Decoy Sites*, PRO.
13. *Cross Channel Attack* (1951), Gordon A. Harrison.
14. HO 186; 1758; *Overlord Security Measures*, PRO.
15. HO 186; 1758; *Overlord Security Measures*, PRO.
16. *Monty, Master of the Battlefield* (1983), Nigel Hamilton.
17. HO 186; 2260; *Coastal areas declared to be regulated*, PRO.
18. ADM 234; 366; *Tiger Report*, PRO.
19. *After the Battle* (1954), No. 44, Winston G. Ramsey.
20. *Cross Channel Attack* (1951), Gordon A. Harrison.
21. *Channel Firing: The Tragedy of Exercise Tiger* (1994), Nigel Lewis.
22. *The Invasion before Normandy* (1989), Edwin P. Hoyt.
23. *The Forgotten Dead (1988)*, Ken Small.
24 *Blitz on Britain (1976)*, Alfred Price.
25. CAB 44; 242; *Overlord*, PRO.
26. Moyra G. *Charlton Diaries*, IWM.
27. CAB 44; 242; *Overlord*, PRO.
28. *The Atlantic War Remembered* (1990), John T. Mason.
29. *Action Stations 5* (1982), Chris Ashworth.

VICTORY CELEBRATIONS

On D-Day 6 June 1944, the invasion armada of the US VII Corps (4th Division) was landing on the Utah sector of the Normandy coast following their departure from South Devon's ports. The thousands of American servicemen, the mass of military equipment carried in all manner of craft, had departed to the far shore. News of the Allied invasion was greeted in Devon with considerable relief and hope for the future. Many Devon people went to church and prayed. There had been no cheering, flagwaving crowds to bid the soldiers *bon voyage*, the invasion force had sailed amid almost total secrecy.

The American troops had followed their predetermined routes from their marshalling area down to the hards and embarked on to their amphibious craft, as they had practised many times before. The way the troops were called to their 'sausages' and the strict security imposed gave no opportunity for any final goodbyes from the people of Devon. In fact the invasion came as a complete surprise to many people, for although they had been aware of the build up of men and supplies, they were surprised when the exodus actually occurred. The immediate interest was now directed to the fighting in Normandy, and expectations were high as the Allied forces began to advance, but not without resistance from the German army.

The D-Day sailings took the civilian inhabitants by complete surprise. This classic photograph was most likely taken in the marshalling area designated K2.

The coastal areas in Southern England were still under a visitors' travel ban. Three weeks after D-Day a woman had been prosecuted in Plymouth for defying the government order, although three weeks later the ban was lifted allowing freedom of movement.

Whatever hopes people had of a rapid victory against the Germans they were dashed when, within a week of the D-Day landings, the first V1 attacks occurred. The first of these pilotless explosive projectiles fell to earth in Sussex. Three days later a heavy and sustained bombardment by Hitler's secret terror weapon began. Three weeks after the first V1 attacks, the government organised a scheme for the

Evacuees arriving at Torquay railway station at the time of the V1 raids on London and South East England in the summer of 1944.

evacuation of schoolchildren from the areas that were being bombarded. One of the consequences was that Devon again was a reception area for evacuees. Kingsbridge arranged to receive 174 children, and Ashburton offered billets to another 150 evacuees.

The war was now in its fifth year and many evacuees had returned to their homes, others had stayed on, contented and enjoying the Devon way of life. One evacuee living on a farm in Torrington had been taught to milk cows and by feeding the calves by hand learnt that they had teeth which could be very painful!

Eggs were collected twice a day by putting a hand under the hen, sometimes getting pecked. When not at school, life out in the open was spent watching the cutting of hayfields using two horses pulling a grass-cutting machine. Then with an eight-foot-wide rake with large wheels at each end, the hay would be collected going backwards and forwards across the fields.

Meals were eaten in the farmhouse kitchen on a scrubbed wooden table, with chairs all around, and two high-backed chairs at each end. The room was built with thick stone walls, and had a flagstone floor. On one side of the kitchen was a large open fireplace with irons and rachets, with a kettle that could be lowered on to the fire. A bread oven was build into the side of the fireplace.

Life on the farm meant having delicious home-cooked meals. Bread was baked twice a week, the dough mixture left to rise by the fireplace. Then the oven would be lit and the house would become filled with the wonderful aroma of freshly-baked bread. Each meal was in itself a feast; pasties, chicken broth, rabbit stew or tasty meat pies. There was apple jelly and cream or fruit pies made with thick crusty pastry and filled with heaps of blackberries and apple, and always a plate of scones or cakes.[1]

Official notification was given in the third week of July 1944 that those inhabitants who had been compulsorily evacuated from their homes in the South Hams area would be able to return. Prior to this announcement public demands had been made for the return of the land. The US Range Commander accepted responsibility for clearing the area. The make-safe operations began with 154 American servicemen from an engineering unit being ordered to fulfil this task.[2] There had already been the tragic deaths of two boys from Loddiswell, with another seriously injured, by an anti-tank grenade that they had found in a field used by American troops. The American-built bunkers and pillboxes that the troops on exercise attacked with live ammunition were now no more than twisted concrete ruins. Vast quantities of rusting barbed-wire piled up like old rope coils were deposited all along the deserted shore, in other areas of the beach were the remains of tubular steel scaffolding. In the aftermath of the pre-invasion exercises Slapton beach was an awful sight.

The complexes of barbed-wire, erected to enable the assault troops to learn how to overcome this form of beach defence, now had to be dismantled. The beach was pegged out in lanes using white tape and systematically checked with mine-detectors and probes.

Throughout the Battle Training Area there were masses of barbed-wire, tank obstacles and other military detritus. Mortar shells, charges of TNT, unspent bullets and other items of equipment were scattered across the area and all would need to be cleared. Inland, the once lush fields were pitted with craters caused by exploding shellfire from army and naval artillery. Roads were damaged, surfaces broken up by the heavy tracked vehicles of the invasion forces. Country lanes were impassable, often deliberately blocked with huge quantities of earth. Slapton Bridge was demolished.

Before the pre-invasion exercises all buildings of historic interest had been marked with yard-wide strips of white tape intended to prevent the buildings from being damaged. Slapton church, hidden from the sea, was hit by a shell that exploded on the roof of the south nave damaging stained glass windows and stone architecture. A naval shell had also exploded on the Church House Inn.

All houses had at sometime been occupied by servicemen. The interior wood-work, gates and posts had been removed from some properties, other buildings had the electrical wiring ripped out. Some houses were completely gutted and rooms were littered with empty tins and food containers. Surprisingly, the amount of damage by gunfire was small. Hedgerows and walls were broken through and sustained considerable structural damage. Now nature had taken over in many places with weeds often waist high.

The Germans were withdrawing from Normandy and the Allies were advancing towards Paris. In a remote part of north-west Devon the villages of Holsworthy organised a 'Victory Garden Week' including maypole and furry dancing. The villagers danced up, down and around the village streets and danced at night in the village hall.

Holsworthy had been involved in many Home Front activities throughout the war. This small community had accommodated evacuees from London, Plymouth and Exeter. The village was popular with the American servicemen who were camped in the area. Holsworthy for its size was renowned for its wartime-saving drives, perhaps its greatest effort the collection of salvage, a worthy wartime activity, that won them the prize in an all-Devon competition.

People of all ages worked throughout the war in Devon: the telegraph boy for Croyde who delivered the important post office telegrams, was described as nimble, upright and sturdy, and celebrated his ninetieth birthday early in August.

Although life was quieter, death on occasions still prevailed in Devon. It came as a disaster at Corbyn's Head, Torbay on 11 August 1944 when men of the Home Guard 10th Torbay Battalion were at an evening practice shoot using a 4.7-inch gun. For some reason the gun misfired killing five members of the Home Guard and one regular soldier. Four other men were seriously injured. The men who were killed are buried in the Heroes Corner at the Torquay Cemetery.[3]

The summer was fine, the Devon harvests were encouraging. At Bideford, farmers reported the oats were free from rust, the barley cereal was good indicating an

COLERIDGE PLACE, Strete.

Situated in the South-West battle training area.

STOLEN

from the above address between December 23rd, 1943 and October 5th, 1944. The following articles, mostly agricultural implements.

A substantial reward will be given to anyone who can give the information that will lead to a conviction. The following articles were safely locked in garage and loft on the above premises.

One "Allen" motor mower with knife, one "Atco" lawn mower and carrier, one lawn mower with roller, one galvanised wheel barrow on rubber tyre, one emery wheel, two wooden wheel barrows, four garden seats, three bass brooms, six besom brooms, two galvanised dust bins, two large green tarpaulins, six lengths of armoured rubber hose pipes, one hundred and thirty feet of white rubber hose pipe, six sets of fittings for same, two brass syringes, two "knapsack" sprayers and fittings, four bill hooks, one heavy crowbar, twenty four wattle hurdles, two hand saws, one cross-cut saw, one drum containing paraffin oil, one drum containing lubricating oil, twenty four pounds of grease, twelve yards of cocoanut matting, six rolls of wire fencing, three rolls of smooth wire, one gross of galvanised nails, four galvanised pails, new, one water tank on wheels, twelve balls of tarred string, twelve tins of weed killer, twelve galvanized wire guards for peas, four large zinc watering cans, three stirrup pumps, four pounds of nails, four pounds of staples, one hammer, one screwdriver, 2 "Springboc" rakes, one nine tread step ladder, one pair high step ladders, a portion of extension ladder, an assortment of agricultural paints and brushes, three new coal shovels, one croquet set in box, two new wooden doors, two oak benches, twenty four wood planks, one galvanised door mat, three salmon rods, two trout rods, one telescope landing net, one brass door knocker taken off Lodge door.

A rare newspaper photograph records the visit of Major Glen Miller and his band to the Odeon Cinema, Plymouth, on 28 August 1944.

excellent year for beer. At Weare Giffard both the oat and wheat yields were good. The cider apple crop in Devon was exceptional, up 50 per cent on the previous year; there was however an acute shortage of labour in the cider factories.

During the war top dance bands with their vocalists and soloists were often idolised and adored in much the same way as film stars. The big band era was at its peak, swing music and jitterbugging becoming increasingly popular, with the American servicemen influencing the younger generations in wartime England. Glen Miller and his band reigned supreme, producing hit records one after another, two of the many being *Moonlight Serenade* and *In the Mood*. Many well known musicians joined the American forces and toured with a band. Artie Shaw and his band were scheduled to travel to Appledore, North Devon. This great musician became ill, but his band arrived at Plymouth and was then based at the US naval base at Exeter, where it gave a series of concerts. Major Glen Miller, with the American band of the AEF (Allied Expeditionary Force), arrived in the UK during June 1944 and was based at Bedford. This forty-piece band played at various USAAF air bases and made regular broadcasts from Bedford and London. The broadcasts to the Allied forces were transmitted from Start Point, Devon with the BBC engineering staff taking great care with the Glen Miller broadcast so it could be picked up by wireless sets used by the troops in the field and Allied forces situated in Southern England in hospitals and camps.

On 28 August 1944 Major Glen Miller and the full band of the AEF flew from Bedford to RAF Harrowbeer, Yelverton. The band was transported to Plymouth, staying at Queen Anne's Battery. On the day of their arrival the dance band section was in concert at the US Naval Hospital Manadon (Plymouth). Meanwhile the string section, comprising twenty-one musicians (from many of the finest American symphony orchestras), played to two thousand servicemen at the US Navy's Shapters Field near Plymouth.

Later at 10.15pm Glen Miller and the full band of the AEF played to an audience of four thousand British and American servicemen at the Odeon Cinema, Plymouth. The servicemen arrived from all parts of Cornwall and Devon to attend the concert. The atmosphere in the city on this occasion was like a pre-war film premiere, with military and civil police forming a cordon to control the large crowds. Among the many current well known members of the band, was Sergeant Ray McKinley and The Crew Chiefs, a popular talented five man vocal group, and the singer Sergeant Johnny Desmond who many commentators thought had a superior singing voice to the current American idol, Frank Sinatra. The tour was brief, the band was forced to stay at Plymouth because of bad weather, returning to Bedford on Wednesday 30 August 1944.[4]

Changes were taking place in Devon on the Home Front, reflecting the wartime situation. The 'Invasion Committees' that had been set up in 1940 at the time of threatened enemy invasion were being disbanded. As the risk of enemy action in

Britain receded the Home Guard was also being stood down in Devon. A way of life of patriotic duty, comradeship and sociability ended with final parades, march pasts, speeches, dinners and concerts, with the promise of future Home Guard reunions. Part of the spirit of wartime England died with the disbandment of the Home Guard.

Even so, the war effort still needed to be sustained and saving drives were being promoted with Devon people persuaded to invest their money in Government War Savings. During 1944 the promotion was 'Salute the Soldier Week' with financial objectives set to equip an army unit with arms or equipment.

An entirely different war effort was pursued at Harberton Junior Church School where the pupils went out and collected 2559 cabbage white butterflies; those children who collected the most butterflies received savings stamps.

At what was Slapton battle area, a few farmers had started to return to their farms. They found hundreds of acres of land full of docks, horseradish and couch grass, all having gone to seed, all needing to be cut down and burnt. Hedges, walls and barns were flattened, boundaries between farms had disappeared.

It was thought Chillington would be the first village to be re-occupied but it was East Allington that was showing the first signs of 'liberation', as smoke was to be seen coming out of several chimneys. Some villagers could not always find the keys to their doors.

To assist the villagers in the domestic regeneration of their household, gifts of buckets, mats, even gaily-coloured quilts, and cooking utensils, all unobtainable from the shops, were being distributed much to the annoyance of the residents of properties who lived 'across the road' and were not evacuated. The first church service at East Allington parish church since the return home was held on 10 September and a hundred people attended. The church had been cleaned and tidied up, but a pile of sandbags remained outside the church door.

Late in the summer of 1944, when the black out was all but over, some Devon communities became a twilight world as the government insisted on there being a 'dim out'. Now for so many of the young generation in Devon, for the first time in their life they saw a lighted shop window at night.

October was mayor-choosing time in Devon. At Totnes the mayor was elected for the eighth successive time, but it was farewell to the Lord Mayor of Plymouth; Lord Astor having held this office throughout the war years.

Dartmouth's post-war ambitions were to incorporate Kingswear and Slapton into their own Borough. The wartime mayor referred to a Dartmouth Airport and among the proposals was the recurring plan to build a bridge across the River Dart.

The WVS organised a party for the elders of Dartmouth at the Guildhall, ninety people attended. The tea was served on two long tables and beside each plate was a small brightly-coloured wrapped parcel containing two ounces of tea and a small quantity of sugar. The old folk were entertained by a display of dancing and

Below right: Land Girls being driven into what was the Slapton Battle Training Area, summer 1944, to help farmers get the land back into condition.

Below left: Building a rick on a farm near Slapton, summer 1944. These Land Girls lived in a hostel and were taken by lorry to the farm.

Before and after: photographs of the Royal Sands Hotel, Slapton. In pre-war days this famous hotel, built right on the beach, was host to many famous guests. In 1944, following the withdrawal of troops from the Battle Training Area, it lay in ruins, the victim of mines and live firing from seaborne exercises.

before leaving each person was given a present. Every lady received a face cloth and a piece of soap, the men cigarettes and matches.[5]

The first church service at Blackawton parish church since the villagers had returned to their homes was held on 5 November 1944. Help was needed to restore the church. When the clergy had left the area late in December 1943, the church was locked and surrounded by barbed-wire. On returning the barbed-wire had been cut and door lock smashed open. The organ was damaged, the church lamp broken, the altar ornaments, linen and communion cross had been stolen. Later a dance was held at Totnes and the proceeds were given as a contribution for the restoration of the church. A generous gift was also received by the vicar and parochial church council from St Mark's Church, Huddersfield which sent a very fine jewelled altar cross and a pair of candlesticks.

Villagers who had been evacuated from the South Hams area were slowly resettling into their homes. There were many problems regarding financial compensation, the American forces had offered some assistance, more as a goodwill payment, and various claims were being submitted. Many inhabitants believed the government had not fulfilled its promise regarding compensation payments. A workforce of some two hundred workers arrived in the South Hams to repair the 881 damaged properties.

In order to commemorate the evacuation a memorial to the villagers was proposed, to be erected on a site between Strete and Torcross. A competition was advertised for the submission of designs for a suitable memorial. Ninety-one entries were submitted, the final selection being made by a committee of residents who lived in the evacuation area.

The last year of the war began with snow falling over South Devon. Inside the roofless St Andrew's Church, Plymouth, a carpet of white snow covered the church floor. Where in Devon no snow had fallen, a heavy frost made everywhere look white.

A small celebration was held in Plymouth when the fifth anniversary of the opening of the wooden tea hut on the GWR North Road Station was commemorated. Since it had opened the volunteers had served 4.8 million free cups of tea to service people.

North Devon was experiencing arctic conditions with snowfalls so heavy it was difficult to distinguish the outline of many buildings. The sun shone, but the snow did not thaw. At Ilfracombe, council workmen went out and cleared the snow off the streets, but with strong winds, the snow began to drift and soon the streets of the town were layered with snow again. The severity of the weather made it very difficult for people in rural areas to obtain provisions, food became short, and essential coal deliveries were restricted. The village of Parracombe was cut off, and an SOS sent out to obtain help. The River Taw partly froze and the huge Barnstaple market had only four stallholders.

During the bitterly cold weather, Ilfracombe's British Legion held a smoking concert. Traditionally, smoking concerts were an all-male social occasion when a group of men met up to talk, eat and drink and to be entertained. On this occasion 180 members and their guests sat in a decorated room. After their meal, they drank and smoked their cigars, pipes or even cheap Woodbine cigarettes. In the smoky atmosphere, the members raised their glasses filled with ale or stout for the royal toast.

Lighting at night was still restricted at the small fishing port of Brixham where the town was so visible from the sea. Brixham had been allocated fifty pre-fabricated houses, with local servicemen being given priority in applying for them. Nearby at Preston Sands, Paignton, the beach huts were being given a fresh coat of green paint after their wartime use for the storage of paper and cardboard for the local council. The weather was still cold in February 1945, but visitors to Paignton continued to arrive in increasing numbers up to the Easter holiday. The large numbers of visitors to Paignton was good news for the hotel and boarding-house trade. Local people were complaining that the midday bus schedules made it impossible for those who went to their work by bus to travel home and return to work within the stipulated lunch-hour break. There was a shortage of buses in the area with priority given to people having to go to work.

Torbay said its goodbyes to the wartime evacuees from Guernsey who were returning home to the Channel Islands. The Belgian fishing community at Brixham were also preparing to leave and were given a farewell social evening by the local fishing fraternity. Some Belgian families decided not to return to their country but to stay in Brixham.

The burnt-out shell of the Women's Institute building at Strete, South Devon. It stood on the clifftop near the centre of the Battle Training Area.

A revealing statistic was discovered almost by chance when, at the 1944 Christmas pantomime dress rehearsals at the Palace Theatre, Plymouth, 1200 Plymouth children were invited to attend. Among the gathering of children was a surprising number of orphans. This stimulated an investigation throughout the city confirming that there were a thousand orphans living in wartime Plymouth.[6]

Post war prospects and plans continued to be discussed. Proposals were made for an industrial area to be established in North Devon with a railway line between Filleigh and Blackmore Gate. Wartime production in North Devon was remarkable. Messrs Prideaux, using mainly women war workers, produced 90 000 mortar bombs, and essential parts for Valentine tanks; Pilton Bakeries produced over 700 000 lbs of bread for the armed forces. Brindley's engineering company was involved with overhauling starter batteries for Spitfires, Beaufighters and Halifax bombers and manufactured precision parts for military equipment. Hampton & Sons at Barnstaple, manufactured 68 000 camouflage nets, and well over half a million haversacks of different sizes. Other items made were 8000 silk parachutes, mosquito nets and thousands of anti-flash gauntlets. Dents processed 800 000 sheepskins to produce jackets for the Army and RAF. These are examples of the vital wartime production activities within one area of Devon.[7]

Easter 1945, and the war on the Home Front was continuing to cause casualties. Three of the in-patients at Bideford Hospital were people who had accidentally fallen over Bideford Quay during the black out. On each occasion, the tide was out.

Victory in Europe Day (VE Day) was proclaimed on 8 May 1945. The official cease-fire was to end a minute after midnight on the 9 May 1945. Devon communities had already made their plans as to how the joyous news would be officially greeted and in what form the victory celebrations would take place.

At Torrington, North Devon, the arrangements were that as soon as notification of VE Day was received a public announcement would be made by a loudspeaker van touring the streets asking the people to assemble in the town's square at a specific time, and for people to wear their uniforms. Members of Torrington Town Council would accompany the mayor to the square where a proclamation would be made followed by a united service of thanksgiving, then festivities would be held for the rest of the day.

It rained at Totnes on VE Day but this did not stop the crowds coming out on to the streets. The bells rang out, and the people put out the flags and the bunting on their homes and across the streets. In the afternoon townspeople listened to the Prime Minister's broadcast, then at 4pm the civic leaders, all dressed in their magnificent robes and regalia, assembled and the proclamation of peace was read out. For the first time since the beginning of the war some of the towns' shop windows were lighted. Totnes parish church, the Plains and Chateau Ville were floodlit, a remarkable sight in red, white and blue lighting. At 11pm a huge bonfire was lit and fireworks were let off, the reflection of the flames on the River Dart was an unforgettable occasion. People danced in the streets until 3am the following morning with many people managing to fall in the leat.

Across the moors at Tavistock, flags and bunting hung over all the town's buildings and across the streets. All the Allied nations' flags were flown, the stars and stripes and the hammer and sickle of the USSR flew side by side. Nearby at

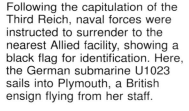

Following the capitulation of the Third Reich, naval forces were instructed to surrender to the nearest Allied facility, showing a black flag for identification. Here, the German submarine U1023 sails into Plymouth, a British ensign flying from her staff.

Plymouth 1945: children celebrate around a victory bonfire.

Below left: A snapshot of servicemen and girls celebrating VE Day at Salcombe.

Below right: VE Day at Dartmouth: bunting and flags on Crowthers Hill.

the village of Horrabridge people celebrated with a huge bonfire topped with a German swastika.

How many people lasted the day at Bere Alston has never been recorded, for here one mile from the boundary of Cornwall, a huge barrel of cider donated by a local person was rolled out and set up outside the parish hall for all to drink, free of charge.

Every Devon community appeared to have its own bonfire with some form of effigy, usually of Hitler, placed on the top. The huge bonfire built at Plymouth Hoe was fuelled by wood taken from the barrage balloon site near Smeaton's Tower. The City Fathers however were not amused when the Plymouth Corporation deckchairs were used to maintain the fire.

VE Day celebration sports,
Barnstaple.

Joyful VJ Day crowds fill the
Guildhall Square, Plymouth.

Right: A VE Day street party,
Barnstaple.

Below: Dartmouth. A VE Day street
party.

All the vessels in Plymouth Sound were bedecked with flags. Plymouth Hoe was
packed with people either watching or dancing. There was also dancing down
below on the historic Barbican by Sutton Pool.

At Tiverton, there were impromptu street parties. A local dance band played to
the crowds of people, as it was driven around the town on the back of a lorry.

The universal memory of the celebrations at this time is of the street parties
that were held throughout the kingdom. Devon upheld the tradition in the most
joyous way. Street parties large or small, informal or organised, were held
throughout the joyful days of May and were great occasions for both children and
adults. Tables, trestles, chairs and forms were obtained from the homes, halls,
lofts, sheds and schools; they all came out on to the streets. Bleached white table
cloths or cotton bedsheets were laid over the tables and plates piled high with
sandwiches of plum jam or fish paste, alongside jellies, blancmanges, homemade
buns, and decorated cakes.

Above: Mrs Marshall, Mrs Croker, Mrs Morgan, Mrs Croxton, Mrs Wannell and Mrs Goodchild, dressed up for VE Day celebrations, Tiverton.

Left: A victory celebration tea party, Middlemead Road, Tiverton.

Sunnybank, Barnstaple. VE Day street party.

Each street party held in Devon was the best. As the sandwiches and jelly were being devoured, someone would play an accordion or a piano. A conjurer would appear at some parties, or a clown, or dancing troupe, to entertain the children.

After the street parties at Bideford, celebrations continued for both adults and children who were given free trips around Bideford Bay in an amphibious craft, other people were taken up the River Torridge in a tank landing craft. At Barnstaple a local man, captured in North Africa and held a prisoner of war in Germany, returned home and organised a street party in thanks for his safe homecoming.

Throughout Devon servicemen who had been German prisoners of war were returning home. In contrast many Devon communities were saying goodbye to their evacuees. The 554 evacuees in the Bideford area began their return journey, although not all the evacuees went back, some deciding they preferred the quality of life that Devon offered them. These young people eventually found work, some married and settled in the county. Other evacuees had no homes or relatives to return to.

Tea and sports. VE Day celebrations in St Katharine's Road, Exeter.

Salisbury Avenue, Hele, Torquay.
Note - as with many of the street
party celebrations, the party-goers
are mainly women and children. At
this time men were mostly still on
'active service'.

A VE Day party, Mount Gould,
Plymouth.

A victory street party, Plymouth.

One large group of men who remained in Devon were the Axis prisoners of war. The fighting in Europe following the Allied landings and subsequent advances resulted in the capture of large numbers of prisoners of war, many of whom were sent to camps in Devon. Italian POW camps had long been established in the county and the Italian soldier in his brown-coloured patched overalls was a familiar sight in the Devon countryside working on the land and helping with the harvest.

Windsworth Tower Camp at Beaworthy was an Italian camp. In the north-west of Devon a German camp (No 43) was opened at Exhibition Field, Holsworthy. Other camps holding German prisoners were at Bamber Road, Cruwys Morchard, Tiverton and at Hazedene Camp, Elburton, Plymouth. Military prisoners were also held at Sidmouth County Hotel, Bickley Camp, Yelverton and Toner camp, Hallwill.

As the war progressed a more liberal policy was implemented towards certain categories of British held POWs. Eventually, some 'trustees' were allowed to be accommodated on farms and to make regulated visits to the local towns. Fraternisation with members of the communities occurred, officially approved or not.[8]

Many such prisoners were to remain in Devon long after the war and some were to marry into local families and themselves to become Devonians.

At Holsworthy, the German POWs and the locals worshipped at the village church side by side. Two German POW's escaped from the Holsworthy Camp; by wearing civilian clothes and, carrying cleverly forged documents, they managed to travel to Plymouth before being recaptured.

The euphoria of Victory in Europe eventually subsided. It was still wartime as the fight against Japan continued with thousands of Westcountrymen still serving in the Far East.

Servicemen who returned home to wives and families were faced with the chronic shortage of suitable accommodation. The end of the European war also meant families were returning to South Devon from shipyards in the North of England where they had been transferred at the beginning of the war. As a temporary measure a civilian camp was opened for them at Lee Mill, a small village between Plymouth and Ivybridge. The camp had been a National Fire Service training centre, but would now provide accommodation for 125 families, with its own church and small shopping centre.

Adapting to a peaceful existence in Devon caused many frustrations with the lack of accommodation, shortages and various regulations that were being imposed, but people turned their attention to national politics and to the general election that had been called for on 26 June 1945. This resulted in the Labour party sweeping to power, replacing the wartime coalition government.

Sergeant F. Ducker of Oreston, returning home to his family from a German POW camp, summer 1945.

The newly elected Prime Minister, Clement Atlee, announced to the nation on 14 August 1945, the final surrender of Japan.

Many people in Devon were unaware of the Japanese capitulation. Barumites arrived at work to find that everywhere was closed down for two days as part of the VJ celebrations. The public response to the ending of the war against the Axis powers varied throughout the county. Many communities had spent up all their emotional energy in celebrating VE Day, others had waited until the conquest of Japan before celebrating, for their loved ones were still fighting in the Eastern theatres of war, and the Japanese were holding many British prisoners in unspeakable conditions.

Throughout the period of the victory celebrations, there were also many people mourning the loss of a close relative, killed or reported as missing. Whatever satisfaction these people felt regarding the Allies' victory, it was tempered by the grief they felt.

At Dawlish, South Devon, the VJ celebrations produced the greatest crowds ever seen there. The throngs converged on the main beach where a great bonfire was lit, fireworks were let off and somehow rockets were fired from passing train. As the bonfire on the beach began to burn out, the mass of people moved to the town and danced throughout the night on the lawns.

VJ Day at Totnes was a repeat of VE Day, with a thanksgiving service, a town parade, street parties, but the addition of a victory parade.

People were sleeping at South Brent, when someone sounded a siren and woke up the villagers. Church bells were rung and immediately a great fire was built to be lit the following night. The Longbridge at Barnstaple on VJ Day was superbly illuminated with coloured lights. The town rejoicing became packed with servicemen who had arrived by the lorry load to join in the celebrations.

Well before the year's end the Americans had gone back home, the US naval base at Plymouth, and later the base at Salcombe closed. The small Devon village of Woolsery was remembered when evacuees presented the villagers with an oak seat as an appreciation of the kindness shown to them by the inhabitants. The monument commemorating the evacuation of the inhabitants of the villages in South Hams was unveiled.

With victory achieved, the people of Devon were now, like the rest of the nation, entitled to an extra half ounce of tea, currently rationed to two ounces per week per person. Individuals were having to apply for their new ration books, and food would remain rationed for much longer than people would realise. This did not really matter, for people were now looking for yesterday's dreams to be fulfilled.

Chapter 8 — References
(PC = Personal Communication)

1. PC: Mr G. Baker.
2. *Stars and Stripes*, Aug. 1944, IWM.
3. PC: Mr R. Coleman.
4. *Next To A Letter From Home* (1986), Geoffrey Butcher.
5. WVRS Archives, London.
6. *Western Evening Herald*, 1945.
7. *North Devon Journal*, 1945.
8. HO 215; 201; *POW Camps*, PRO.

APPENDICES

Appendix A
The Home Guard Battalions of Devonshire
31.10.44

1. Loyal City of Exeter
2. Clyst
3. Cullompton
4. Barnstaple
5. Bideford
6. Chulmleigh
7. Okehampton
8. Holsworthy
9. Newton Abbot
10. Torbay
11. South Hams
12. Dartmouth
13. Totnes
14. Moorside
15. Plympton
16. Plymouth
17. Dockyard
18. Saltash
19. Seaton
20. Tiverton
21. 33rd GPO
22. Southern Railway
23. Drakes
24. Hartland
25. Ilfracombe

T.A. Association Administration,
Devon Battalions, 23 Longbrook Street, Exeter

Appendix B
Women's Voluntary Groups in Devon
(Sample taken from contemporary document. Many others existed throughout the county)

Organisation	Ladies	Attending
Guildhall Working League	45	including ex Mayoresses. (Mrs M. A. Clegg, 14 St Hilary Tce
War Aid Supply Depot	45	Lady Tozer
Women's Voluntary Service	30	Mrs M. A. Hordley, J.P.
War Work parties of Anglican Churches	8	Mrs C. Martin, St. Andrew's.
War work groups of Nonconformist Churches	8	Mrs B. N. Phillips, 74 Addison Road, Plymouth.
Jewish Ladies	3	Miss H. Cohen, Highbury, Mannamead, Plymouth
Ladies of Royal Marines	3	Mrs Glunicke, Royal Marine Barracks.
Ladies of the RAF	3	Mrs Boyce, Headquarters, 19 Group, RAF Plymouth
Salvation Army Groups	2	Lieut Commissioner Mrs N. Evans, Abbotsfield, Seymour Road, Plymouth.
Girl Guides and Rangers	4	Mrs Vernon Ledger, Norbiton Hse, Albany Place, Plymouth.
Ladies of Mercantile Asscn (helping at N, Rd Canteen)	2	Mrs S. G. Richards, 10 Home Park Avenue, Plymouth.
Townswomen's Guilds	3	Mrs A. Shearne, 1 Hartley Avenue, Plymouth.
Sir Francis Drake Bowling Club (helping at N. Rd Canteen)	2	Mrs N. Holt Griffiths, Anoon, The Drive, Gartley, Plymouth
Service Ladies helping at North 2 Road Canteen	2	Mrs Pinsent, Grand Hotel, P.
United Co-op Women's Guild Executive	10	Mrs G. A. Glover, 44 St John's Road, Plymouth.
Joint Co-op Women's Guilds Executive	10	Mrs D. E. Came, 3 Hastings Tce, Plymouth.
Dickens Fellowship (helping at N. Rd Canteen)	2	Mrs S. S. Hutchings, 92 Alexandra Road, Mutley, P.
Ladies of Argyle Supporters' Club helping at North Road Canteen	2	Mrs Wallace, 29 Treverthien Tce, Stoke, Devonport.
Mrs Crimp, organising North Road Canteen Helpers	1	Mrs A. H. Crimp, 107 Browning Rd., Devonport.
Miss Bayly, of Executive of Services Welfare Fund	1	Miss E. M. Bayly, J.P. Inceworth, Hartley, P.
Mrs Dauks (Bishop's wife) Service Women's Club, 84 Old Town Street (G.F.S.)	1	Miss M. Wilton, Secretary
YMCA Service Women's Hostel, Mount Wise, Devonport	1	Miss D. Lance
Council of Social Service	4	Miss M. A. Glover, Morley Chas., Morley Street, P.
Women's Branch, British Legion	5	Mrs Paynter, 35 Rosebery Ave, St Judes, Plymouth.
Toc H Hostel 46 Union Street, Stonehouse, P.	2	Mrs J. T. Gillespie, Highfield, Venn Cross, Hartley, P.
Temartens, Westwell Park Chas. (Canteen)	1	Secretary
Canteen for Naval Workers, Central Hall, Fore Street, D.	2	Mrs E. D. Rogers, J.P., 239 Victoria Road, St Budo'
Royal Sailors' Rest, Fore Street, Devonport	2	Miss Wilson
Concert Parties for Troops	2	Mrs R. H. Wagner, 1 Park Pl. Stoke, Devonport.
Primrose League, Sutton Division	2	Mrs Snelling, Conservative Office, 17 Lockyer St, P.
Voluntary Helpers with Mobile Canteens	2	c/o J. Bowering, Esq., 6 Thornhill Vls, P.

Note; Red Cross, St John's, Civil Nursing Reserve and Civil Defence are included in official Civil Defence Units for the Inspection

Appendix C
Provision of Air Raid Shelters, Paignton, 1942
(from a contemporary document)

PUBLIC AIR RAID SHELTERS SITUATED IN THE URBAN DISTRICT OF PAIGNTON

No.	Type	Situation	Accommodation
1.	Surface	Victoria Park Sports Ground	50.
2.	...	...	50.
3.	...	Victoria Park Car Park	50.
4.	...	...	50.
5.	...	...	50.
6.	...	Station, Central Car Park	50.
7.	...	...	50.
8.	...	...	50.
9.	...	Palace Avenue Gardens	50.
10.	...	...	50.
11.	...	Torquay Road (Near Manor Road)	50.
12.	...	Torquay Road (Near Seaway Road)	50.
13.	...	...	50.
14.	...	Paignton Green (South)	50.
15.	...	...	50.
16.	...	... (North)	50.
17.	...	... (South)	50.
18.	...	Preston Green (North)	50.
19.	...	... (South)	50.
20.	...	Goodrington Park	50.
21.	...	...	50.
22.	...	Goodrington South Sands	50.
23.	...	Totnes Road (Tweenaways)	50.
24.	...	Dartmouth Road (Three Beaches)	50.
25.	...	Totnes Road (Primley)	50.
*26.	Old Vaults below garden	Kirkham Street	75.
27.	Surface	The Old 'Clink', (Near Littlegate Road)	10.
28.	...	Winner Hill Road	50.

*It is now being considered whether this Shelter should be closed owing to its condition.

Appendix D
A sourced reference of air attacks or where stray bombs were known to have dropped on or near a Devon Community (non-definitive)

Abbreviations

AIR = AIR 28; 261; Public Record Office.
CDT = Records of the Civil Defence, Torquay.
EM = Book – *Exmouth Milestones*.
EPR = Exeter Police Records.
HO = PRO – *Home Office Class*. Piece.
MHS = Ministry of Home Security Weekly Reports, PRO 210.
PRO = Public Record Office, Kew.
SCD = Southern Command (Wartime) Diaries, PRO.
TT = *Totnes Times*.
WDR = West Devon Records, Plymouth.

Date	Location of Raid	Source	Date	Location	Source
	1940		27 August 40	Braunton	*North Devon Journal*
5 July 40	Spasmodic bombing over Devon	MHS	28 August 40	Plymouth	WDR
6 July 40	Barnstaple	SCD	29 August 40	Kingswear	CDT
6 July 40	Galmpton	CDT	30 August 40	Ugborough	TT
6 July 40	Plymouth	WDR	2 September 40	South Molton	SCD
7 July 40	Plymouth	WDR	2 September 40	Uffculme	SCD
7 July 40	Teignmouth	MHS	3 September 40	Exmouth	SCD
8 July 40	Plymouth	WDR	3 September 40	Sidmouth	SCD
10 July 40	Marldon	CDT	4 September 40	Modbury	SCD
10 July 40	Plymouth	WDR	5 September 40	Plymouth	WDR
11 July 40	Churston Ferrers	CDT	5 September 40	Tamerton Foliot	SCD
12 July 40	Plymouth	WDR	5 September 40	Torquay	SCD
13 July 40	Ivybridge	SCD	6 September 40	Exeter	EPR
13 July 40	Modbury	SCD	11 September 40	Plymouth	WDR
15 July 40	Plymouth	WDR	11 September 40	Dawlish	SCD
15 July 40	Brixham	CDT	12 September 40	Paignton	CDT
19 July 40	Plymouth	WDR	12 September 40	Honiton	SCD
19 July 40	Yealmpton	MHS	12 September 40	Uffculme	SCD
19 July 40	Widecombe	MHS	13 September 40	Okehampton	SCD
20 July 40	Plymouth	WDR	16 September 40	Exeter	EPR
28 July 40	Mansands	CDT	17 September 40	Plymouth	WDR
31 July 40	Tiverton	Tiverton Museum	25 September 40	Plymouth	WDR
			27 September 40	Barnstaple	SCD
7 August 40	Exeter	EPR	30 September 40	Eddystone Lighthouse	Trinity House
13 August 40	Plymouth	WDR	1 October 40	Okehampton	SCD
13 August 40	Modbury	SCD	9 October 40	Plymouth	WDR
13 August 40	Ivybridge	SCD	10 October 40	Plymouth	WDR
13 August 40	Okehampton	SCD	16 October 40	Plymouth	WDR
14 August 40	Plymouth	WDR	20 October 40	Kingsbridge	SCD
15 August 40	Instow	SCD	22 October 40	Plymouth	WDR
15 August 40	Appledore	SCD	28 October 40	Exeter	EPR
15 August 40	Woolacombe	SCD	1 November 40	Plymouth	WDR
15 August 40	Axminster	SCD	6 November 40	Plymouth	WDR
15 August 40	Honiton	SCD	7 November 40	Barnstaple	SCD
15 August 40	Ottery St Mary	SCD	8 November 40	Cullompton	SCD
16 August 40	Exeter	EPR	9 November 40	Eddystone Lighthouse	Trinity House
18 August 40	Seaton	SCD	10 November 40	Westward Ho!	SCD
19 August 40	Crediton	SCD	18 November 40	Plymouth	WDR
20 August 40	Newton Abbot	MHS	18 November 40	Bovey Tracey	SCD
20 August 40	Black Torrington	SCD	18 November 40	Gittisham	SCD
20 August 40	Brixham	CDT	27 November 40	Brixham	CDT
21 August 40	(RAF) Exeter	AIR	27 November 40	Plymouth	WDR
25 August 40	Plymouth	WDR	27 November 40	Dartmouth	SCD
26 August 40	Tavistock	SCD	28 November 40	Exeter	MHS
27 August 40	Bere Alston	*Tavistock Times*			

28 November 40	Exeter	MHS
28 November 40	Exmouth	MHS
11 December 40	Chittlehampton	SCD
12 December 40	Kingsteignton	SCD
15 December 40	Plymouth	WDR
22 December 40	Okehampton	SCD
23 December 40	Buckfastleigh	SCD
28 December 40	Plymouth	WDR
28 December 40	Billacombe	SCD
28 December 40	Brixham	SCD
30 December 40	Eddystone Lighthouse	Trinity House

1941

4 January 41	Exmouth	Exmouth Library
5 January 41	Sidbury	MHS
9 January 41	Plymouth	WDR
10 January 41	Exmouth	EM
11 January 41	Plymouth	WDR
12 January 41	Plymouth	WDR
12 January 41	Hartland Lighthouse	Trinity House
12 January 41	Stoke Gabriel	TT
13 January 41	Plymouth	WDR
15 January 41	Plymouth	WDR
16 January 41	Exeter	EPR
17 January 41	Brixham	CDT
18 January 41	Exmouth	EM
19 January 41	Plymouth	WDR
27 January 41	Plymouth	WDR
1 February 41	Exmouth	EM
13 February 41	Plymouth	WDR
19 February 41	Plymouth	WDR
27 February 41	Brixham	CDT
2 March 41	Lynton	MHS
4 March 41	Exeter	EPR
12 March 41	Brixham	CDT
12 March 41	Galmpton	CDT
14 March 41	Plymouth	WDR
20 March 41	Plymouth	WDR
21 March 41	Plymouth	WDR
23 March 41	Eddystone Lighthouse	Trinity House
3 April 41	Plymouth	WDR
3 April 41	RAF Exeter	AIR
5 April 41	RAF Exeter	AIR
7 April 41	Plymouth	WDR
10 April 41	Plymouth	WDR
11 April 41	Paignton	CDT
12 April 41	RAF Exeter	AIR
13 April 41	RAF Exeter	AIR
14 April 41	RAF Exeter	AIR
15 April 41	Plymouth	WDR
17 April 41	RAF Exeter	AIR
21 April 41	Salcombe	Bundes Archive
21 April 41	RAF Exeter	Bundes Archive
21 April 41	Plymouth	WDR
22 April 41	Plymouth	WDR
22 April 41	Torquay	CDT
22 April 41	Start Point Lighthouse	Trinity House
23 April 41	Plymouth	WDR
25 April 41	Dartmouth	MHS
28 April 41	Plymouth	WDR
29 April 41	Plymouth	WDR

29 April 41	RAF Exeter	AIR
30 April 41	Plymouth	WDR
30 April 41	Berry Pomeroy	TT
3 May 41	West Prawle	MHS
4 May 41	Plymouth	WDR
4 May 41	Torquay	CDT
4 May 41	Braunton	NDJ
5 May 41	Honiton Clyst	SCD
5 May 41	Exeter	EPR
5 May 41	Plymouth	WDR
6 May 41	Plymouth	WDR
6 May 41	Exeter	EPR
7 May 41	Plymouth	WDR
7 May 41	Teignmouth	MHS
7 May 41	Ugborough	TT
8 May 41	Brixton	WDR
9 May 41	Plymstock	WDR
9 May 41	Plymouth	WDR
9 May 41	Dartmouth	MHS
9 May 41	RAF Exeter	AIR
10 May 41	RAF Exeter	AIR
10 May 41	Broadsands	CDF
11 May 41	Brixham	CDT
11 May 41	Dartmouth	MHS
11 May 41	Plymouth	WDR
12 May 41	Plymouth	WDR
12 May 41	RAF Exeter	AIR
13 May 41	Staverton	TT
13 May 41	Netherton	TT
13 May 41	Berry Pomeroy	TT
14 May 41	Harberton	TT
14 May 41	Harberton Ford	TT
15 May 41	Teignmouth	MHS
15 May 41	Dittisham	TT
16 May 41	Plymouth	WDR
19 May 41	Brixham	CDT
20 May 41	Torquay	CDT
24 May 41	Churston	CDT
26 May 41	Plymouth	WDR
28 May 41	Exmouth	EM
4 June 41	Budleigh Salterton	MHS
11 June 41	Brixham	CDT
11 June 41	Dawlish	MHS
11 June 41	Teignmouth	MHS
11 June 41	Exeter	EPR
17 June 41	Torquay	CDT
4 July 41	Plymouth	NDR
4 July 41	Budleigh Salterton	MHS
5 July 41	Teignmouth	MHS
5 July 41	Cornwood	HO 198; 194
9 July 41	Plymouth	WDR
9 July 41	Kenton	MHS
24 October 41	Teignmouth	MHS
25 October 41	Bideford	*North Devon Journal*
22 November 41	Ugborough	MHS
5 December 41	Plymouth	WDR

1942

12 February 42	Torquay	CDT
12 February 42	Exmouth	EM
12 February 42	RAF Exeter	MHS
7 March 42	Exmouth	MHS
7 March 42	Teignmouth	MHS
18 March 42	Torquay	CDT
27 March 42	Torquay	CDT
27 March 42	Brixham	CDT

31 March 42	Exmouth	CDT
2 April 42	Torquay	CDT
17 April 42	Budleigh Salterton	MHS
23 April 42	Exminster	MHS
23 April 42	Diptford	TT
23 April 42	Dartington	TT
23 April 42	Harberton	TT
23 April 42	Bishopsteignton	MHS
23 April 42	Exeter	
23 April 42	RAF Exeter	SCD
23 April 42	Totnes	TT
23 April 42	Berry Pomeroy	TT
24 April 42	Newton Abbot	MHS
24 April 42	Exeter	EPR
25 April 42	Exeter	EPR
25 April 42	Newton Abbot	SCD
25 April 42	Hope (RAF Bolt Head)	SCD
26 April 42	Exeter	EPR
1 May 42	RAF Bolt Head	SCD
3 May 42	RAF Chivenor	SCD
3 May 42	Exeter	EPR
3 May 42	Ide	SCD
6 May 42	Brixham	CDT
14 May 42	Brixham	CDT
16 May 42	Plymouth	WDR
29 May 42	Blackawton	TT
29 May 42	East Allington	TT
7 June 42	Torquay	CDT
18 June 42	Brixham	CDT
28 June 42	Colyton	SCR
29 June 42	Plymouth	WDR
1 July 42	Teignmouth	MHS
12 July 42	Brixham	CDT
26 July 42	Beesands	MHS
26 July 42	Stokenham	Not Confirmed
29 July 42	Brixham	CDT
1 August 42	Teignmouth	MHS
3 August 42	Torquay	MHS
3 August 42	Paignton	CDT
7 August 42	Torquay	CDT
12 August 42	Seaton	MHS
13 August 42	Teignmouth	MHS
13 August 42	Stoke Gabriel	TT
24 August 42	Dittisham	HO 192; 889
2 September 42	Teignmouth	MHS
4 September 42	Torquay	CDT
4 September 42	Paignton	CDT
8 September 42	Salcombe	MHS
17 September 42	Seaton	MHS
18 September 42	Kingswear	HO 192; 351
19 September 42	Salcombe	MHS
19 September 42	Slapton	MHS
13 October 42	Dartmouth	MHS
14 October 42	Berryhead Lighthouse	Trinity House
15 October 42	Dawlish Warren	MHS
16 October 42	Cornworthy	MHS
16 October 42	Stoke Gabriel	TT
21 October 42	Totnes	MHS
25 October 42	Torquay	CDT
26 October 42	Seaton	MHS
26 October 42	RAF Dunkeswell	SCD
3 November 42	Teignmouth	MHS
3 November 42	Dawlish	MHS
3 November 42	Torquay	CDT
30 November 42	Sidmouth	MHS

30 November 42	Honiton Clyst	MHS
30 November 42	Whimple	MHS
30 November 42	RAF Exeter	SCD
30 November 42	Dawlish	MHS
17 December 42	Stoke Fleming	MHS
30 December 42	Paignton	CDT
30 December 42	Exeter	EPR
30 December 42	Torquay	CDT

1943

2 January 43	Kingsbridge	MHS
6 January 43	Kingsbridge	MHS
8 January 43	Torquay	CDT
10 January 43	Teignmouth	HO 192; 905
10 January 43	Dawlish	MHS
21 January 43	Brixham	CDT
21 January 43	Brixham	CDT
26 January 43	Averton Gifford	MHS
9 February 43	Salcombe	*Kingsbridge Gazette*
13 February 43	Dartmouth	MHS
13 February 43	Torquay	CDT
13 February 43	Plymouth	WDR
13 February 43	Paignton	CDT
16 February 43	Kingsbridge	MHS
16 February 43	Okehampton	HO 192; 908
26 February 43	Exmouth	EM
12 March 43	Salcombe	HO 192; 909
13 March 43	Kellaton	MHS
15 March 43	Eddystone Lighthouse	Trinity House
18 March 43	Brixham	CDT
18 March 43	RAF Kingswear	SCD
23 March 43	Dartmouth	MHS
30 March 43	Salcombe	MHS
30 March 43	RAF Bolt Head	MHS
30 March 43	Marlborough	MHS
29 April 43	Plymouth	WDR
17 May 43	Teignmouth	MHS
29 May 43	Torquay	CDT
29 May 43	Brixham	CDT
13 June 43	Plymouth	WDR
13 June 43	Plymouth	WDR
12 August 43	Plymouth	WDR
12 August 43	Wrangton	SCD
16 November 43	Plymouth	WDR

1944

28 March 44	Plymouth	WDR
29 April 44	Plymouth	WDR
29 May 44	Torquay	CDT

Appendix E
Admiralty Report on Coastal Batteries, 1940

COPY   <u>SECRET.</u>

<u>1st Sea Lord.</u>

      R.N. and R.M. personnel are not being transferred from the East and South East coasts to the South West, but those manning eight batteries are being left in their present positions in order that the Army personnel which would have relieved them may man guns in the South West.

2.   This R.N. and R.M. personnel will be at one week's notice for withdrawal from 31st July. Army personnel will man all future Coast Defence batteries.

3.   It has been ascertained from H.Q. Home Forces that manning of new batteries in the South West is intended to proceed as follows:-

By 1st August (4–4.7" batteries + 4 more on E. and S.E. Coasts)	Lyme Regis Exmouth Teignmouth Appledore	
By 15th August (18–4" batteries + 10 more on other coasts)	Swanage Abbotsbury Seaton Sidmouth Dawlish Salcombe Looe Par Penzance	Hayle Newquay Padstow Barnstable Ilfracombe Minehead Port Talbot Llanelly Carnarvon

4.   A further 20–4" batteries are expected to be manned by 1st December, but sites for these have not yet been determined.

5.   Torpedo tubes are now in action at:—

        Portland
        Dartmouth
        Fishguard

They will be in action shortly at:—

        Torquay
        Falmouth
        Liverpool

6.   Warhead mines have been supplied to 18 ports on this coast and are being laid now.

            (Sgd.) C. H. L. WOODHOUSE
                  for Director of Local Defence.

Appendix F
North Devon Defence Plans, 1940

DEVON SUB AREA OPERATION INSTRUCTION NO. 7.

Reference Map Sheet 118 1" to 1 mile.

1. The following considerations affect the defence of the NORTH COAST of DEVON.:—

    (a) The most likely landing places for seaborne or airborne troops is between HELE BAY and WESTWARD HO!—other localities are most unlikely.

    (b) The immediate hostile objectives are considered to be BARNSTAPLE and BIDEFORD, the former being the most important.

    (c) The first and most important line of defence is the Coast, and every effort will be made to prevent the enemy landing or debouching from the beaches or quays.

    (d) Should the enemy establish himself on the Coast, he must be prevented from securing BARNSTAPLE or BIDEFORD.

2. O.C. 50th WARWICKS is responsible for reconnaissance and co-operation of defences of the Coast line but special areas of responsibility are allotted as under:—

AREA	TROOPS
(a) HELE BAY and ILFRACOMBE.	10th East Surrey Regt. 11th Devon Regt.,
(b) WOOLACOMBE BAY, CROYDE BAY, SAUNTON SANDS, CHIVENOR AERODROME, RIVER TAW (Rt Bank), BARNSTAPLE,	50th R. Warwicks.
(c) WESTWARD HO!, SOUTH GUT, APPLEDORE, INSTOW SANDS, RIVER TORRIDGE, BIDEFORD.	No. 8 A.M.P.C.

3. With a view to the immediate construction of defensive work, O.C. 50th WARWICKS will arrange for a reconnaissance to be carried out and will forward a report showing the number and location of constructive works and R.E. material required under the following headings:—

    (a) Pill boxes for machine guns.
    (b) Tactical wire for defence of beaches.
    (c) Permanent obstructions to beach exits.
    (d) Wire required, also picquets—
        (i) for Defence of beaches.
        (ii) for Platoon localities.

PORTS, BEACHES and LANDING GROUNDS.

A. SEABORNE LANDINGS.

The following are points where a seaborne landing is thought possible, together with the Corps Beach numbering of each:—

(i) LIKELY LANDING PLACES

WIDEMOUTH SANDS	6324	45b.
BUDE HAVEN	6329	
(incl. CROOKLETS)		46.
WESTWARD HO! SANDS	8753	50e.
INSTOW SANDS	9053	51a.
SAUNTON SANDS	8858	51b.
CROYDE BAY	8761	52
WOOLACOMBE BAY	8965	53

(ii) OTHER POSSIBLE LANDING PLACES

CRACKINGTON HAVEN	5719	45a.
NORTHCOTT MOUTH	6331	47a.
SANDY MOUTH	6332	47b.
COMBE	6334	48a.
STANBURY MOUTH	6335	48b.
MARSLAND MOUTH	6440	49.
WELCOMBE MOUTH	6440	50a.
SPEKE'S HILL MOUTH	6646	50b.
MOUTH MILLS	7349	50c.
BUCKS MILLS	7946	50d.
HELE BAY	9870	54a.
WATERMOUTH BAY	9970	54b.
COMBE MARTIN	0169	54c.
HEDDON'S MOUTH	0971	54d.

(iii) PORTS

BUDE	6329
*CLOVELLY	7547
APPLEDORE	9052
BIDEFORD	8948
INSTOW	9052
FREMINGTON	9555
BARNSTAPLE	9955
ILFRACOMBE	9570
*LYNMOUTH	1671

(N.B. CLOVELLY and LYNMOUTH are suitable for small ships only.)

B. AIRBORNE LANDINGS—The following are feasible landing grounds for troop-carrying aircraft (excluding aerodromes), together with the Serial number given in N.D.S.A. S/22 of 3/9/40:—

(i) Landing Ground Reserved for R.A.F.   SERIAL NO.

PICKWELL DOWN	9063	13

YOULSTON OLD PARK	0458	27.

(ii) <u>Landing Grounds Obstructed.</u>

WESTWARD HO! SANDS		1
INSTOW SANDS		2
SAUNTON SANDS		3
CROYDE BAY		4
WOOLACOMBE BAY		6
BRAUNTON GT. FIELD	9158	5
BEAFORD MOOR	0136	7
HOLLOCOMBE MOOR	0334	8
PICKWELL DOWN	9063	13
MULLOCOT CROSS	9466	14
CORNBOROUGH RACE COURSE	8550	19
LYNTON GOLF COURSE	1369	32

(iii) <u>Landing Ground not Obstructed (as being more than 5 miles from Beach or aerodrome or as due to be ploughed shortly.)</u>

STIBB CROSS	8536	11
BELLE VUE	9643	12
BITTADON	9663	15
GORMON'S DOWN	0361	22
PARRACOMBE COMMON	1267	23
BRENDON COMMON	2066	24
YARD DOWN	1657	25
EAST ANSTEY COMMON	3050	26
WELSFORD MOOR	7143	28
COMMON MOOR	7923	29
HIGHBOROUGH FARM	7843	34
WITHERIDGE MOOR	2836	35

It is appreciated that 'crash' landings are possible in almost any part of the Sub Area in addition to the places listed above.

(iv) Places suggested by R.A.F. as being likely places for parachutists aiming at CHIVENOR AERODROME and control of River TAW Estuary:—

Point   –   454 at 9160
ASH WARREN   –   9459

STATES OF READINESS

1. <u>NORMAL</u>

   (a) All troops holding defensive positions on beaches and at aerodromes will "STAND TO" from one hour before sunrise until one hour after.

   (b) During remaining hours of darkness, beaches and cliffs where landings are possible will be patrolled either by regular troops or by H.G.

   One third of the garrison of beaches and aerodromes will be ready for immediate action.

   Very foggy weather will be regarded as darkness, and very active patrolling will be carried out.

   (c) Where H.G. are solely responsible for beaches, they will provide picquets and patrols by night and observation by day.

Appendix G
Top Secret Plans for Exercise 'Tiger'

TOP SECRET
TOP — SECRET

8475 /a

HEA[   ]S
SOUTH[   ]MD
23 MAR 1944 FIRST UNITED STATES ARMY
SALISBURY APO 230

HEADQUARTERS

: SECRET :
:Auth: CG, First US Army:
:Date: 21 Mar 44 :
:Initials: :

Register No PG-1503

Copy No. 14 of 26 Copies.

353(C)

21 March 1944

SUBJECT: Amphibious Exercise TIGER

TO   : Commanding General, VII Corps

1 spare copy

1. Information.

In preparation for forthcoming operations, Force "U" will conduct an amphibious training exercise during the period 26 – 30 April 1944. The exercise will be known as TIGER and will be held on the SLAPTON SANDS Training Area.

2. Purpose.

The purpose of Exercise TIGER is to conduct a rehearsal of Force "U", Operation OVERLORD, in which actual plans, formations and conditions are adhered to as closely as limitations of equipment and facilities will permit. Emphasis is to be placed on the establishment and maintenance of communication between all supported and supporting forces. Camouflage discipline will be stressed in the concentration area and during the exercise proper.

3. Scope.

The exercise will be conducted to include the following operations:

a. Accomplishment of all pertinent instructions contained in Section V, "Preparation for Movement" of ETO-POM-SSV dated 10 January 1944 (corrected).

b. Processing of all participating troops through concentration and marshalling areas.

c. Embarkation at proper scales.

d. Movement overseas under control of US Navy.

e. Execution of prearranged Naval Fire Support Plan and Air Support Plan.

f. Debarkation and assault of SLAPTON SANDS beaches.

– 1 – (over)

TOP — SECRET

Ltr. Amphibious Exercise TIGER (Cont'd).

        (3) <u>Phase III</u> – Operations during this phase will include consolidation and extension of the beach head line, concentration of forces involved in preparation for return movement to home stations or marshalling areas as ordered by T/C, SOS.

        (4) <u>Phase IV</u> – Completion of unloading and continuation of operation of beach maintenance area.

    b. <u>Phase I.</u> Operations during Phase I will be conducted under the supervision of the SOS.

        (1) <u>Preparation for Movement.</u>

          (a) Movement to the concentration area will be governed by movement instructions to be issued by the Transportation Corps, SOS, based on VII Corps Plan.

          (b) Prior to departure from home stations all units will comply with par. 107, POM-ETO-SSV, dated 10 January 1944 ·(Revised).

        (2) <u>Concentration and Embarkation.</u>

          (a) Concentration will take place in the Dartmouth, Plymouth East Area. Embarkation will be out of Dartmouth, Brixham, Torquay and Plymouth East.

          (b) Details for the concentration and embarkation of Force "U" will be determined by the SOS in conjunction with The CG, VII Corps and appropriate US Naval and British authorities.

          (c) Unit overstrength and residual personnel will be handled in accordance with paras. 70, 71, and 73, ETO-POM-SSV.

    c. <u>Phase II.</u>

        (1) CG, VII Corps will prepare and submit to this headquarters by 7 April 1944, a tactical exercise on SLAPTON SANDS Training Area for Phase II. This exercise will approximate the Force "U" assault plan for Operation OVERLORD as closely as the area will permit and will include participation by elements of the 101st A/B Division. In the event it is considered impractical to drop these elements they will be moved into position by motor. Position areas selected should be on the western edge of the SLAPTON SANDS area out of the impact area.

        (2) Emphasis will be placed on the establishment, maintenance and testing of all means and channels of communication.

        (3) Service ammunition will be fired.

Appendix H (map)
Locations of Main Aerial
Attacks on South Devon, 1940–44

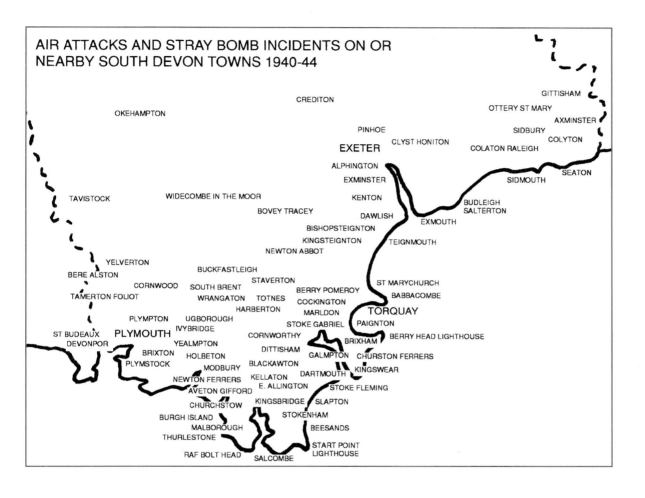

AIR ATTACKS AND STRAY BOMB INCIDENTS ON OR
NEARBY SOUTH DEVON TOWNS 1940-44

Appendix I
Facsimile Page from the Sonderfahndungsliste

The notorious 'Black Book' listed 2820 people who were to be arrested or taken into protective custody (concentration camps) following the proposed German invasion. They included Lady Astor and members of the Transport and General Workers Union, Plymouth.

842

Paignton

Personenverzeichnis:
B. 71

Peterborough

Fundstellen:
V e r e i n :
Geschäftsstelle der Transport and General Worker Union, gewerkschaftl. marxist. Arbeiterorganisation, Church Street 10, RSHA IV A 1, Stapo Bremen.

Plymouth

Fundstellen:
V e r e i n :
Geschäftsstelle der Transport and General Worker Union, gewerkschaftl. marxist. Arbeiterorganisation, Courtenay Street 25, RSHA IV A 1, Stapo Bremen.
Personenverzeichnis:
G. 116

Portland

Personenverzeichnis:
F. 145

Portsmouth

Fundstellen:
V e r e i n :
Geschäftsstelle der Transport and General Worker Union, gewerkschaftl. marxist. Arbeiterorganisation, Kingston Road 57, Victoria House, RSHA IV A 1, Stapo Bremen.

Port Talbot

Fundstellen:
V e r e i n :
Geschäftsstelle der Transport and General Worker Union, gewerkschaftl. marxist. Arbeiterorganisation, Talbot Road, Central Buildings.

Preston

Fundstellen:
V e r e i n e :
Geschäftsstelle der Transport and General Worker Union, gewerkschaftl. marx. Arbeiterorganisation, RSHA IV A 1, Stapo Bremen.
Geschäftsstelle der Transport and General Worker Union, gewerkschaftl. marx. Arbeiterorganisation, Guildhall Street 30, RSHA IV A 1, Stapo Bremen.

Princetown

Personenverzeichnis:
M. 105

Putnay b. Lond.

Personenverzeichnis:
B. 130

Appendix J
Order for the Torquay Home Guard, 1940

```
                    TORQUAY BATTALION HOME GUARD.

              NO. 1.PLATOON.        PLANTOON HEADQUARTERS,
                                    ST. MARYCHURCH TOWN HALL
                                    TORQUAY.

     VERY IMPORTANT.                       October 10th 1940.

                  It has been found impracticable for the Platoon Staff to
         warn each individual for Duty or Parades, and so from this date on, members of
         the Platoon must be asked to look in at the Platoon Headquarters at some time
         during each day, to see if they are required for any such duty or parade.

                  Orders will be posted on the  "Routine Order" Board daily,
         giving the above detail.
                       As much notice as is possible will be given, and if any
         member finds it impossible to perform the duty allotted to him, he must at once
         inform the Platoon Clerk, (Mr. Burt) at either Platoon Hd. Qrs. or to him at the
         Public Library, Telephone 3221.

                  It is emphasized to all members of the Platoon, that, although
         the Home Guard as a whole is under the jurisdiction of "Military Law", they are
         placed on their honour as volunteers, to carry out any duty they are asked to
         perform, in a smart and soldier like manner and in a Cheerful Spirit.

                            MOBILIZATION ORDERS.

                  Until any orders are issued to the contrary, No. 1 Platoon
         has been allotted Action Positions as follows, in the event of Hostilities
         developing:

              No. 1. Section ....Babbacombe Beach
              No. 2. Section ....Watcombe "Road Defence Posts".
              No. 3. Section ....In Reserve(at Oddicombe-Babbacombe).
              No. 4. Section ....Oddicombe Beach.

                  The "ALARM" may be taken to be,continuous SHELL OR
         MACHINE-GUN FIRE,OR INTENSE BOMBING FROM AIR LAND OR SEA anywhere in the area of
         TORQUAY. On the "ALARM", sections will proceed, uniformed, armed and equipped,
         without delay to their positions under the orders of the respective Section
         Commanders.
                  The present Platoon Hd. Qrs. will be established as the
         PLATOON BASE on Mobilization.

                            (Sd.) F. J. March
                            Platoon Commander.
```

Appendix K
Evacuation Plans for London Schoolchildren, 1940

A six day task of evacuating 120 000 children from the London area began
13 June 1940.

Villages in the Barnstaple, Torrington, Bideford and South Molton areas were
to receive the following numbers of children:-

Bishops-Nympton	108	Witheridge	148
East Buckland	26	East Worlington	56
West Buckland	60	Rackenford	67
Charles	56	Rose Ash	67
Chittlehampton	207	Romansleigh	26
Filleigh	67	Mariansleigh	50
North Molton	174	Meshaw	30
Burrington	133	Knowstone	45
Chulmleigh	286	East Anstey	40
Chittlehamholt	52	West Anstey	36
Satterleigh and Workliegh	42	Molland	47
Georgenympton	40	Twitchen	24
King's Nympton	113	Reference: *Western Times* 14:6:1940	

BIBLIOGRAPHY

Ashworth, Chris, *Action Station 5: Military Airfields of the South West*. Patrick Stephens, 1982.

Bass, Richard T. *Spirits of the Sand*. Lee Publishing, 1992.

Bass, Richard T. *Precious Cargo*. Lee Publishing, 1993.

Beauman, Bentley K. *Greensleeves*. Seeley Service, 1991.

Beck K. and Copsey J. *The Great Western in South Devon*. Wild Swan Publishing, 1990.

Bowan, Martin. *B24 Liberator, 1939–1945*. Patrick Stephens, 1989.

Burton, S. H. *The South Devon Coast*. Laura Werner, 1954.

Burton, S. H. *Devon Villages*. Robert Hale, 1973.

Butcher, Geoffrey. *Next to a Letter from Home*. Mainstream Publishing, 1986.

Bradbeer, Grace. *The Land Changed Its Face*. David & Charles, 1973.

Calder, Angus. *The People's War: Britain 1939–1945*. Jonathan Cape, 1969.

Clamp, Arthur L. *The Hope Cove Area During the Second World War, 1939–1945*. Arthur L. Clamp, 1992.

Clamp, Arthur L. *Dartmouth and Kingswear During the Second World War, 1939–1945*. Arthur L. Clamp, 1993.

Coleman, R. *378 Battery Coast Artillery*. Coleman, 1989.

Collier, Basil. *The Defence of the United Kingdom*. HMSO, 1957.

Coulter, J. L. S. *The Royal Naval Medicine Service, Vol. 1*. HMSO, 1954.

Colville, John. *The Fringes of Power*. Hodder & Stoughton, 1985.

Darwin, Bernard. *War on the Line*. Southern Railway, 1946.

Day, Kenneth F. *Days on Dartmoor*. Devon Books, 1987.

Denes, Garbor. *The Story of the Imperial*. David & Charles, 1982.

Denny, Joyce. *Henrietta's War*. Penguin, 1939.

Doughty, Ken. *The Day the Bombs Fell on Aveton Gifford*. Aveton Gifford, 1993. Parish Project Group, nd.

Edwards, Anne. *Royal Sisters Elizabeth & Margaret, 1926–1956*. Collins, 1990.

Ellis, Major L. F. *The War in France and Flanders 1939–1945*. HMSO, 1953.

English, E. T. *Pilgrim to Plymouth*. Plymouth Guild of Social Service, 1967.

Firebrace, Aylmer, Sir. *Fire Service Memories*. Andrew Melrose, 1949.

Ferguson, Sheila and Fitzgerald, Hilda. *Studies in the Social Services*. HMSO, 1978.

Fleming, Peter. *Invasion 1940*. Rupert Hart Davis, 1957.

Fletcher, Bannister, Sir. *A History of Architecture of the Comparative Method*. The Athlone Press, 1961.

Foreman, John. *Battle of Britain*. Air Research Publications, 1988.

Freeman, Ray. *Dartmouth: A New History of the Port*. Harbour Books, 1987.

Fyson, Nance Lui. *Growing Up in the Second World War*. Batsford, 1983.

Galland, Adolf. *The First and the Last*. Eyre Methuen, 1953.

Gardiner, Juliet. *"Over Here"*. Collins, 1992.

Gill, Crispin. *Sutton Harbour*. Sutton Harbour Company, 1970.

Gillman, Peter. *Collar the Lot*. Quartet Books, 1980.

Gosling, Ted. *Around Seaton and Sidmouth*. Allan Sutton, 1991.

Graves, Charles. *Women in Green: The Story of the WVS in Wartime*. William Heinemann, 1948.

Green, S. M. *The Story of the Exeter Blitz*. A. Wheaton, 1946.

Hames-Hayter, Jane. *A History of Chagford*. Phillimore, 1981.

Hamilton, Nigel. *Monty, Master of the Battlefield*. Hamish Hamilton, 1983.

Haugland, Vern. *The Eagle Squadrons*. David & Charles, 1979.

Harrison, Gordon A. *Cross Channel Attack*. Washington, USA, 1951.

Hawkins, Mac. *Somerset at War*. Dovecote Press, 1988.

Herington, P. *Australia in the War*. Australia, 1982.

Higgins, Tony. *The Free French in Kingswear*. Dartmouth, 1992.

Hinsley, F. H. et al. *British Intelligence in the Second World War* (Vol 3, part 1; Vol 3, part 2). HMSO, 1988.

Hinsley, F. R. H. and Simkins, C. *British Intelligence in the Second World* (Vol 4). HMSO, 1990.

Howard, Michael. *British Intelligence in the Second World War* (Vol 5). HMSO, 1990.

Hoyt, Edwin P. *The Invasion Before Normandy*. Robert Hale, 1987.

Hummelchan, G. *German Schnellboote*. Profile Publications, 1973.

Jones, R. V. *Most Secret War*. Hamish Hamilton, 1978.

Killridge, Alan. *Passenger Steamers on the River Tamar*. Twelveheads, 1984.

Kingdom, A. R. *The Bombing of Newton Abbot Station*. ARK Publications, 1991.

Lambert, John and Ross, A. *Allied Coastal Forces of WW2*. Conway Maritime Press, 1990.

Lawrence, Malcolm. *A Touch of Genius*. J. M. Dent, 1988.

Lewis, A. H. *Memoirs of Royal Naval Experiences*. IWM, nd.

Lewis, Nigel. *Channel Firing: The Tragedy of Exercise Tiger*. Viking, 1989 (reprinted 1994, Harbour Books, Devon).

Longmate, Norman. *How We Lived Then*. Hutchinson, 1971.

Longmate, Norman. *The Americans in Britain.* Hutchinson, 1975.

Mais, S. P. B. *Glorious Devon.* GWR, 1934.

Mason, Francis. *Battle over Britain.* McWhirter Twins, 1969.

Mason, John T. *The Atlantic War Remembered.* Air Life Publications, 1990.

Messenger,Charles. *The Commando's 1940–1946.* Charles Kimber, 1946.

Morgan, Frederick, Sir. *Overture to Overlord.* Hodder, 1950.

Morgan, Jane. *Agatha Christie.* Collins, 1984.

Morrison, Samuel Eliot. *History of United States Naval Operations in World War 2* (vol xi). Little Brown, 1962.

Morley, Sheridan. *A Talent to Amuse.* Michael Joseph, 1964.

Murch, David and Muriel. *The American Forces at Salcombe and Slapton during World War 2.* David Murch, 1984.

Nowarra, J. Heinz. *Focke-Wulf.* Haynes, 1988.

Nowarra, J. Heinz. *BF109.* Haynes, 1989.

O'Brien, Terence H. *Civil Defence.* HMSO, 1953.

Pack, S. W. C. *Britannia at Dartmouth.* Alvin Redman, 1966.

(Pigeons). *Pigeons in World War II.* Racing Pigeon, 1950.

Pike, John. *Torquay: The Place, the People.* Torquay, 1992.

Plummer, Russell. *The Ships that Saved an Army.* Patrick Stephens, 1990.

Prawle, Gerald. *The Secret War, 1939–1945.* White Lion, 1956.

Price, Alfred. *Blitz on Britain.* Ian Allen, 1976.

Radnor, John. *It all Happened Before. The Home Guard through the Ages.* George S. Harap, 1945.

Ramsey, Winston G. *The Blitz: Then and Now* (Vols 1, 2, 3). Battle of Britain Prints Publications, 1987, 1988, 1990.

Ramsey, Winston G. *After the Battle.* Battle of Britain Prints, 1984.

Ries, Karl. *The Luftwaffe.* Batsford Books, 1987.

Robinson, John Martin. *The Country House at War.* Bodley Head, 1989.

Roskill, S. W. Captain. *The War at Sea 1939–1945* (Vol 1). HMSO, 1954.

Rothnie, Nial. *The Baedeker Blitz.* Ian Allen, 1992.

Rusbridger, James. *Who Sank Surcouf?* Random Century, 1991.

Russell, Percy. *Dartmouth.* B. T. Batsford, 1950.

Savignon, Andre. *With Plymouth Through Fire.* S. E. Ouston, 1968.

Schenk, Peter. *Invasion of England.* Conway Maritime Press, 1990.

Schweitzer, Pam. *Goodnight Children Everywhere.* Age Exchange Theatre Trust, 1990.

Stevenson, Derek. *Five Crashes Later.* William Kimber, 1988.

Small, Ken. *The Forgotten Dead.* Bloomsbury, 1988.

Taylor, F. *The Goebbels Diaries.* Sphere Books, 1982.

Teague, C. Dennis. *A History of RAF Station Harrowbeer 1944–1946.* D. Teague, nd.

Thomas, Peter. *Fire on the Wind.* Peter Thomas, 1992.

Titmus, R. M. *Problems of Social Policy.* HMSO, 1950.

Treece, Marcia. *According to our Cloth.* Marcia Treece, 1984.

Trewin, J. C. *Portrait of Plymouth.* Robert Hale, 1990.

Turner, E. C. *The Phoney War on the Home Front.* Michael Joseph, 1961.

Turner, Kathy. *Around Kingsbridge.* Alan Sutton, 1988.

Twyford, H. P. *It Came to our Door.* Underhill, 1949.

Wakefield, Kenneth. *The First Pathfinders.* William Kimber, 1981.

Walford, Eddie. *War Over the West.* Amigo Books, 1989.

Walker, Frank. *The Mystery of X5.* William Kimber, 1988.

Waller, Janet. *Women in Wartime.* MacDonald, 1987.

Ward, Sadie. *War in the Countryside.* Cameron Books, 1988.

Wasley, Gerald. *Blitz: An Account of Hitler's Aerial War Over Plymouth, March 1941.* Devon Books, 1991.

Way, Chris. *The Big Bands Go to War.* Mainstream Publishing, 1991.

Whiting, Charles. *The Three Star Blitz.* Leo Cooper, 1987.

Whitley, M. J. *German Destroyers of World War Two.* Arms & Armour Press, 1991.

Wills, Henry. *Pillboxes.* Leo Cooper, 1985.

Winslow, T. E. *Forewarned is Forearmed.* William Hodge, 1948.

Wintle, Frank. *Plymouth Blitz.* Bossiney Books, 1981.

Wood, Derek. *Attack Warning Red.* MacDonald & Jane's, 1976.

Woodward, F. W. *Citadel.* Devon Books, 1987.

Worrall, Geoff. *Exeter Airport.* Devon Books, 1988.

Worrall, Geoff. *Target Exeter.* Express & Echo (Exeter), 1992.

Young, John M. *Britain's Sea War.* Patrick Stephens, 1989.

INDEX

Page numbers in italic type refer to illustrations or information contained in the captions.

Abercrombie, Professor L.P. 144
Aircraft (Allied)
    B17 Flying Fortress 112
    Blenheim bomber 90
    Boston bomber 93
    Bristol Beaufighter *95*
    Dakota C-47 167
    Fairey Swordfish *14*, 15
    Gloucester Gladiator 62, *63*
    Hadrian glider 167
    Hawker Hurricane 63
    Liberator PBY 4-1 *166, 167*
    Liberator PBY-5A 167
    Lysander 51
    Mosquito 159
    Spitfire 62, 90, 93, 110, 112, 149
    Spitfire Mk XIV 167
    Sunderland 20, 31, *32*, 63, 66, 72, 109
    Thunderbolt 157, *159*
    Typhoon 167
    Wellington 167
Aircraft (Axis)
    Dornier Do17E *98*, 104
    Dornier Do217 104, 158, 159
    Focke-Wulf FW190 *109*, 110, *112, 114,*
    115, 117, *119*, 121
    Heinkel HeIII 63, 70, 73, *74*, 104, 127
    Junkers Ju88 63, *64*, *75*, 91, 102, 104
    Messerschmidt 410 149
    Messerschmidt Me109 109, 110
Air Raid Precautions (ARP) 13, 16, 18, 19, *21*,
    33, 72
Air raid shelters 33, 37, 70, 114, 122, 164
    Anderson 147
    Morrison 97, 121, 147
Air Raid Wardens Service 18, 21, 23, 34
Alderney 62
Allied Expeditionary Force 172
Alphington 91, 109
Alverdiscott 67
Appledore 3, 38, 51, 53, 70, 109, 125, 127
Ashburton 34, 170
Ashwater 89
Assembly areas 147, *151*, 152, 153, *161*, 162, *163*,
169
Astor, Lady 8, *81*, *82*, 166
Astor, Lord 8, 72, *81*, 166, 173
Atlantic convoys 62
Atlee, Clement 182
Australian Forces 90
    See also RAAF
Auxiliary Coastguards 57
Aveton Gifford 115-16
Aylesbeare 97

Babbacombe 532, 90
Baden-Powell, Lady 117
Baedeker (raids) 24, 96, 97, *98*, 99, 104, 105
Barnstaple 1, 3, 9, 16, 29, 50, 51, 91, 127, 143, 176,
178, 182
    Pannier Market *10*, 127, 175
Barrage balloons 23, *62*, 63, 95
Bastard, Colonel R. *58*
Bath 99, 105
Battle of Britain 48, 61
Battle of the River Plate 36, *37*, 94
BBC 34, 72, 74, 115, 172
Beaworthy 181
Belgian Forces 90
Begian refugees 43, 44, 92, 175
Belgium 40
Bere Alston 177
Bibby Line 45

Bideford 3, 29, 38, 50, 51, 69, 93, 109, 116, 123, 127,
128, 147, 171, 176, 179
Billy Cotton Band 74, 75
Birmingham 74
Bishopsteignton 97
Bittaford 27
Black out 11, 19, 20, 30, 31, 35, 37, 61, 74, 173
Black US troops 145
Blackawton 133, 135, 136, *138, 139*, 140, 174
Blackpool 131
Blackshirts 8
Bolt Head 11, 112
Boyd, Lieutenant Tom 94
Bradley, Lt-General Omar 166
Branscombe 53, 114
Braunton 3, 124, 130
Bristol 18, *61*, 74
Bristol Blitz 24
British Fascist Party *8*
British Legion 40, 175
Brixham 3, 38, 40, 43, 44, 45, 54, 55, 64, 107, 137,
145, 146, 150, 153, 155, *164*, 175
Broad Sands 53
Brownston 122
Buckland 89
Buckland Abbey 6
Buckland Brewer 116
Bude 50, 51
Budleigh Salterton 53, 114
Bulkworthy 116
Burgh Island 56
Burrator Reservoir 127

Campbell, Sir Malcolm 125
Canada 42
Canadian Forces 43, 46, 90, 130
Chagford 13
Chain Home (*see* Radar)
Chamberlain, Neville 22
Channel Islands 58, 59, 94, 175
Chawleigh 69
Chillington 140, 173
Chittlehamholt 69
Chittlehampton 69
Christie, Agatha 40, 110
Churchill, Winston 36, *37*, 40, 46, 58, 59, 81, *82*, 91,
114, 176
Churston 150
Clannaborough 69
Clovelly 107, 142
Clyst St Mary 97
Coastal batteries 53, 54, 56
Coastal Command 31, 63, 66
Coastal defences 50-51, 53, 54, 55, 56, 60, *123*
Coastguards *See* Auxiliary Coastguards
Combe Martin 3, 30, 127
Combined Operations Experimental Establishment
(COXE) 125, 127
Commandos 58, 59, 94
Compulsory Evacuation Order 131
Corbyn's Head 43, 171
Cornwall *1*, 31, 85, 88, 121, 135, 141, 152, 177
Coventry Blitz 66, 71
Coward, Noel 120
Crediton 3, 27, 42, *50*, 145
Crew Chiefs, The 172
Crossing, William 107
Croyde 171
Croyde Bay 27, 51, 130
Cruwys Morchard 181
Czech Forces 90, 93

Dambuster raids 127
Dartington *26*, 27
Dartmoor 16, 38, 56, 57, 86, *91*, 107, 127, *128*, 150
Dartmouth 12, 15, 16, 17, 18, *21*, 25, 26, *32*, 33, *35*,
36, 40, 41, 44, 47, 53, 55, 58, *64*, 70, 109, 111, 115,

116-17, 120, 131, 135, 145, *146*, 147, 149, 150, 153,
154, 157, *158, 159*, 161, 167, 173, *177, 178*
    Castle 54
    Royal Naval College *See* Royal Navy, HMS
    Britannia
Dawlish 27, 61, 114, 182
'Dig for Victory' campaign 60
D'Oyly Carte, Rupert 52
D-Day *3*, *125, 130*, 146, 153, *156, 160, 161*, 162, *164*,
165-7, 169
de Gaulle, General Charles 46
de Gaulle, Philippe 117
Decoy sites *149*, 150
Denmark 96
Desmond, Sergeant Johnny 172
Devers, Lt-General Jacob *129*
Devon County Council 24, 93
Devon pasty scheme 116
Devonport 2, 3, 6, 17, 18, 29, 36, *45*, 46, 47, 63, 67,
72, 73, 75, 78, 80, 82, 85, 88, 94, 120, 147
    Drill Hall *8*, 45
Directorate of Miscellaneous Weapon
Development (DMWD) 125
Dittisham 110, 143, 146
Drake, Sir Francis 6, 72
Drewsteignton 57
Dunkeswell *166*, 167
Dunkirk 4, 40ff., 144

East Allington 134, *139*, 140, 173
East Cornworthy 150
East Prawle 52
E Boats *46*, 117, 120, 155, 157, *158*, 165
Eden, Sir Anthony 40
Edward VII 133
Edward VIII 11
Elizabeth, wife of George VI 11, 72, *73*, 105
Essex 24
Evacuees 23, 24, 25, *26*, 27, 28, 36, 37, 70, 90, 94,
182
    Exeter 171
    London 21, *22, 26, 27, 28*, 61, *170*, 171
    Plymouth 88, 94, 144, 171
Exercise Duck (*see* Operation Duck)
Exercise Fabius *160*, 161
Exeter 1, 2, 4, 5, 6, 7, 8, 27, 31, 36, 42, 54, 64, 69, 70,
89, 121, 124, *127*, 128, 145, *179*
    Cathedral 5, 60, 94, 99, 101, 102, *104*, 105, 114,
140
    Deller's Cafe 5, 93, 105
    Nadderwater 104
    Redhills 104
    Theatre Royal 120
Exeter Blitz 5, 24, 93-106
Exeter City Council 102, 105
Exminster 97
Exmoor 10, *57*, 70
Exmouth 1, 8, 18, 21, 22, 37, 40, 53, 55, 61, 90, 93,
114, 117-20

Fenton, Lieutenant Leslie 94
Filleigh 89, 176
Fire brigades (AFS) 74, 80, 100, 101, 147, 181
Fleet Air Arm 15
Fort Benning 144
Fortescue, Earl 134
France 40, 42, 104, 109, 112, 125
Franco-German Armistice 46
Free French Forces 43, 46, 47, 59, 90, 117, *118, 158*
French refugees 44, 45, 92
Fritz-X bomb 158

Galmpton 38, 63
Gaumont British News 27, 145
George V 9, 11
George VI 11, 72, *73*, 105
Georgeham 130

German Forces 43, *46*, 47, 48, 49, 56, 58, *61*, 62, 144, 169, 171
German Invasion Headquarters 'Sealion' 64
German, Sir Edward 6
Germansweek 109
Germany 1, 8, 13, 17, 32, 33, 40
GI brides 145
Goebbels, Dr Joseph 1, 81, 96
Goering, Reichsmarschall Herman 1, 66, 96
Goodrington 54
Goodrington Sands 53
Government Agriculture Scheme 38
'Great Panjandrum' *126*, 127
Great Torrington *See* Torrington
Great Western Railway (GWR) 7, 36, 41, 45, 54, 117, 118, 175
Guernsey 58, 59, 122, 175

Haldon 11
Hallwill 181
Hamoaze 146, *157*
Harberton 173
Hards 146, *149*, 150, *151*, 152, 153, *154*, 159, *164*, *165*
Hatherleigh 69
Henty-Greer, Lieutenant 109
Hermann, Hauptmann Hajo *63*
Hess, Rudolph 90
Hillary, Richard 113
Himmler 1
Hitler, Adolf 1, 8, 40, 48, 62, 70, 96, 97, 169
Holland 40, 47, 59, 60, 104
Holsworthy 150, 171, 181
Home Guard 40, 49, 50, 51, 53, 54, 55, 56, 57, *58*, 60, 65, 69, 115, 127, *128*, 131, 140, 171, 173
Honiton 103, 145, 167
Hope Cove *54*
Horns Cross 51, 116
Horrabridge 177

Ide 104
Ilfracombe *4*, 10, 21, 28, 29, 34, 35, 37, 42, 51, 61, 65, 69, 70, 109, 114, 124, 127, 175
Indian Forces 56
Instow 3, 51, 125, *126*
Internment camps 32
Irwin, Lieutenant 94
Ivy Boys *See* US Forces, 4th Infantry Division
Ivybridge 87, 181

Japan 91, 181, 182
Japanese Forces 91, 94
Joe Loss Band 59
Joyce, William 8

Kamm Huber line 96
Kennedy, John F. *166*
Kennedy, Joseph Jnr *166*
Kent, Duke of *71*
Kingsbridge 15, 23, 25, 26, 55, 56, *61*, 65, 88, 94, 114, 122, 124, 133, 139, 147, 170
Kingswear 36, 41, 52, 54, 55, 94, 109, 117, 118, *154*, 165, 173
Kirk, Admiral Alan 166
'Knickebein' 71

Land Army Girls *See* Women's Land Army
Landing craft *155*
Lapford 3
Lawrence, T. E. 8
Lee Mill 181
Liberty Ships 130
Lifton *58*
Lighthouses 112
Lincombe 130
Liverpool 145
Lloyd George 10
Local Defence Volunteers (LDV) *See* Home Guard
Loddiswell 56, 170
Lodger Restrictive Order 90
London 21, 23, 24, *26*, 27, 61, 78, 80, 153, *170*
   See also Evacuees
London Blitz 24, 61, 71
Lord Lieutenant of Devon 134

Lubeck 96, 97
Luftwaffe 13, *62*, 63, *64*, 66, 69, 70ff., 91, 93, 95ff., 115ff., 142, 149, 158, *160*
Lundy 70
Lustleigh *27*
Lydford 49
Lyme Bay 48, 51, 155, 157, *158*
Lynmouth 35

Martinhoe 70
Mary, Queen, wife of George V 9
Mary Tavy 38
McAndrew, Vernon 59
McKinley, Sergeant Ray 172
Merchant Navy 39
   See also Shipping
Mexico 145
Middlesex 24, 25, *27*
Miller, Glen 172
Minefields 50, 53, 54, 133, 141
Minehead 35
Modbury *2*, *56*, 88, 122
Montgomery, Brigadier (later Lord) Bernard *14*, 16, 131, 153
Moretonhampstead 12, 22, 34
Morgan Giles Shipyard 38, 117, *118*
Mortehoe 3, 51
Mortehoe *56*
Mosley, Sir Oswald 8
Mothercombe *56*
Motor Launches 37, 38, 58, 94
Motor Torpedo Boats (MTBs) 54, 117, *118*, 155, 157, *158*, 165
Mountbatten, Lord Louis 18, 81
Mulberry harbours 46
Munich crisis 13, 27

National Fire Service *See* Fire brigades
Newton Abbot 1, 11, 16, 28, 30, 34, 64, 145
Newton St Cyres 3, 89
New Zealand Forces 90
Nicholson, Flight Lieutenant 113
Nissen huts 117, 124, 143, *146*
Normandy 46, 131, 145, 153, 155, 162, *163*, 165, 167, 169, 171
Northam 53

Okehampton 108, 121
   Royal Artillery Camp 51, *128*, *133*
Omaha Beach 153, *160*
Operation Barbarossa 70
Operation Beaver 153
Operation Bolero 145
Operation Cyclone 45
Operation Duck 142, 153, *154*
Operation Dynamo 40
Operation Fortitude 149-50
Operation Fox 153
Operation Muskrat 153
Operation Overlord 123, 141, 145, *147*, 157, 167
Operation Sealion 48
Oran, Morocco 46
Oreston 88, 158, 182

Paignton 1, *9*, 17, 24, 27, 32, 40, 45, 88, 109, 114, 117, 120, 147, 153, 175
Parracombe 175
Pas de Calais 150
Pearl Harbor 91
Pipe Line Under The Ocean (PLUTO) 127
Plymouth 1, 5, 8, 9, 10. 11, 13, 15, 16, 20, 23, 24, *25*, *33*, 34, 36, 37, *43*, 44, 45, 47, 55, 57, 58, *64*, 65, 100, 103, 117, 121, 142, 143, 145, 147, 149, 152, 153, 155, 157, *160*, 161, 165, 166, 169, *172*, 175, 176, *180*, 182
   Breakwater 32, 63, 159
   Elburton 181
   Guildhall 77
   Manadon 172
   Marsh Mills 42
   Millbay 8, 42, 45, 71, 72
   Mutley 6
   Queen Anne's Battery 141, 146, 172
   RM and Naval Barracks 76
   Shipbuilding 38
   St Andrew's Church 75, *82*, 175
   St Augustine's Church 22, 76, 80

Stoke 79
Stonehouse 85
Sutton 8
Sutton Harbour 3
   The Hoe *17*, 42, *60*, *72*, 90, 107, 177, 178
   Tinside 9, 10, 107
Plymouth Argyle 4, *5*, 10
Plymouth Blitz 24, 66, 69-91, 101, 107, 115, 144
Plymouth Sound 43, 46, 49, *55*, 63, *72*, *161*, 178
Plympton 87, 88
Polish Forces 45, 46, 51, 90
Portland 52, 64, 165
Portsmouth 45, 142
Powder Mills 107
POWs, British 182
   German 181
   Italian 181
Prawle Point 19, 67
Prien, Gunther 33
Princetown 16, 107
Prudential Assurance Co. 27, *28*

'Q' sites 97
Quonset huts 124

Rabbits 38, 107
Radar 53, 91, 110
   Chain Home 52, 91
   RDF (RADAR) 19
Raeder, Admiral 47
RAF 34, 37, 58, 96, 113
   Bases
      Bolt Head *51*, 91, 93, 111, 112, 167
      Chivenor 54, 91, 125, 167
      Cleave 50
      Exeter 32, 54, 62, 63, *64*, 90, 91, *95*, 112, 167
      Haldon 90
      Harrowbeer 88, 90, 167, 172
      Mountbatten 8, 31, 66, 109, 146
      Roborough 51, 62, *63*, 80
      St Eval 31
      Torre Abbey 90
      Warmwell 64
      Winkleigh *51*, 54
      Yelverton 90
   Squadrons
      87 Squadron 62
      147 Squadron 62
      152 Squadron 62, 64
      213 Squadron 63, 64
      225 Squadron 51
      276 Squadron 90
      317 Squadron 93
   See also Aircraft, Motor Launches
Rationing
   Clothes 90, 107, 143
   Food 36, 60, 69, 103, 107, 113, 143
   Petrol 23, 30, 136
Red Cross 124
Rediffusion Broadcasting System 72
Regiments
   Devon 22
   Durham Light Infantry 42
   East Kent 55
   East Yorks 15
   King's Own Scottish Borderers 15
   Lincolns 15
   Middlesex 15
   6th Devons 21
   50th Warwickshire 50
Regional Commissioner
   for South West 78, 122, 131, 133
   Scheme 18
Renault-Routre, Colonel Gilbert 59
Reynolds, Sir Joshua 87
Ribbentrop, von 11, *12*
River Dart 12, *27*, 36, 41, 54, 59, 94, 109, 111, 117, 143, 146, 165, 173, 176
River Exe 117
River Gara 131
River Lynher 56
River Plym 56
River Tamar 56, 73, 88, 146, *150*, *151*
River Taw 51, 175

River Teign 57
River Torridge 51, 123, *124*, 179
Roborough 88
Rodier, Sub-Lieutenant Mark 94
Roosevelt, F.D. 91
Rostock 96, 97
Royal Artillery 51, 107
Royal Australian Air Force 20, 31, *32*, 66
Royal Dockyard *See* Devonport
Royal Engineers 55, 70, 76
Royal Marine Corps 18
Royal Marines 42, 45, 57
Royal Navy 44, 130, 133, 137
    Naval bases
        HMS *Britannia* 15, 16, 18, 26, 55, 81,
        111, 116, 124
        HMS *Drake* 78
    See also Shipping
Royal Observer Corps 51, 52, 110
RSPCA 139
Russia 70, 82, 114
Russian Forces 96

Saint Nazaire 45, 94, 96
Salcombe 4, *11*, 43, 55, 60, 65, 88, 91, 121, 122
124, 131, 145, 147, 153, *160*, 161, *177*, 182
Salisbury 74
Saltash 141
Saltern Sands 53
Saltram House 146
Sandford 3, *50*
Sark 59
Saunton 51, 124, 128
Seaton 4, 32, 33, 114, 150
Secret Intelligence Service (SIS) 59
Shebbear 89
Shipping
    British Merchant vessels
        Arandora Star 32, 33
        Brighton Belle 41
        Devonia 4, 41, 42
        Glen Avon 41
        Inverdargle 35
        Lady Cable 41, 42
        Lancastria 45
        Mew (steam ferry) 41
        Seymour Castle 41
        Sir John Hawkins (tender)42
        St Andrew 45
        Victoria and Albert 18
        Waverley 42
    German Naval vessels
        Graf Spee 36
        Schleswig Holstein 16, 17
        Tirpitz 94, 109
    Royal Naval vessels
        HMS *Ajax* 36
        HMS *Azalea* 155
        HMS *Campbeltown* 94
        HMS *Campeador* 59
        HMS *Cicala* 117, 165
        HMS *Courageous* 14, 15, 29
        HMS *Exeter* 36, *37*, 94
        HMS *Harstad* 120
        HMS *Hood* 72
        HMS *Impulse* 30
        HMS *Javelin* 67
        HMS *King George V* 158
        HMS *Lord Hailsham* 120
        HMS *Prince Philip* 109
        HMS *Revenge* 15
        HMS *Royal Oak* 33
        HMS *Saladin* 58, 155
        HMS *Scimitar* 58, 155
        HMS *Sheffield* 15
        HMS *Snaefell* 42
        HMS *Southampton* 15
        HMS *Trinidad* 80
        HMS *Veteran* 124
        HT *Dorsetshire* 13, 45
        HT *Lancashire* 13, 14
        HT *Somerset* 13, 45
        MT *Clan MacAlistair* 14
    US vessels
        USS *Arkansas* 12

USS *Bayfield* 157
USS *New York* 12
USS *President Warfield* 123, *124*
USS *Wyoming* 12
Other vessels
    FS *Belfort* 117
    FS *Paris* *45*, 46
    Herzogin Cecilie 11
    La Part Bleu 65
    Meknes 46
    Moldavia 120
    Research 111
    Slamat 13
    SS *Koscirsz* 46
    Surcouf 46, 47
Shute, Neville 125
Sidmouth 19, 36, 37, *53*, 67, 69, 114, 149, 181
Smeatharpe 167
Slapton *3*, 36, 115, 124, 131, 134, 140, *141*, 142,
147, 171, 173
    Beach/Sands *14*, *15*, 16, 19, *42*, 55, 170
    Royal Sands Hotel 15, 133, *154*, *174*
Slapton Battle Training Area 130, 131, 153, *154*,
155, *156*, 157, 159, 171, 173, *174*, *175*
South Brent 34, *61*, 182
South Hams 2, 15, 16, 24, 25, 30, 42, 170-75, 182
    Evacuation of 131-42
South Molton 3, 10, 30, 61
Southampton 149
Southern Command Weapon Training School,
Woolacombe 125
Southern Railway 9
Spain 14
Spanish Civil War 14, 62
Special Operations Executive (SOE) 59
Sperrle, Feldmarschall Hugo 62
Stalin, Joseph 114
Start Bay 131
Start Point 48, 49, 57, 59, 120, 155, 172
Stoke Fleming 115, 124
Stokenham 133, 134, 135, 136, 140
Stop-line defences 47, 48
Strete 55, 124, 131, 137, 140, 154, *171*, 175
Surrey 24
Swindon 74

Tavistock 16, 30, 34, 35, 40, 42, 60, 69, 88, 90,
92, 121, 176
Teignmouth 1, 11, 16, 24, 27, 38, 41, 54, 55, 63,
110, *114*, 115, 117, 121, *123*, 124, 147
Territorial Army 19
Thompson, Colonel Paul W. *129*
Thornbury 89
Thurlestone 107
Tiger (Exercise) 153, 155, 157, *158*, *159*, 167
Tiverton 8, 19, 34, 69, 93, 124, 145, 178, *179*, 181
Torbay (area) 4, 12, 89, 110, 152, 155, 161
    See also Brixham, Paignton, Torquay
Torcross 55, 115, 131, 133, 140, 175
Torpoint 157
Torquay 1, 4, 7, 8, 11, 27, *28*, 30, *31*, 40, *49*, 53,
55, 59, 60, 61, 64, 92, 93, 103, 109, 110, 115, 117,
121, 143, 145, 146, 147, 153, *162*, *164*, *170*, 171,
180
    Imperial Hotel 10, 12, 34, 120
    Marine Spa *7*, 12
    Palace Hotel 113
    Palm Court Hotel *7*
    St Marychurch 53, 121-2
    Torre Abbey Sands *7*
Torquay United 12
Torrington 37, 51, 53, 109, 128, 150, 176
Totnes 27, 34, 61, 81, 97, 109, 143, 146, 150, 173,
174, 176, 182
Trek out
    Exeter 104
    Plymouth 85-8, 89
Turnchapel 66, *67*, 88, 146

U Boats 23, 29, 32, 33, 49, 60, 94, 112, 124, 167,
176
Ugborough 27, 30
Upottery 167
US Forces 91, 93, 109, 129, 131, 133, 137, 140-42,
144, 147, 150

USAAF 96, 157
    Eagle Squadron 111, 112
    Fleet Air Wing 7, *166*
    36th Fighter Group 157
    78th Fighter Group *159*
    101st Airborne Division 167
    439th Troop-Carrying Group 167
US Army 123, 124
    Cavalry Reconnaissance 145
    Divisional Signals 145
    1st Army Group *166*
    121 Eng. Combat Battalion 121
    42nd Field Artillery Battalion 145
    44th Field Artillery Battalion 145
    227 Field Artillery Battalion 121
    1st Infantry Division *160*
    4th Infantry Division 143-67
    29th Infantry Division 121, 130, *133*,
    141, 142
    175th Infantry Regiment 130
    704th Ordnance Company 145
    4th Quartermaster Company 145
    US 1st Army 153
    US V Corps 153
    US VII Corps 153, 169
US Navy 123, 124
    Naval bases *146*, 182
    Naval Construction Battalion 124
Utah Beach *163*, *164*, 165, 167, 169

V1 Flying Bomb 97, *166*, 169
V2 Rocket 97
VE Day 176-80, 182
Vichy Government 46
Victoria Cross 109, 113
VJ Day 178, 182

Warner's Holiday Camps 32
Weare Giffard 172
West Prawle 52
Western Morning News 76
Western Times 92
Westleigh 3
Westward Ho! 45, 51, 125, 127
Weymouth 40, 48, 165
Whitestone 104
Widecombe 107
Widemouth 51
Williamson, Henry 8
Women's Land Army (WLA) 34, 38, *173*
Woodbury 97
Woolacombe 3, 16, 51, 125, 130
    Assault Training Centre 122, 124, 128, *129*,
    130, 131, *132*, 142, 145, 153
Woolsery 182
Wrangaton 27
WVS 14, 25, 30, 88, 103, *104*, 109, 115, 116, 122,
133, 135, 136, 137, 173

X-GERAT 71, 96, 105

Yelverton 57, 88, 107, 181